THE NATIONAL GEOGRAPHIC TRAVELER
SYDNEY

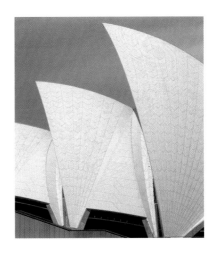

THE NATIONAL
GEOGRAPHIC TRAVELER

SYDNEY

Evan McHugh

Contents

How to use this guide 6–7 About the author 8
Sydney areas 41–172 Excursions 173–204 Farther Afield 205–30
Travelwise 231–64 Index 265–69 Credits 270–71

Page 1: Sydney Opera
House
Pages 2–3: Sydney to
Hobart Yacht Race
Left: Sydney Surf
Boat Carnival

How to use this guide

See back flap for keys to text and map symbols

The *National Geographic Traveler* brings you the best of Sydney in text, pictures, and maps. Divided into three sections, the guide begins with an overview of history and culture. Following are eight area chapters with featured sites chosen by the author for their particular interest and treated in depth. Each chapter opens with its own contents list for easy reference. Two final chapters suggest excursions from Sydney.

A map introduces each area of the city, highlighting the featured sites and locating other places of interest. Walks and a drive, plotted on their own maps, suggest routes

for discovering the most about an area. Features and sidebars offer intriguing detail on history, culture, or contemporary life. A More Places to Visit page generally rounds off the chapters.

The final section, Travelwise, lists essential information for the traveler—pre-trip planning, getting around, communications, money matters, and emergencies—plus a selection of hotels and restaurants arranged by area, shops, entertainment, and activities.

To the best of our knowledge, site information is accurate as of the press date. However, it is always advisable to call ahead.

Color coding

58

Each area of the city is color coded for easy reference. Find the city area you want on the map on the front flap, and look for the color flash at the top of the pages of the relevant chapter. Information in **Travelwise** is also color coded to each area.

Museum of Contemporary Art

🅰 Map p. 71
✉ 140 George St., The Rocks
☎ 9241 5892 (recorded information)
www.mca.com.au
$ $$
🚈 Circular Quay Station
⛴ Circular Quay

Visitor information

Practical information is given in the side column by each major site (see key to symbols on back flap). The map reference gives the page number where the site is shown on a map. Further details include the site's address, telephone number, entrance charge in a range from $ (under $4) to $$$$$ (over $25), days closed, and nearest public transportation stop. Other sites have visitor information in italics and parentheses in the text.

TRAVELWISE

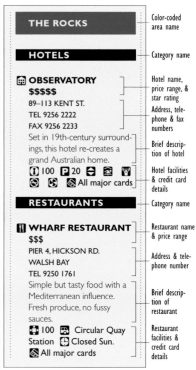

Color-coded area name

Category name

Hotel name, price range, & star rating

Address, telephone & fax numbers

Brief description of hotel

Hotel facilities & credit card details

Category name

Restaurant name & price range

Address & telephone number

Brief description of restaurant

Restaurant facilities & credit card details

Hotel and restaurant prices

An explanation of the price ranges used in entries is given in the Hotels & Restaurants section (see pp. 239–57).

AREA MAPS

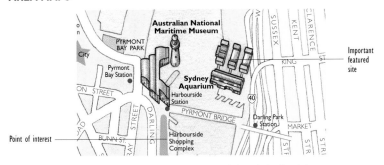

- A locator map accompanies each area map and shows the location of that area in the city.

WALKING TOURS

- An information box gives the starting and ending points, time and length of walk, and places not to be missed along the route.

EXCURSION MAPS

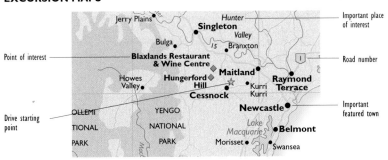

- Towns, cities, and sites described in the Excursions and Farther Afield chapters (pp. 173–230) are highlighted in yellow on the map. Other suggested places to visit are also highlighted and are shown with a red diamond symbol.

THE NATIONAL
GEOGRAPHIC TRAVELER

SYDNEY

About the author

Evan McHugh is a native of Sydney and has traveled throughout Australia, Europe, and the United States. He has worked as a journalist on a range of subjects including technology, travel, and literature with the national newspaper, the *Australian,* and for the television program *Beyond 2000.* He is currently Features Editor of the Ansett Airlines magazine *Panorama,* and writes a weekly column for the *Australian* on the more offbeat aspects of home-ownership and renovating.

He has written two novels, *Short Sharp Sweet* and *The Sailor's Widow,* and assisted Aboriginal designer John Moriarty, whose designs are featured on two Qantas 747s, in the writing of his biography.

McHugh's interests include gardening and fixing up old houses. He is a tennis player and a very competitive yachtsman. Like most Australians, he loves summer, beaches, and barbecues.

Michelle Wright assisted in researching hotel and restaurant selections.

History & culture

Sydney Harbour Bridge and the Australian maritime flag

Sydney today

STAND ON THE BUSY PROMENADE OF CIRCULAR QUAY, WITH THE CITY OF Sydney behind you, the Opera House on the right, and the harbor sparkling between the ferries edging to the wharves in front, and you get a sense of standing at the birthplace of a nation.

A little over 200 years ago, on January 26, 1788, the flag that marked the beginning of European settlement in Australia was planted on this very spot. The First Fleet—11 sailing vessels battered by eight months at sea during their voyage from England—dropped anchor in the cove right in front of you. All around, the ships' crews, convicts, guards, and soldiers pitched their tents.

Today, most people enter Australia by air, yet the place where one has a true sense of arrival remains Circular Quay. On the left is the Sydney Cove Overseas Passenger Terminal, where visitors from around the world have been arriving for two centuries. On the right, its creamy white curves etched against the blue of sky and water, the Sydney Opera House is one of the jewels of 20th-century architecture.

Yet it also speaks of the city's maritime history. The "sails" of the Opera House, unfurled against the waves that lap around them on three sides, whisper of voyages in square-rigged tall ships, convict transport vessels, and flying clippers. On weekends, when pleasure craft skim past its feet, the building could be voyaging still.

Circular Quay is the ideal starting point to discover the city: ferries in front of you; buses, trains, and taxis behind; and a lot of sights within easy walking distance. But pause a moment, take time to orient yourself before venturing into this vibrant city to discover its past as well as its present. Then be ready to explore the history, the indigenous culture, the waterways, the natural environment, or the modern global city that Sydney has become.

You might think that you can see Sydney's major sights—the Opera House, the harbor, Bondi Beach—in less than a day and not miss a thing. Actually, no. You can't get a real taste of the city without visiting Lion Island and Pittwater, or seeing the bizarre and beautiful flora and fauna. Then there are some of the best wines and food in the world to taste and diamonds, opals, or indigenous art and artifacts to buy.

For entertainment, choose from a performance in the Opera House, the outdoor events of the Sydney Festival, or watch half a million people line the streets for the spectacular Gay and Lesbian Mardi Gras (see pp. 140–41). Discover how friendly and full of life the people are in the cafés, pubs, restaurants, and streets; walk, swim, sail, dance, have a picnic, or just sit and watch life in all its richness wander past.

See it all in a day? Ideally, you should allow a year. That way you can experience the full range of the seasons, the full calendar of annual events, and have just enough time to really embrace the lifestyle and amenities that make this city such a fun and stimulating place to be. Beyond the obvious attractions, the internationally known sights, there are literally dozens of things to visit and do.

Sydney covers more than 600 square miles (1,550 km). Physically, its boundaries have expanded to engulf other towns and cities around it. Parramatta (see pp. 188–89), 12 miles (19 km) to the west, is now an inner suburb. Newcastle (see p. 214) and Wollongong (see p. 224), around 100 miles (160 km) to the north and 50 miles (80 km) to the south respectively, are now considered commuter suburbs—part of what has been called the New-Syd-Gong urban conglomeration. Many office workers travel from the Blue Mountains to reach the city each day. The population within commuting distance of the Central Business District (CBD) is in the region of five million. And it is a diverse assortment of people, with more than 140 different nationalities represented.

George Street, in The Rocks, is one of Sydney's oldest streets, with several historic, 19th-century buildings.

LIFESTYLE

The people of Sydney enjoy a lifestyle that is the envy of many other cities. Sydney is circled by national parks and no fewer than six major waterways (some far larger than Sydney Harbour) within 60 miles (96 km) of the city center. As for the climate, it varies from hot to cool; compared to most cities there is no winter—just a season where you'll need a coat in the evening and maybe a sweater during the day. Consequently, most of the recreational activities tend to be outdoors—barbecues, picnics, trips to the beach, boating, sports, or simply walking.

It is this outdoor lifestyle that encourages the informality and friendliness so noticeable in Australians in general and Sydneysiders in particular. It's hard to be insular when little time is spent behind closed doors. An example: If you happen to be in the city on a balmy summer evening, take a taxi down to Mrs. Macquarie's Point, at the eastern head of Farm

Cove across from the Opera House. On the lawns facing the cove people are having picnics, fishing, or just strolling up and down. It's nighttime and no one is worrying about being attacked or robbed.

CITY AREAS

Unknown to much of the population, the sections of the city are not so different from those chosen by the Aboriginal people who first inhabited the area. There is also a certain

High-spirited vacationers hold their own unofficial Christmas celebrations on Bondi Beach.

amount of "tribalism" to the different sectors of the city. For example, an expression you may hear is "OTB." It means Over The Bridge, and refers to the reluctance people from the southside have to going anywhere on the northside of the city—even those who were born there and have moved into the Inner

City. There are people who live in the affluent Eastern Suburbs who don't believe anyone of consequence lives west of Rushcutters Bay; those who live between Rushcutters Bay and Kings Cross believe you can't get a good cup of coffee west of Darlinghurst. The people of the Northern Beaches are considered to be rather like New Age Californians—tanned, healthy, keen on dolphins and crystals—while those on the Southern Beaches are thought to identify with the less sophisticated 1950s and '60s.

The Westies are divided into two: the Westies proper—the vast swath of bedroom communities stretching to the Blue Mountains, and the Inner West—the suburbs close to the city on its western side. In these inner suburbs the radicals, the grunge elements, and the agitators gather in their cafés near the University of Sydney to discuss issues and make plans.

In the Blue Mountains, where it gets cold enough to convince you there are four seasons in a year (sometimes it even snows), the property prices are cheaper and artists and writers can afford a drafty garret in which to shiver and think.

These are incredibly broad generalizations (just try them on a local and see), but they're a good start. If you overlay all this with the multicultural elements of the city, the picture becomes a little more detailed: Greek, Italian, Chinese, Vietnamese, and Indian neighborhoods. There are communities of Pacific Islanders, Aborigines, Balkans, Spanish, Africans, Japanese, and Lebanese, as well as Christian, Jewish, Muslim, and Buddhist places of worship. It goes on and on.

The remarkable thing about this diversity is the peaceful manner in which everyone lives side by side: no walls, soldiers, riots, or tensions. Even the sizable gay community goes largely unmolested. Certainly there are isolated unpleasant incidents, but the prevailing attitude can best be described in ten words— respect, tolerance, and understanding for every race, religion, and creed.

Within this kaleidoscope of cultures and cuisines is an easygoing, outgoing population that can hardly believe its luck. It is not uncommon to dine at an upscale restaurant and find on its menu influences from nearly every inhabited continent. Asian visitors have looked on in amazement at noodle bars full of Australians hungrily and expertly wielding chopsticks. In some of the city's restaurant strips, you can choose from up to a dozen different national cuisines. Sydneysiders love food.

LEISURE TIME

Not surprisingly, a great deal of Sydney's leisure activity is outdoors, with sports such as cricket, rugby league and rugby union, Aussie rules, and soccer in the lead. Basketball and baseball are becoming increasingly popular, too. On any weekend you'll find thousands of people out on Sydney Harbour in powerboats, sailboats, and even kayaks. And then there's the beach. Walking is also extremely popular, whether on the various coastal walks, the harbor walks, or longer options in the national parks that surround the city.

Sydneysiders love to unwind after work. Friday nights in the city's pubs and bars are a boisterous affair as office workers and laborers alike relax and socialize over a few beers. In summer particularly, you'll find people spilling into the streets, noisily discussing the week's events, the weekend's plans. Many pubs have beer gardens that take advantage of the

Special interests

Sydneysiders have a diverse range of interests and are generally very willing to share them with like-minded visitors. So whether you are keen on aviation, trains, or quilting, there is sure to be a club or company that can cater to your needs.

To make finding a particular organization easier, all Sydney phone numbers are now available on the Internet. The white pages (www.whitepages.com.au) list all business and home numbers alphabetically; the yellow pages (www.yellowpages.com.au) list businesses by activity. The phone numbers are also linked to a street directory.

Tourism NSW (Sydney Visitor Centre, The Rocks, Tel 13 2077; www.tourism.nsw.gov.au) has an extensive database that may be useful, as well as a full calendar of events. ∎

The cliffs above Farm Cove are a prime spot for wedding photos.

balmy climate and the desire locals have to get out into the warm night air. There will often be barbecue and bistro facilities, and you'll see children running around in the garden while mom and dad line up for dinner.

The people of Sydney are inordinately proud of their city, with good reason, and they never tire of hearing visitors praise it. "Sydney is the best address on earth" they will tell you. One of the city's best known contemporary artists, Ken Done (1940–), who specializes in brightly colored, simplistic images of the city's landmarks, even went so far as to put the slogan on a T-shirt.

As a journalist with the *Australian Magazine,* Miriam Cosic, who moved to Sydney from Australia's other major city, Melbourne, put it: "When Melbourne people talk about Australia, they mean Australia. When Sydney people talk about Australia, they mean Sydney." Not only that, Sydney now considers itself so cosmopolitan that it identifies more closely with New York, Paris, or London than it does with Melbourne, Brisbane, or Canberra.

VISITORS' SYDNEY

Sydney is as relaxing a place to visit as it is to live in. The level of personal security is on a par with or better than other major cities. This is not to say that there is no crime, nor that pickpockets don't congregate around tourist areas.

It is also a relatively easy city to navigate. Most sights are within walking distance of each other; if not, there is plenty of public transportation. Everyone speaks English and most people are friendly and helpful. Sydneysiders are not quickly offended and it is almost impossible to commit a cultural faux pas.

Bear in mind that there is an egalitarianism in Australia not found in many other countries. The flip side of this, though, is that Australians have a healthy dislike for anyone in authority or who behaves with a superior attitude. Talk down to someone for example, even if they are providing a service, and you may be surprised

at the consequences. On the positive side, most people you meet will assist you out of a genuine desire to be helpful. This means you only need tip when you are in a restaurant, and you don't have to do that if you don't like the service. And a word of advice: "g'day" is an informal greeting, not a farewell. Say "g'day" to an Australian at the end of a conversation and he or she will probably look bemused.

As much a part of Sydney as its museums, theaters, and galleries are its beaches, waterways, and nature reserves. The city also invites you to participate in its lifestyle. So when visiting Bondi, don't just take a photo, kick off your shoes and wiggle your toes in the sand. Go for a swim or follow the spectacular headland walk that winds away to the south. In the harbor, pick one of the numerous venues that offers a view of the water and a sumptuous meal to boot. Rent a yacht. Perhaps arrange to spend a night on the water and awake to the gentle rocking of your boat and

the sight of the harbor in all its glory. Above all else, remember that this city is meant to be enjoyed.

A FEW PRECAUTIONS

One of the most attractive features of Sydney is its proximity to the countryside and its wildlife (see pp. 198–203). In the national parks that surround the city, kangaroos jump and kookaburras laugh. In the seas, whales spout and dolphins leap. However, there are

Much of Sydney's social scene revolves around a refreshing drink taken in one of the city's many pubs.

some hazards to watch out for. These include sharks, bluebottles, blue-ringed octopuses, spiders, snakes, mosquitoes, magpies, bush fires, "widow-makers" (see p. 19), rips (see p. 19), heatstroke, sunstroke, sunburn, and dehydration. Most of these, though, can be avoided with a little common sense.

In January 1994, bush fires spread to Como, a southern suburb of Sydney, devastating houses and gardens.

Sharks probably loom largest in most people's imagination. There are sharks in Sydney Harbour and swimming in open water isn't recommended. However, most of the popular harbor beaches are netted, as are the popular ocean beaches, which are closely patrolled by aircraft and lifeguards.

Bluebottles—small marine stingers with an inflated "sail" and long blue tendrils—usually blow in to land when there is an onshore wind, and you'll see them washed up on the beach if they are about. Although painful, their sting is not fatal and the best remedy is to pour vinegar over the affected area, or buy a cream called Stingoes from the drugstore.

Blue-ringed octopuses are found in rock pools. They are fairly timid, but if you do come across one, under no circumstances attempt to pick it up as its bite is fatal.

There are two venomous spiders you should be wary of: funnel-webs, which have a fatal bite, and red-backs, whose bite can be fatal to a small child. Both are found under rocks or wood in damp areas. If you are bitten, immobi-

lize the affected area, apply a pressure bandage, and seek medical treatment immediately. Also be prepared to administer cardiopulmonary resuscitation as long as necessary.

Not all snakes are venomous, but it is best to give any snake a wide berth. Treat a snake bite in the same way as a spider bite.

Sydney's mosquitoes do not carry any nasty diseases, although there are concerns about the debilitating Ross River Fever. However, mosquitoes can be annoying when you are outdoors and insect repellent is recommended, especially when you are out in the evening.

Visitors from cooler climates may find it takes some time to adjust to the heat and sun of a Sydney summer. Always wear a hat, put on sunscreen, drink plenty of fluids, and if it is very hot, slow down. Heat stress can lay low even the fittest people.

Safe hiking
In spring, keep a look out for magpies as they can be territorial at this time and may swoop, clack their beaks, and sometimes actually strike. Wear a hat.

A number of precautions should be taken with regard to bush fires during the summer (Nov.–Jan.). On entering a national park, check

the level of fire danger on the indicator boards or with a ranger. If the danger level is extreme and there is a high wind, seriously consider curtailing any extended bush walking. At any hint of smoke, immediately move to safe ground. In the event of a total fire ban, open fires of any description, including barbecues, are forbidden anywhere in the Sydney area. If you are caught by advancing fire, do not try to outrun the flames; find an open area if you can, or find any depression in the ground that can afford some shelter, cover yourself as much as possible, and let the fire pass over you. If you are in a vehicle, stop in an open area, get down on the floor, and cover yourselves with clothing until the fire has passed. If you are in a house, stay there. And if you are given instructions by emergency services personnel, do what they tell you.

Another danger of walking in the national parks is that gum trees sometimes shed their dead branches, known as "widow-makers," without warning. If you go camping, always check the branches above the tent.

Safe swimming

Most of Sydney's ocean beaches are patrolled by lifeguards and safe swimming areas are designated by pairs of flags. Always swim between the flags and if the beach is unpatrolled take great care. The main danger is a rip, an area where water carried in by waves flows back out to sea. Rips are typically channels of deeper water with few if any breaking waves. This makes them inviting to swimmers lacking confidence to face the surf, which is why they claim so many lives. If you get caught in a rip, the most important thing is not to panic. By trying to fight the current you can rapidly become exhausted. If possible, swim across the current until you are out of the rip, then make your way back to shore through the surf. Otherwise, relax and float, raising an arm or shouting to signal for help.

To get a tan, 15 minutes a day is plenty. Half an hour of hot sun on sensitive skin can leave you very uncomfortable for days afterward.

Depending on what your day will involve, it is a good idea to put together a small survival kit to carry with you. This should include a hat, sunscreen, sunglasses, a bottle of water, and mosquito repellent. ■

Food & drink

NEARLY EVERY ETHNIC GROUP TO ARRIVE IN SYDNEY HAS BROUGHT ITS own cuisine, and many of the foods are ideal for the Sydney climate—crisp and tangy, perfect for freshening your palate on a warm sunny day. Salads have always been popular, but the addition of chili, lemongrass, or coriander has added another dimension to the experience.

These days, the fashion in Sydney is to rely on good-quality ingredients rather than heavy sauces and layers of flavor, and the result is not dissimilar to the eclectic bistro-style foods of London or New York. Add a strong flavor of Asia and you have the "Modern Australian" interpretation of nouvelle cuisine. Don't be surprised to find Japanese sushi or Thai beef salad on the same menu as risotto and pasta. Keep an eye out, too, for bush foods. In some restaurants you will be able to tuck into the national specialties, kangaroo and emu, as well as crocodile, buffalo, and camel. All delicious. Then there are such items as loquat (a small, plumlike fruit) ice cream and lilli pilli jam, made from the Australian fruit resembling a bunch of grapes.

ETHNIC DIVERSITY

To get an idea of the range of cuisines found in Sydney, visit Cleveland Street with its Turkish pizzas and Lebanese restaurants, or Darlinghurst's Italian restaurants. Leichhardt (named after Ludwig Leichhardt, an explorer who disappeared in 1848) is a long way west of Darlinghurst, but the Italian cafés here are great—even if you don't like the coffee, watching the people on parade is worth the price of a cup. Alternatively, try the Spanish restaurants on Liverpool Street in the city, Chinatown just around the corner, the Japanese restaurants in North Sydney and Crows Nest, or the Thai restaurants on King Street, Newtown. There are also Vietnamese restaurants in Cabramatta and Korean in Campsie.

A range of eating experiences can be had on or near the water in The Rocks, Darling Harbour, and the Eastern Suburbs, as well as at Sydney Fish Market. Don't forget the idea of packing a picnic and heading for one of the waterside parks. If you're on a budget, you can have a pleasant time at the tables set outside at the northern end of the Opera House complex.

TOP CHOICES

All the following restaurants are covered in the Hotels and Restaurants section of Travelwise, but some names to remember are Forty One (that's the floor of the building it's on, and the view is only surpassed by the food), Tetsuya's (book well in advance), Bennelong Restaurant (the restaurant at the Opera House), Darley Street Thai (the last word in sumptuous Thai food), the Bathers Pavilion (breakfast or a long lunch watching the boats drift by), and the Nielsen Park Kiosk in Vaucluse. Others to note are the Imperial Peking, Kables, Rockpool, Wockpool, Paramount, Suntory, and Unkai. And there are some fantastic places missing from this list. Choose any of these, however, and be assured of a vacation memory.

ALFRESCO

Sydney's climate makes it ideal for dining outdoors, day or night. Many restaurants, from the most upscale to the humble suburban eatery, have outside seating somewhere on their premises. Some, such as the Sydney Cove Oyster Bar, for example, have almost all of their tables outside where the views and the balmy evenings can be enjoyed. Other restaurants are so open in design that you might as well be outside.

When making a reservation, you will probably be asked if you would like to sit inside or out. And if you walk into a restaurant that doesn't appear to have outside seating, it's always worth asking because you'll often find that there's a spot tucked down a side passage somewhere.

Nearly every pub in the city has a beer garden; even those in the heart of the business district will try to squeeze a couple of tables onto the sidewalk. Others have space on their

Sydney Fish Market is a treat for lovers of seafood.

Sausages and steaks, washed down with beer or wine, are popular choices at barbecues.

roof where you can enjoy your refreshment under the sun and stars.

One of the city's most impressive pubs is the Newport Arms, up in the Northern Beaches. In The Rocks you'll find several beer gardens in the pubs along George Street, as well as the rooftop garden at the Glenmore Hotel on Cumberland Street. Don't be surprised to see customers spilling out onto the street where there is no other option.

NATIVE FARE

Perhaps the most recognizable contribution that Australia has made to world cuisine is the curious substance known as Vegemite. How anyone could actually consume this sharply flavored, vile looking black paste confounds many. Australians, on the other hand, are raised on the stuff and can't get enough of it.

Try it if you want, perhaps on toast, or console yourself with the knowledge that there are more palatable items you can seek out. Seafood is the obvious place to start. If you can find it, abalone from South Australia is in great demand. Most of it is exported, particularly to Japan.

More readily available is a fish called barramundi, native of the estuaries of northern Australia. It is a great game fish, but, more importantly, excellent to eat. Barramundis are now farmed, and while those caught in the wild are said to taste better, these come a very good second. The fish farms in the waters of Tasmania are also producing delicious Atlantic salmon.

Closer to home, rock oysters from along the N.S.W. coast are highly prized and readily available. Usually termed Sydney Rock or Wallis Lake oysters, they are likely to be found on almost every restaurant menu. However, you can save a lot of money if you buy them from one of the many retailers at the Sydney Fish Market.

You won't be disappointed by the produce from King Island, which is situated in the storm-swept Bass Strait between the Australian mainland and Tasmania. The "must tries" are King Island beef, cheese (such as brie and camembert), and cream. If you don't see these items on menus, they can be found in delicatessens and the David Jones Food Hall (see p. 108) in the city.

Friends meet for pre-performance drinks at the Concourse Restaurant at the Opera House.

B.Y.O.

Outside many restaurants are the letters B.Y.O. or B.Y.O. Only, which indicate that the restaurant permits you to Bring Your Own beverages. N.S.W. restaurants are required to have a license to sell alcohol, but they are permitted to serve it if you bring it with you. Even when licensed, most restaurants will let you bring beverages in. In either case they may charge a small corkage fee per person.

WINE & BEER

The wine lists of most restaurants in Sydney are almost exclusively comprised of Australian wines. And why not? In Europe, the United States, and Japan, the wines from nearly every state of Australia are recognized as among the best and most consistent found anywhere (see pp. 212–13).

You may see wine from other countries in the best restaurants, or in those that specialize in a regional cuisine.

If homesick for your local brew, you'll probably find it in one of the larger liquor stores around the city, especially if it's a premium beer. Guinness is widespread in pubs, while the likes of Lowenbrau, Heineken, Miller Genuine Draft, Carlsberg, Corona, and even Boddington's Pub Ale can be found at liquor supermarkets such as Kemeny's on Bondi Road and Camperdown Cellars (several stores across the city).

As for the local beers, the big names in the premium market include Hahn and Crown Lager, while light beers such as Hahn Premium Light and Cascade Premium Light make pleasant drinking if you are watching your alcohol intake.

The major brewers are adding to their range at an impressive rate, but keep an eye out for some of the microbrewery beers. In The Rocks, there are some nice lagers and ales to be tried at the Lord Nelson (see p. 76), and Scharer's Little Brewery in Picton (southwest of Sydney) is worth a visit if you're in the area. Order beer by the brand and glass size: A "middy" glass holds 10 fluid ounces (284 ml), while a "schooner" glass contains 15 fluid ounces (426 ml).

And for nondrinkers, there's a huge range of exotic fruit drinks to choose from: fruit pulp with ice, fruit with milk, etc. ■

History of Sydney

IT IS STILL BEING DEBATED EXACTLY HOW LONG AUSTRALIA HAS BEEN inhabited by Aboriginal people, who are believed to have arrived from Southeast Asia. Conservative estimates by anthropologists, based on carbon dating of charcoal from fires and food remains at known sites, put it at 40,000 to 50,000 years.

Whatever the time scale, scholars estimate that before the arrival of the First Fleet in 1788 there were about 3,000 people living in the Sydney region. They were split into three main language groups: the Dharawal in the south, the Dharug to the west, and the Ku-ring-gai to the north. The region between Botany Bay and Sydney Harbour was populated by a dialect group of the Dharug, who called themselves the Eora.

People from the different areas—the coast, the wooded plains, the mountains—used different tools and weapons as appropriate to the terrain: clubs, spears, axes, throwing sticks (a hunting tool, heavier than but similar to a boomerang), baskets, canoes, or fishhooks.

Within these regions, small groups of about 50 people, representing different families, had their own areas where they hunted and gathered food. Each of these groups also displayed slight language differences, although they had little difficulty understanding each other. Despite their attachment to particular areas for finding food, groups traveled widely throughout the region and moved around for ceremonies. This suggests

there was considerable social, if not economic, interaction.

Aboriginal life was governed by tribal law that was enforced by the elders (both men and women) of each group. Punishment could be severe, with wrongdoers often being repeatedly speared by the offended parties. Initiation ceremonies marking the transition to adulthood were also brutal. One ceremony witnessed in Sydney in 1795 involved the removal of a front tooth from each initiate. Scarification of the face and body was also widely practiced.

FIRST EUROPEANS

For the Aboriginal people living in the Sydney region, the first contact with Europeans came in 1770, when the English navigator James

Fireworks over the harbor marked Australia's bicentennial in 1988. Similar displays occur every New Year.

Cook, captain of the bark *Endeavour,* dropped anchor at Botany Bay and took on water and botanical specimens. Cook's exploration of the entire east coast is marked by some as the "discovery" of Australia, even though the Dutch had known of the north and west of the country for centuries. They named it New Holland. Searching for the Great South Land, Magellan suspected he had passed it on his voyage of 1519 to 1522, and Makassar seafarers from the Indonesian archipelago had been trading with the Aborigines of the north for centuries.

Cook's arrival at Botany Bay, however, proved to be the vanguard for the permanent European settlement of the country. Cook and his botanists, Joseph Banks and Daniel Solander, reported that the coastal district was sparsely inhabited by Aborigines, having encountered no more than "30 or 40 together" (although the true number was in the thousands). As a result the country was considered (erroneously) *terra nullius*—no man's land. Banks suggested that a penal colony should be established there to alleviate the problem of overcrowded prisons in England.

Not until more than 200 years later was this error of ownership rectified when what has become known as the Mabo Case was conducted before the Australian High Court and the legal existence of native title finally recognized. The case involved an Aboriginal man named Eddie Mabo (and others) who had enjoyed the use of parts of an island off the Queensland coast but never held native title. It was established that, because they and their progenitors had inhabited the island in an unbroken line since before white settlement, they had a right to claim ownership. The implications for the rest of the country were momentous, not just because it meant other Aborigines could claim similar titles, but because it meant that a lot of assumed ownership by the Crown and the total control of the various Land Titles acts were thrown into question. But by then, of course, the Europeans were well and truly established.

FIRST SETTLEMENT

By any fair assessment, the first 20 years of settlement in Sydney were not a success. The First Fleeters nearly starved, the convicts were horribly mistreated, the marines were there against their will, and the first free settlers resented the dictatorial military governors. In addition, the Aborigines, who were more numerous than the first governor had been led to believe, were driven from their lands and faced death either from introduced disease or at the hands of the new arrivals. If storms didn't destroy the colonists' meager crops, fire did. Several food stores also burned down and

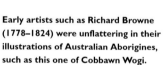

Early artists such as Richard Browne (1778–1824) were unflattering in their illustrations of Australian Aborigines, such as this one of Cobbawn Wogi.

floods destroyed boats and property. At one point, all the colony's cows escaped (they were found years later in a fertile area now called "Cowpastures"). Eventually, though, the catalog of disaster and misery ended in outright rebellion.

The story of Sydney's European settlement starts with the First Fleet. Eleven ships were assembled in Portsmouth, England, to transport more than 1,350 convicts and marines on an eight-month, 13,905-mile (23,500-km) voyage to the other side of the world. Under the command of Capt. Arthur Phillip, they arrived in Botany Bay in January 1788. Shortly behind them, two French vessels under the Comte de la Pérouse, after whom a suburb in the city is named (see p. 158), entered the same bay.

Not finding the bay to his liking, however, Phillip ventured northward along the coast to a bay that Captain Cook had sighted in 1770 and named Port Jackson (Sydney Harbour) after the judge advocate of the fleet at the time. Phillip described it as "the finest harbour in the world," and immediately decided to move the colony there. The English Union

Jack was hoisted in Sydney Cove on January 26, 1788, the date celebrated ever since as the anniversary of Australia's foundation.

Not one ship visited the fledgling colony in its first year, and as each of the original vessels departed on other missions, the settlers' sense of isolation deepened. The prospects for farming around Sydney Cove were not good either, with poor, sandy soils thinly covering the yellow sandstone of the rugged headlands.

With no roads through the inhospitable country, it was natural to use the waterways to explore the area. Within the first year the harbor waters had been navigated inland to the present day Parramatta (Aboriginal for "head of the river," or "place where eels lie down"). Here the settlers found more fertile soils and were able to plant wheat, corn, and other crops.

By this time, however, stocks had shrunk considerably. The fleet's flagship, *Sirius*, had been sent in October 1788 to obtain supplies from Cape Town and did not return until May in the following year.

By now the Aboriginal people had been exposed to smallpox. Lacking any resistance to this and other European diseases, the death toll was appalling. Throughout the Sydney region the population is believed to have fallen

imminent arrival of the Second Fleet, carrying several hundred more hungry convicts.

Nevertheless, despite further difficulties in the early years—disastrous floods, fires in the granaries, attacks by the natives—the colony gradually built up its resources, and as its population grew, it became clear that there was no going back.

to one third, with social structures and the traditional way of life devastated.

Meanwhile, the settlers had their own problems. In January 1790 an expected supply ship failed to arrive, and rations were reduced to half. On April 5, Phillip estimated that the colony—more than a thousand people—had enough food to last just six weeks, and further reduced the rations. The following week, two convicts were sentenced to one thousand lashes each. Their crime? Stealing food. Early in May, the first convict died of hunger. Starvation and disease were to remain a threat to the new settlement for almost two decades.

It wasn't until June 1790 that the long-awaited *Lady Juliana* arrived, carrying much needed supplies, as well as more convicts. But she also brought bad news, reporting the loss of another supply ship that had struck an iceberg east of the Cape of Good Hope and had to return to port. The crew also reported the

The settlement of Sydney, seen from the west side of the cove, is depicted in this watercolor by J. Eyre (circa 1806).

On November 1, 1792, the brig *Philadelphia* from the United States became the first foreign ship to arrive in Sydney with goods to trade—cured beef, wines, gin, rum, tobacco, and tar. Then in January 1793, the first free settlers arrived aboard the *Bellona*; she also carried official permission from the English government for commissioned officers to receive grants of land. Among these officers was Lt. John Macarthur, who immediately claimed 100 acres (40 ha) near Parramatta, which he called Elizabeth Farm (see p. 189) after his wife.

No longer merely a penal colony, Sydney was on its way to becoming one of the most prosperous of Britain's dominions. However, this put the new settlers on a collision course with the colony's military governors.

Hyde Park Barracks (circa 1820), painted by Joseph Lycett, is one of the finest surviving buildings of early Sydney.

EARLY 19TH CENTURY

During the colony's early years, the military and a handful of unscrupulous traders (including Macarthur) managed to gain monopolies in a number of desperately needed commodities. One of these, rum, had virtually become the currency of the colony, especially among the convicts. The governors, meanwhile, were so autocratic that the free settlers began to complain about the lack of even the most basic freedoms that they enjoyed in England.

Macarthur, who had become a captain in the New South Wales Corps, was sent back to England in 1801 to answer charges of causing trouble for Gov. Phillip Gidley King (1758–1808), former second lieutenant on the flagship *Sirius*. King became lieutenant governor of the colony and finally governor from 1800 to 1806.

The charges were dismissed in 1804, but Macarthur took the opportunity to purchase a number of prime Spanish merino rams and ewes, and these founded the flocks that were to fuel much of the prosperity of Australia during the 19th century.

In Macarthur's absence the Vinegar Hill Rebellion took place near Parramatta on March 4–5, 1804. It involved 260 Irish convicts rebelling against their harsh treatment. Although quickly put down and the ringleaders hanged, the uprising heralded the storm that was to envelop the entire colony.

In 1805, amid growing tensions in the Sydney colony, English naval officer Capt. William Bligh (1754–circa 1817) was appointed governor as successor to King. When he arrived in 1806, he set about breaking the power of the monopolists and stopping the barter in rum. In 1807 he outlawed the barter in goods of any description. This brought him into open conflict with Macarthur who, on January 26, 1808 (coincidentally the 20th anniversary of the founding of the colony), led the Rum Rebellion. It took until October for news of the rebellion to reach England, and another year for Bligh's successor to be appointed and make the journey to Sydney.

When the new governor, Lachlan Macquarie (1761–1824), arrived in the colony, he was appalled at what he found. Sydney was in a state of foment, the few buildings were ramshackle or derelict, and exploration only reached 30 miles (50 km) inland—thwarted by the seemingly impenetrable barrier of the Blue Mountains.

Macquarie was a man whose vision was matched only by his ego. However, no governor has left such an indelible mark on the city of Sydney. In the decade of his government (1810–1821), Macquarie constructed more than 200 major public buildings and established the Royal Botanic Gardens. He was assisted by English-born architect Francis Howard Greenway, who was transported to Australia in 1812 for forgery.

No less important was the road building that linked towns such as Parramatta and Windsor and the farmlands to the southwest and northwest. Perhaps Macquarie's greatest achievement, however, was the construction of a road through the Blue Mountains in 1813, opening up vast areas of rich farmland that lay on the other side.

Meanwhile, in the colonial office of London there were concerns about the cost of Macquarie's increasingly extravagant projects. He found himself under growing pressure to curb his expenditure, and in 1820 his resignation was accepted. The following year, hundreds of people turned out to bid the governor and his wife farewell.

Although Macquarie's successors spent money more carefully, by now the colony was generating enough wealth to fund its own development and to demand services and facilities to support its endeavors. Thus Gov. Ralph Darling, who was in office from 1825 to 1831, found himself embarked on the major engineering feat of the 1820s: the convict-built Great Northern Road leading north to the Hunter Valley that enabled produce from the farms to be transported back to Sydney.

The 1830s saw rich landowners constructing magnificent harborside estates, some of which survive to this day (see Vaucluse House, p. 148, and Elizabeth Bay House, p. 146). In 1840, transportation of convicts to Sydney ceased, though felons continued to be sent to Australian settlements in Tasmania and on Norfolk Island. In 1842 a partially elected legislative council was instituted and Sydney was incorporated as a city.

So, less than 60 years after it had been established, Sydney had become a prosperous trading port and the center of a rich agricultural economy.

As good as life was, however, it was nothing compared to what was to follow after the discovery of gold became known. In 1823 gold had been found in the Bathurst region west of the Blue Mountains. It was kept a secret, however, as landowners with agricultural interests were fearful they would lose laborers in the face of more lucrative competition. When word finally got out, though, in 1851, the rush was on.

LATE 19TH CENTURY

From the 1850s until the early 1900s, new fields of gold were discovered all over New South Wales. In the 1880s the richest lead, silver, and zinc deposits in the world at that time were found at Broken Hill in the far west of the state. With these discoveries came a period of growth and prosperity, and the fruits of that prosperity are everywhere to be seen around the city of Sydney.

The substantial buildings in Martin Place (see pp. 50–51), including the former General Post Office (G.P.O.), date from these years, as does the University of Sydney (1853) with its Great Hall designed by Edmund Blacket (1817–1883). Many of the city's major buildings—the Australian Museum (see pp. 62–63), the Town Hall (see p. 112), the Queen Victoria Building (see p. 111), and the Art Gallery of New South Wales (see pp. 56–59)—are also from this period. The handsome houses of inner suburbs such as Woollahra, Paddington (see pp. 136–37), and Stanmore, with their elaborate Italianate facades and wrought-iron and leaded windows, reflect the desire of well-to-do Sydneysiders to display their wealth.

The city's newfound wealth also saw the need for improved security for the colony, and over a period of several decades steps were taken to fortify parts of the harbor. The striking Fort Denison (see p. 97), rising in the middle of the harbor, was completed in 1857.

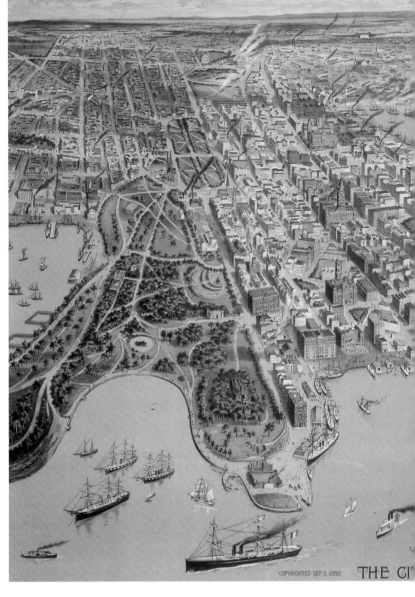

COPYRIGHTED SEP 3 1888 THE CI

A lithograph of the City of Sydney in 1888 by M.S. Hill shows the growth of the settlement based on wealth created by gold and wool.

Prior to that the island on which the fort was built had been called (somewhat unimaginatively) Rock Island. During the first year of the colony, wrongdoers were abandoned there for a week or two to contemplate their misdeeds.

The year 1857 marked the colony's worst shipping disaster. Approaching the harbor one night in bad weather, the crew of the passenger vessel *Dunbar* mistook a gap in the line of cliffs facing the sea (called The Gap) for the entrance and the ship was driven onto the rocks. Many of the passengers were returning to Sydney from England, where they had been spending their newly acquired wealth (see pp. 102–103).

Despite such setbacks, the years leading up to the turn of the century marked Sydney's

SYDNEY BY M.S.HILL, SYDNEY

coming of age. The population was growing rapidly as new settlers, attracted by gold, arrived. Numerous municipal councils were constituted and the first railway opened in 1855. The Royal National Park was dedicated in 1879, making it the second oldest national park in the world after Yellowstone in the United States.

In 1888 it was hard to believe that the thriving city of Sydney had only been in existence for a hundred years. The centenary was marked by the laying out of Centennial Park. This area, originally swampland and the colony's first major water source, has since been developed into one of the city's best recreational assets. A century earlier, a member of the First Fleet, Capt. Watkin Tench (circa 1758–1833) of the Marine Corps, had expressed the hope that the expedition would lead to the establishment of a new empire. He would have been impressed at what had been achieved in the space of just one tumultuous century.

Perhaps even more extraordinary, just 13 years after the centenary, on January 1, 1901, Sydney and the rest of the country celebrated the formation of the Commonwealth of Australia. Appropriately, the federation documents were signed in a ceremony at Centennial Park. And as part of the celebrations of the nation's bicentennial, in 1988, the Federation Pavilion was built on the exact spot of the 1901 signing.

FEDERATION TO WORLD WAR II

Just as the increasing wealth of Sydneysiders was expressed in the opulence of their houses during the second half of the 19th century, in the wake of nationhood the architecture of many Australian homes reflected national pride. The style that dominated in Sydney at the turn of the century actually came to be called Federation. It was characterized by large houses standing on sizable blocks of land (the extension of the railway system made it possible to live farther from the city) with gardens full of Australian native plants.

The houses themselves typically featured wide verandas, carved detail, and Australian motifs. Look for kangaroos, kookaburras, and gum leaves in leaded windows in suburbs such as Mosman, Haberfield, and Strathfield.

Yet, despite enjoying its status as a new nation, Australia still retained close ties with the country that established it—its highest court of appeal was the Privy Council in England. And when England was threatened by war, the Australian people stood ready to support it. Thousands of young men from Sydney and every other city and town across the country answered the call to World War I. Many never returned.

In 1914, the cruiser H.M.A.S. *Sydney* took part in Australia's first major naval victory during an engagement with the German cruiser *Emden*. *Sydney*'s mast is now located on Bradleys Head (see p. 93) in the harbor. In 1915, Australian troops suffered severe losses while attacking Turkish positions on the cliffs of Gallipoli. The incident has become Australia's defining moment in war. During the campaign, 7,594 people were killed and 19,500 wounded. The remembrance day for Australians killed in all wars is held on the anniversary of the first Gallipoli landing—

A dawn service is held annually on April 25 at the Cenotaph, Martin Place, to recall Australians' sacrifices in war.

April 25. It is called Anzac Day, after the Australian and New Zealand Army Corps. All over Australia, parades, dawn services, and wreath-layings are held at memorials in towns and cities.

After the war not even Sydney's wealth could protect it from the financial storm that swept the world during the Great Depression. From 1929, the worsening crisis saw more than a third of the Australian work force unemployed. In Sydney, cliff caves around the harbor formerly used by Aborigines now sheltered many of the homeless.

For East Timor we forget

Amid the atmosphere of crisis, the Sydney Harbour Bridge (see pp. 86–89) was opened in 1932. It was one of the largest construction projects undertaken to that date and finally linked the north and south shores of the harbor, giving a considerable boost to the development of the city's northern suburbs.

When World War II broke out in 1939, Australian men and women found themselves fighting at much closer quarters than they had during World War I. The Japanese push south through the Pacific and Southeast Asia was halted in the waters and jungles adjacent to the country's north coast—the Coral Sea and Papua New Guinea respectively.

The arrival of U.S. trading vessels in Sydney's early days had assisted the fledgling settlement's chances of survival. In 1942, it was America that once again came to Australia's aid as the country was threatened by the advancing Japanese. The decisive battle of the Coral Sea in early May 1942 halted the Japanese advance. Nevertheless Sydney was attacked by three Midget submarines later in the month.

Part of one of the submarines can be seen at the Naval Museum on Garden Island (see p. 97), and most of another is at the Australian War Memorial in Canberra (see p. 230). The third submarine disappeared without a trace. In June 1942, Japanese submarines also fired on the Eastern Suburbs. No one was injured but property values fell, a rare occurrence in this affluent area.

POSTWAR ERA

The United States' support during World War II marked the beginning of closer relations between the two countries, and greater recognition of Australia's position in the Asia–Pacific region. The end of the war also heralded an era of mass immigration from Europe as people left the shortages and

Sydney has one of the world's most multicultural societies. Today, many Sydney children are likely to be a mixture of two or three different races.

devastation there in search of a better life. The spread of communism in Europe in the late 1940s and early 1950s added to the flow.

For Sydney, this meant a rapid growth in population and a building boom in the 1950s. Vast outer suburbs of cheaply built "fibro" houses (fibrous cement sheets nailed to wooden framing) were constructed to accommodate the thousands of people arriving every day. In the 1960s, sturdier dwellings of red brick and red tile were mass produced. The Australian dream came to be a quarter-acre block with a three-bedroom house, a dream most of the population was able to achieve, as by now unemployment was virtually nonexistent.

The downside to the dream, however, was the monotony of the suburbs; while life was generally good, it was not particularly stimulating. New arrivals from Europe may have felt they had landed in a city that at first glance resembled paradise, only to find it was a cultural wasteland. Fortunately, many brought

their culture with them. A new word entered the vocabulary: multiculturalism.

During World War II, the Korean and Vietnam Wars, and peacetime, through to the present day, U.S. warships have been visiting Sydney in quantity, their crews contributing greatly to the "worldliness" of the colorful suburbs in the vicinity of the naval base on Garden Island, just east of the Central Business District. In a sense they have maintained the regular contact between the two countries that goes back to the first trading vessel in 1792, the whaling ships of the 19th century, and the clippers bringing gold-hungry prospectors.

The end of the Vietnam War in 1975 brought another wave of immigration. Boatloads of Vietnamese refugees made their way to Australia to escape the hardships of their homeland.

SYMBOLS OF THE 20TH CENTURY

On October 20, 1973, the Sydney Opera House was officially opened on Bennelong Point. The setting is appropriate. Bennelong was one of the first Aboriginal people befriended by the settlers, so the site provides links both to Sydney's European beginnings and its indigenous culture. With the opening of the Opera House, the arts in Sydney gained a focus and a profile. Ever since, the artistic community has grown in size and confidence, to the benefit of the entire city. At the same time the Opera House has given Sydney a unique identity.

In the years since the Opera House was built, Sydney has become a financial powerhouse for its region, and a multicultural metropolis pulsating with youthful energy. It is given to bursts of extravagance that can be overwhelming at times (witness the frequency and scale of its fireworks displays and the unbridled hedonism of the Mardi Gras parades), but you can't fault the enthusiasm.

Residents have little doubt that it was no accident that Sydney was selected to host the 2000 Olympics. The modern games are a spectacular event and Sydney is a spectacular city. The two were made for each other. ■

A sculpture in Darling Harbour, with references to boomerangs and the Sydney Opera House, captures the spirit of the 2000 Olympic Games.

The arts

YOU COULD BE FORGIVEN FOR THINKING THAT, GIVEN ITS GEOGRAPHICAL distance from the major world centers of performing arts, Sydney might be rather light on live drama, opera, music, and dance. The reality, however, is very different.

For a start, Sydney is the headquarters of the National Institute of Dramatic Art (NIDA), whose alumni have included Mel Gibson, Academy Award-winner Geoffrey Rush, Cate Blanchett, and Judy Davis. It is not uncommon to catch the likes of Rush in productions by Sydney's two main theater companies—the Sydney Theatre Company (venues at the Wharf Theatre in The Rocks and the Opera House Theatre) and Company B (at its theater in Belvoir Street, Surry Hills, just south of the city).

Names visitors may not be familiar with include Richard Roxburgh (whose Hamlet was simply awesome), Jacqueline McKenzie (just as good as Ophelia in a run that was a complete sellout), Ruth Cracknell (the grand dame of Australian theater), Max Cullen, and Miranda Otto. These and many others are on a par with the big names and cover a repertoire that ranges from William Shakespeare to Tennessee Williams and Henrik Ibsen, from Anton Chekhov to contemporary Australian drama by names such as Michael Gow, Tim Winton, and David Williamson. Directors Neil Armfield and Barrie Kosky in particular enjoy pushing theater to its limits.

In the summer, keep an eye out for William Shakespeare's *A Midsummer Night's Dream,* performed outdoors in the Royal Botanic Gardens. Look, too, for the Bell Shakespeare Company, a touring company that stages productions at the Playhouse in the Opera House, the Botanic Gardens, the Wharf Theatre, and the Opera House steps.

The standard of performance in the city is helped by the focus of the Australian film industry in Sydney. The National Film Television and Radio School is based here, and Rupert Murdoch's Fox Studios operates in the former Showground near Centennial Park.

Of course, no visit to Sydney is complete without a night at the opera, or at least the Opera House. The concert halls on Bennelong Point host performances by the Sydney-based Opera Australia that range from the light works of Gilbert and Sullivan to the heavy artillery of Richard Wagner. While the opera company handles the big performances, its smaller division, Oz Opera, mounts smaller-scale productions that are easier to take on tour. Also based at the Opera House is the Sydney Symphony Orchestra (SSO), an accomplished group of musicians under the baton of Dutch conductor Edo de Waart. The youthful exuberance of the Australian Chamber Orchestra, under the young but immensely talented conductor Richard Tognetti, throws caution to the winds and excites concertgoers with its varied and innovative repertoire. Musica Viva Australia, meanwhile, is the world's largest chamber music presenter, and one that can be justifiably proud of its stable of artists. It has an extensive touring program and stages performances in Sydney year-round.

As for dance, classic ballet is well served by the Australian Ballet, which also performs at the Opera House, as does the innovative and provocative Sydney Dance Company. Both companies tour extensively.

A number of smaller organizations ensure there is a never-ending supply of stimulating performances going on around the city. Throw in blockbuster musicals, and numerous appearances by visiting performers and groups, and hardly a night passes when there isn't something worth going out for.

The busiest time of the year, however, is January, when the Sydney Festival (see p. 232) is in full swing. Free outdoor performances of opera, classical music, jazz, and country and western draw thousands of people to The Domain. Major touring companies visit, and there is a packed schedule of events.

Performances at the Bangarra Dance Theatre combine contemporary dance with traditional Torres Strait Islander dance.

ART

Australian art goes back further than the arrival of the First Fleet in Sydney. The Aborigines have inhabited Australia for over 40,000 years, and for them, artistic expression is, and was, a way of life. They painted and engraved all kinds of surfaces and used their art to convey knowledge of sacred sites and tell complex stories.

Today, Aboriginal art has become an essential element in the field of contemporary Australian art as modern artists adapt tradi-

tional painting techniques to new media, tools, and technology.

For more information on Aboriginal art and where to go in Sydney to see and buy it, see pp. 154–55.

European art

The main achievement of 200 years of European art in Australia is the appreciation for the beauty of the environment in which it is created. The dark and tormented soul of the

artist is certainly present, but on balance the great artists of Australia have concentrated on mythologizing the landscape and its people.

From the beginning of the settlement, artists documented the foundation of the colony and the country's unique flora and fauna. In so doing, they found a quality of light and texture in the landscape that challenged their traditional artistic training. The response was the evolution of a uniquely Australian approach within conventional

A brightly colored beach scene called "Leaving from Balmoral" (1998) typifies Ken Done's distinctive style.

forms, and this process of discovery is visible in practically all the large galleries in Australia.

Crucial in the development was the Heidelberg school—a circle of artists, including Tom Roberts (who toured Europe in the 1880s), Frederick McCubbin, Arthur Streeton, Charles Conder, and Hans Heysen.

They painted in the bucolic township of Heidelberg in Victoria between 1888 and 1901, bringing an impressionist's eye to the heroism of Australian life and history at a time when the country was approaching nationhood. The movement was greatly assisted by Sydney artist Julian Ashton (1851–1942), whose art school trained many of the country's artists and who helped establish the Heidelberg school's influence that is still felt today.

However, it was the work of Norman Lindsay (1876–1969), before World War I, that achieved the most notoriety, at least for a while. The combination of his nudes, which celebrated the pleasures of the flesh, and his determination broke down the barriers of a prudishness that, at the time, saw separate beaches for men and women.

Between the two World Wars, several artists were responsible for bringing contemporary art to the fore. They included the internationally recognized Australian artist Sidney Nolan (1917–1992), Albert Tucker (1914–), whose macabre, surrealist works were charged with symbolism, William Dobell (1899–1970), a student of Julian Ashton and an outstanding portrait painter, and Russell Drysdale (1912–1981), whose desolate landscapes and gaunt figures broke with the Heidelberg romanticism. They built on the Heidelberg school's interpretation of light and used surreal perspectives in a local context. In their work you can see the real Australia and its people—sunburned, withered, and yet resilient.

For postwar impressions of the Australian landscape, Frederick (Fred) Williams (1927–1982) is hard to beat. A gentle, thoughtful man, his sensitivity to the sparse vegetation of the arid interior forms an eloquent bridge to the pointillism of Aboriginal art. For sheer love of color and light, seek out Margaret Olley's (1923–) still lifes, and luxuriate in the richness of her art.

Color, light, and texture—embodied in the witty and sensuous work of Brett Whiteley (1939–1992), for example, or the populist art-on-a-T-shirt Ken Done—now form the palette of modern Australian art, where innovation continues within relatively conservative and conventional forms. The country's best known art prize, for example, the Archibald Prize, presented at the Art Gallery of New South Wales, is for portraiture. However, Victoria's Contempora 5 art prize, won recently by Fiona Hall, a talented sculptor working in many different media, bears testament to the breadth of expression to be found in Australian art.

LITERATURE

Even before the arrival of the First Fleet, the seeds of Australia's literary heritage had been sown. The plan to colonize New South Wales had provoked considerable interest and, before they set sail, several of the senior officers had signed book deals with London publishers. One of the best of these is still available in print, *1788*, by Watkin Tench (see p. 31). This is a lively and vivid account of the early years of Sydney and its environs. In the colony's second year of existence, convicts performed its first play, *The Recruiting Officer*, by Irish playwright George Farquhar (circa 1677–1707).

The first Golden Age of Australian literary life spanned the years leading to Australia's Federation, in 1901. Balladeers and storytellers Henry Lawson (1867–1922) and Banjo Paterson (also known as A.B.—Andrew Barton—Paterson, 1864–1941) were engaged in lively debate about the merits of city and country life. Ethel Turner's (1872–1958) *Seven Little Australians* was the Australian equivalent of *Little Women* by American writer Louisa May Alcott.

The richness of Sydney's poetry is embodied in the collection *Sydney's Poems*, issued in 1992 to mark the 150th anniversary of Sydney's incorporation as a city. It includes Kenneth Slessor's (1901–1971) "Five Bells," inspired by the drowning of a friend who fell off a ferry to Kirribilli on the way to a party (see p. 102).

Sydney's most famous literary figure is Patrick White (1912–1990), winner of the Nobel Prize for Literature in 1973. His works include *Voss* (set in part in Sydney and inspired by the explorer Ludwig Leichardt) and *The Tree of Man* (set on Sydney's outskirts and tracing the hardships of a family struggling to survive).

More recently, Robert Drewe's *The Bodysurfers* (published in 1983) is a collection of short stories set in Sydney and other locations that capture the hedonism and guilty pleasures of contemporary Australia. ■

The Opera House, the Royal Botanic Gardens, and the Art Gallery of New South Wales are concentrated in the east of the city. Historic buildings and museums will also show you a side of Sydney you may not have expected.

Circular Quay & east

Tapestry detail, State Library foyer

Circular Quay & east

CIRCULAR QUAY, THE MAIN FERRY TERMINAL, EFFECTIVELY ACTS AS A division between the two sides of the city. The eastern side presents Sydney's most impressive face: The Opera House, the Royal Botanic Gardens, The Domain, Macquarie Street, and Hyde Park stretch back from the harbor. There are also art galleries, cathedrals, and major museums, all on a grand scale. The gardens are among the best in the world and offer spectacular views of the harbor alongside a dazzling and beautiful range of trees and plants. In contrast, the western side, with The Rocks and the docks of Darling Harbour that once housed the convicts from England and where ships loaded or unloaded cargo, is where the daily hustle and bustle of city life takes place.

And it has always been this way. The first Government House was built on the eastern side of the city, and the Royal Botanic Gardens take in the area of the first farm in the colony, itself established on the site of an Aboriginal initiation area.

What is most remarkable is that all these points of interest are contained in an incredibly compact space. A two-hour walk can take you around all the major sights, but, as you will find, you can easily spend several days discovering what this area has to offer. ■

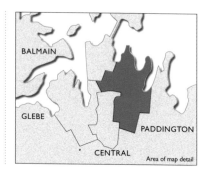

Circular Quay is Sydney's historic heart: It was here that the First Fleet dropped anchor in 1788. Today, the quay is more angular than circular, but it remains the center of daily life.

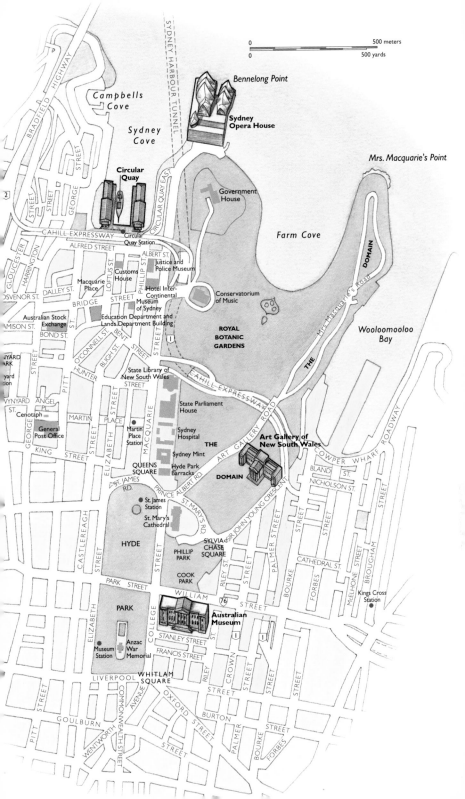

0   500 meters

0   500 yards

Bennelong Point

Sydney Opera House

Campbells Cove

Sydney Cove

Mrs. Macquarie's Point

Circular Quay

Government House

Farm Cove

CAHILL EXPRESSWAY

Circular Quay Station

ALFRED STREET

THE DOMAIN

CIRCULAR QUAY EAST

SYDNEY HARBOUR TUNNEL

BRADFIELD HIGHWAY

GEORGE STREET

GLOUCESTER STREET

HARRINGTON STREET

2

ALBERT ST.

Justice and Police Museum

Customs House

Macquarie Place

Museum of Sydney

Hotel Inter-Continental

Wooloomooloo Bay

GROSVENOR ST.

DALLEY ST.

LOFTUS ST.

PHILLIP ST.

BRIDGE STREET

Australian Stock Exchange

Education Department and Lands Department Building

JAMISON ST.

BOND ST.

Conservatorium of Music

ROYAL BOTANIC GARDENS

O'CONNELL ST.

BLIGH ST.

BENT STREET

HUNTER STREET

PITT STREET

WYNYARD PARK

State Library of New South Wales

THE DOMAIN

MRS. MACQUARIE'S ROAD

CAHILL EXPRESSWAY

VYNYARD STATION

ANGEL PL.

MARTIN PLACE

State Parliament House

Sydney Hospital

Sydney Mint

Hyde Park Barracks

Art Gallery of New South Wales

Cenotaph

General Post Office

Martin Place Station

ELIZABETH STREET

MACQUARIE STREET

THE DOMAIN

ART GALLERY ROAD

GEORGE STREET

KING STREET

QUEENS SQUARE

St. James Station

St. Mary's Cathedral

ST. JAMES RD.

PRINCE ALBERT RD.

ST. MARY'S RD.

SIR JOHN YOUNG CRESCENT

COWPER WHARF ROADWAY

BLAND ST.

NICHOLSON ST.

CASTLEREAGH STREET

HYDE

SYLVIA CHASE SQUARE

PHILLIP PARK

COOK PARK

RILEY ST.

PALMER STREET

BOURKE STREET

FORBES STREET

CATHEDRAL ST.

MEEHONE STREET

BROUGHAM STREET

Kings Cross Station

PARK STREET

WILLIAM STREET

76

Australian Museum

PARK

COLLEGE STREET

Anzac War Memorial

Museum Station

ELIZABETH STREET

STANLEY STREET

FRANCIS STREET

CROWN STREET

RILEY STREET

BOURKE STREET

FORBES STREET

WHITLAM SQUARE

LIVERPOOL STREET

GOULBURN STREET

PITT STREET

WENTWORTH AVENUE

COMMONWEALTH STREET

OXFORD STREET

BURTON STREET

PALMER STREET

BOURKE STREET

The Opera House complex is housed under three "sails": Bennelong Restaurant (left), the Concert Hall (center), and the Opera Theatre (right).

Sydney Opera House

IT IS AS MUCH A WORK OF ART AS A BUILDING. CERTAINLY it is one of the greatest architectural statements of the 20th century, not only the hub of the artistic life of the city, but an expression of its very soul. One million Swedish ceramic tiles form the seamed pattern covering the distinctive "sails," or "shells," and from a distance the building appears to be voyaging on the harbor water.

Sydney Opera House

- ⬛ Map p. 43
- ✉ Bennelong Point
- ☎ 9250 7111, 9250 7777 (box office)
  www.soh.nsw.gov.au
- 💲 $–$$$

Construction commenced in 1959 and was expected to take three to four years to complete, at a cost of seven million dollars. However, things didn't go quite to plan and the building was opened in 1973 by Queen Elizabeth II at a final cost of 102 million dollars. Along the way

Danish architect Jørn Utzon (who had won the competition to design the building in 1957) resigned in the face of constant pressure from engineers, builders, and governments who were becoming increasingly concerned at the cost. Utzon left Australia and has never

returned to see the completed building, although he did accept the keys to the city in 1998.

The Opera House actually consists of three separate buildings—the **Opera Theatre,** fully rigged under the sails on the eastern side; the **Concert Hall** in the sails on the western side; and the much vaunted **Bennelong Restaurant** on the city (southern) side. These accommodate a complex of theaters, performance spaces, restaurants, and cafés. Other smaller restaurants and cafés extend around the western side to the Harbour Restaurant facing Kirribilli to the north. Each year nearly 3,000 performances are staged in the com-

plex, making it one of the busiest arts centers in the world.

If visiting the Opera House during the day, you'll find that most of the interiors are closed and to see them you will need to follow a guided tour. However, take a walk around the base of the building along the eastern and western sides and you'll come across stairs ascending the exterior of the building. These take you up to balconies on the front of the Concert Hall and Opera Theatre sails, with good views of the harbor.

To glimpse some of the interiors, from the land side of the buildings, ascend the Monumental Steps and look into the main foyers of

EARLY TRAGEDY

During the building's construction money was raised to cover the shortfall by holding lotteries (first prize was U.S.$160,000). Graeme Thorne, the eight-year-old son of one of the lottery winners, was kidnapped after the news of his family's good fortune became public. He disappeared on July 7, and was found, murdered, on August 16 after a ransom was paid. ■

both buildings with their massive concrete arches disappearing into the void above.

If attending a performance in the Concert Hall, note the 18 large acoustic discs suspended above the stage and the elaborate Australian wood paneling.

During an intermission in performances in the Concert Hall or Opera Theatre, head up to the northern foyers of both buildings. Refreshments are available here,

but the main attraction is the view through the massive glass panes under the sails. It feels like you're on the bridge of a large ship, which is exactly what Utzon intended.

In January, during the Sydney Festival (see p. 232), free performances are often held on the Monumental Steps. Arrive early and bring a cushion and a sun umbrella, because the events are very popular and the steps and setting sun can be uncomfortable. ■

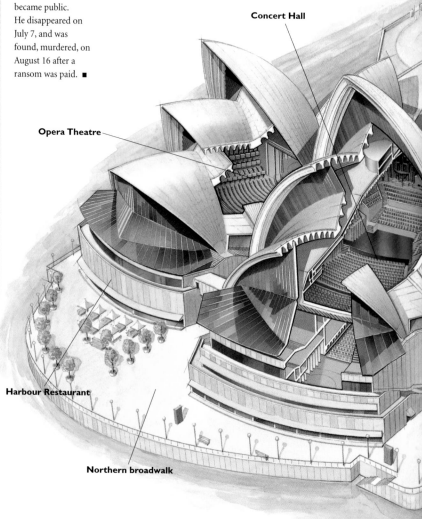

Concert Hall

Opera Theatre

Harbour Restaurant

Northern broadwalk

Opera House Tours

Tours depart regularly from 9 a.m.–4 p.m., from the tours office on the lower level of the Circular Quay concourse. Tours of the backstage area are intermittent, but generally take place on Sun.

$$

Monumental Steps

Bennelong Restaurant

Playhouse

Western broadwalk

Set on the eastern side of Sydney Cove, the Opera House is one of the greatest 20th-century buildings.

The Opera House dominates the view as visitors idle in cafés lining the Circular Quay promenade.

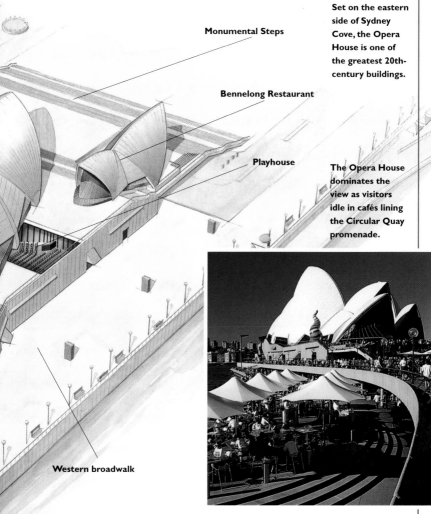

Around Circular Quay

Justice and Police Museum
- 🏛 Map p. 43
- ✉ 1 Albert St.
- ☎ 9252 1144
- www.hht.nsw.gov.au
- 🕐 Closed Mon.–Fri. Feb.–Dec.
- 💲 $

Museum of Sydney
- 🏛 Map p. 43
- ✉ Corner of Bridge & Phillip Sts.
- ☎ 9251 5988
- www.mos.nsw.gov.au
- 💲 $

AT FIRST SIGHT, THE AREA DIRECTLY BEHIND CIRCULAR Quay may appear to be nothing but a concrete jungle, but in fact it is sprinkled with a number of gems that you can explore in as little as two hours or a leisurely day. On the walkway leading to the Opera House, notice the metal plates set into the ground. This is Writers' Walk, commemorating the writings of famous authors, poets, and playwrights who have either visited the city or lived in it.

Behind Circular Quay is the **Customs House** (*Alfred St.*), an imposing structure begun in the 1840s and continually added to until 1917. It now houses cafés, shops, and art exhibitions. Look right and you'll see on the building's western side a Union flag marking the spot where it is believed the English flag was first raised in the settlement.

A block to the east, on the left as you face the Customs House, is the **Justice and Police Museum.** Housed in an attractive collection of buildings that includes the Water Police Court (1856), the museum explores the colorful interaction between the constabulary and wrongdoers throughout Sydney and New South Wales.

The 19th-century Lands Department Building, on Bridge Street, is adorned with particularly beautiful sculptures around the entrances.

Street entertainers perform on the broadwalk of Sydney Cove, with the city in the background. Cruises and ferry services depart from here to all points around the harbor.

Walk a block back from the harbor to the **Museum of Sydney** (MOS), opened in May 1995. The museum is justifiably proud of the fact that it is part of the city's history, built on the site of the first Government House (1788) in the colony. Initially a prefabricated house, the foundations of a later, more permanent Government House (demolished in 1846) are still visible through glass panels in the museum floor. It was the scene of the Rum Rebellion (see p. 28). Themed areas illustrating the history of the city from 1788 to 1850 include the "Environment," "Eora" (the indigenous people of the Sydney area), "Colony" (the first settlement), "Trade" (looking at the commodities that contributed to

Sydney's wealth), and the "Bond store" (an area where stories are told). A must-see can be found on all three levels. When you open the drawers of the "Collectors Chest" you are taken on a journey via images, objects, and text that reflects Sydney's past.

Going west from the museum along Bridge Street, you'll find **Macquarie Place,** yet another of the places the pivotal if egotistical Gov. Lachlan Macquarie named after himself. On Bridge Street, take a moment to admire two buildings on the left: the Education Department (1913) and the Lands Department Building (1876–1890) designed by James Barnet (colonial architect). Here the statues in the porticoes commemorate famous

The Museum of Sydney preserves the foundations of the first Government House and relics recovered from sites around the city.

Australian explorers and legislators. The empty spaces await future luminaries. Macquarie Place, a popular spot for workers to have lunch, has an anchor and cannon from the First Fleet's flagship, H.M.A.S. *Sirius*. In one corner of the postage-stamp-size park is a Francis Greenway-designed obelisk, erected in 1818. It is the point from which road distances to the rest of Australia are measured.

Follow Bridge Street across to Pitt Street and you'll be standing above the **Tank Stream,** a watercourse that once supplied the original colony with water and now runs underground into Sydney Cove. Bridge Street was so named because it was the site of the first bridge in

Inside the ultra-modern Museum of Sydney, a young visitor peers into a drawer of the Collectors Chest to learn about Sydney's history.

the colony, built in 1788 across the mudflats. Along Pitt Street, you'll pass the **Australian Stock Exchange.** Visitors are welcome during business hours and lectures on investment are frequently held for the public.

MARTIN PLACE

Continue two blocks along Pitt Street, away from the harbor. This takes you through the financial section of the Central Business District to Martin Place. Here you'll find the old **General Post Office,** which caused as much controversy over its cost in the 1880s as the Opera House did nearly a hundred years later. Designed by James Barnet, the building was begun in 1866 and completed in 1887, in time for the colony's centenary in 1888. The 200-foot (61-m) clock tower, dismantled in 1942 because of fears it would be used as a navigation aid by Japanese bombers, was rebuilt

after the war. Martin Place is also the site of the **Cenotaph,** where the memories of those lost in war are honored on Anzac Day (April 25) and Remembrance Day (November 11). ∎

Queen Victoria sits proud on the sandstone facade of the General Post Office.

Seahorses

Among the exotic creatures that abound in and around Sydney, one of the most beautiful is the seahorse (*Hippocampus whitei*), which lives in seagrass beds in the many small bays of the harbor. However, they are usually incredibly well camouflaged.

One place where seahorses of a different kind can be easily spotted is Circular Quay. Here ornamental seahorses decorate the railings at the water's edge, and you'll also find some in sculptures in the entrance to the Circular Quay Station. ∎

Royal Botanic Gardens

AFTER VISITING THE OPERA HOUSE, CONSIDER TAKING A look at the Royal Botanic Gardens that sweep around the bay of Farm Cove to the east. Apart from the 7,500 species of trees and plants, there are several food outlets ranging from a kiosk to the well-established and very satisfying Botanic Gardens Restaurant. The balcony is a lovely spot for a post-visit lunch.

Royal Botanic Gardens

Map p. 43

Mrs. Macquarie's Rd.

9231 8125

Government House

Map p. 43

Royal Botanic Gardens

9931 5222

Closed Mon.–Thurs.

The 75-acre (30-ha) gardens, the oldest scientific institution in the country, were established in 1816 by Governor Macquarie on the site of the first farm in the colony. With the harbor as a backdrop, stunning examples of the flora of Sydney and the surrounding region are set against enchanting views of the Opera House, the city, and the water. Numerous sculptures enhance the ambience.

On summer evenings outdoor performances of William Shakespeare's *A Midsummer Night's Dream* (*information and tickets available at the botanic gardens shop*) attract audiences who bring champagne picnics with them.

A special feature of the gardens is the **Sydney Tropical Centre,** which consists of two glasshouses, the Pyramid and the Arc. These maintain the humidity and warmth necessary to nurture tropical and native vegetation. At times the automatic shutters are wide open, which says quite a bit about Sydney's summer.

The **Rose Garden** is full of a mixture of old-fashioned roses and more modern, distinctive varieties. Sadly, you can't take any with you, but there is a section in the Herb

The Sydney Tropical Centre in the Royal Botanic Gardens protects rare ferns, palms, and orchids in the high-tech Pyramid and Arc glasshouses.

Garden where you can rub, pick, and taste to your heart's content. The garden has a fascinating range of herbs and gives details of their medicinal or culinary uses.

The **Succulent Garden** is a walled-in section with a selection of dry-climate plants from around the world, with an emphasis on Australian flora.

Other sections of the gardens to explore include the **National Herbarium of New South Wales,** established in 1985, which has some of the dried specimens collected by Joseph Banks during Cook's visit to Botany Bay in 1770.

A visitor information center and shop provides leaflets detailing walks and features of the gardens. Free guided walks leave the center at 10:30 a.m. and a "train" runs around the gardens.

GOVERNMENT HOUSE

In the gardens just south of the Opera House is Government House, formerly the official residence of the governor of New South Wales. Designed by Edward Blore (1787–1879), architect to England's King William IV and Queen Victoria, it was constructed between 1837 and 1845 in the Gothic Revival style. It replaced the original Government House whose foundations can be seen at the Museum of Sydney (see p. 49).

Far grander are the stables (situated on the approach road from Conservatorium Road) designed by Francis Greenway. They were the cause of controversy when Commissioner J.T. Bigge arrived in 1819 to examine Macquarie's spending and questioned the construction of "such a palace for horses." The stable buildings now house the **Conservatorium of Music** (*Tel 9351 1263*), a music school. Lunchtime concerts are held on an irregular basis. ■

Wollemi pine

One of the most prized specimens in the gardens is found in the **Rare and Threatened Plants Garden,** which was opened in 1998 near the visitor information center. Referred to as the Jurassic Tree because it is related to trees from that period, the Wollemi pine was thought to have been extinct until 1994, when it was discovered by a national parks ranger, David Noble, hiking in the rugged Wollemi National Park near the northern extremity of the city. The director of the Royal Botanic Gardens at the time, Professor Carrick Chambers, compared the discovery to finding a "small dinosaur still alive on earth."

There are thought to be only 39 mature trees—each up to 129 feet (40 m) tall—in Wollemi National Park (the exact location is kept secret), but propagation has ensured that the dangers of flood and bush fire will not mean the loss of the species. ■

The Domain

It's grand to be an unemployed and lie in The Domain
And wake up every second day
And go to sleep again.
—Banjo Paterson, *It's Grand* (1902)

Pass through it at the wrong time of the year, though, or even the wrong time of day, and The Domain doesn't look like much at all. It's just a big field. However, the fact is that since the city's early days, The Domain has been, well, special.

The Domain
 Map p. 43

At certain times, up to a quarter of a million people can throng this field—attending a massive open-air concert as part of the annual Sydney Festival (*Tel 8248 6500;* see p. 232), for example. People have gathered here since the area was made part of the "public domain" in 1810.

Originally it was fenced in (you can still see the gates, dating from 1817, which flank the road on the southern side) and was open during daylight hours only. Since 1860 it has remained open 24 hours a day, at times serving as a resting place for the destitute, as Banjo Paterson attests. The Domain was

also the venue for cricket matches once nearby Hyde Park became too congested.

It was and still is a venue for rallies, protests, and public meetings that have shaped the future of the city and the nation. On Sundays it is a "speakers' corner," with pundits declaiming from boxes.

At lunchtime, The Domain is very much alive with soccer players and joggers. In December and January, the park becomes one of the major venues for Christmas and New Year's celebrations. Carols are sung by candlelight in late December; and in January, every Saturday, jazz, country and western, pop, classical, and opera concerts are staged—all free. Giant video screens and an all-encompassing sound system ensure everyone can see and hear the performances. A highlight of the classical music concert is Ilyich Tchaikovsky's (1840–1893) *1812 Overture*, complete with cannon fire, fireworks, and the sound of the bells of St. Mary's Cathedral on nearby College Street. However, it is the pleasure of an evening of entertainment under the stars that is the main attraction. As Dorothea Mackellar wrote in a poem about a group of children from Woolloomooloo she had seen in The Domain:

Elf light, owl light;
Elfin green sky;
Under the fruit trees, bats flit by.
—*Sydney's Poems* (1919)

It's still like that. ■

Art Gallery of New South Wales

ESTABLISHED IN 1874, THE GALLERY HAS ONE OF THE premier art collections in the country. Its emphasis, as you would expect, is on Australian art, from all periods, but there are also notable pieces of Impressionist and Asian art—a legacy of the local Asian community and generous Asian patrons who have close business relationships with Australia.

An elaborately decorated ritual vessel, dating from the Zhou dynasty, is displayed in the gallery's Asian collection.

The Australian art includes the exceptional Yiribana Aboriginal and Torres Strait Islander Gallery (see p. 157) on level 1, opened in 1994. Exhibitions from overseas galleries are also mounted, many involving the cream of the art world, and others present retrospectives by local artists. Annually, entries in three of Australia's leading art prizes—the Archibald (Jules François Archibald, 1856–1919) for portraiture, the Wynne (Richard Wynne, died 1895) for landscape, and the Sulman (Sir John Sulman, 1849–1934) for watercolor—are displayed and judged, often controversially.

Designed by colonial architect W.L. Vernon, the gallery (extended in 1988) is built on a hillside. The collections are spread over five levels, ascending and descending from level 4. Guides to the gallery can be obtained from the visitor information desk here. Level 5 contains the photography exhibitions.

LEVEL 4

The entrance to the building is on this level, and what an entry it is. Take a moment to admire the grand ceiling before moving on to the 19th-century European and Australian art gallery and the 20th-century Australian collection. You'll also find the gallery gift shop and temporary exhibition spaces on this level. Ask at the main information desk for details of talks and visiting exhibitions.

The 19th-century European Gallery is small, but it contains many outstanding pieces of art. Those of particular interest are Rex Whistler's "Nocturne in Grey and Silver," and works by several of the Impressionists, including Camille Pissarro, Claude Monet, and Henri Toulouse-Lautrec.

From here you can walk straight through to the 19th-century Australian Gallery, which presents some of the most revered works in the country. One of the must-sees is Elioth Gruner's "Spring Frost," which won the Wynne prize in 1919.

Another work not to miss is Charles Meere's "Australian Beach Pattern" (1940), which is reproduced on the cover of Robert Drewe's *The Bodysurfers* (see p. 40).

Art Gallery of New South Wales
- Map p. 43
- Art Gallery Rd., The Domain
- 9225 1744
- www.artgallery.nsw.gov.au
- Sydney Explorer, Martin Place Station

Opposite: Henry Moore's sculpture "Reclining Figure, Angles" (1980), outside the Art Gallery of New South Wales

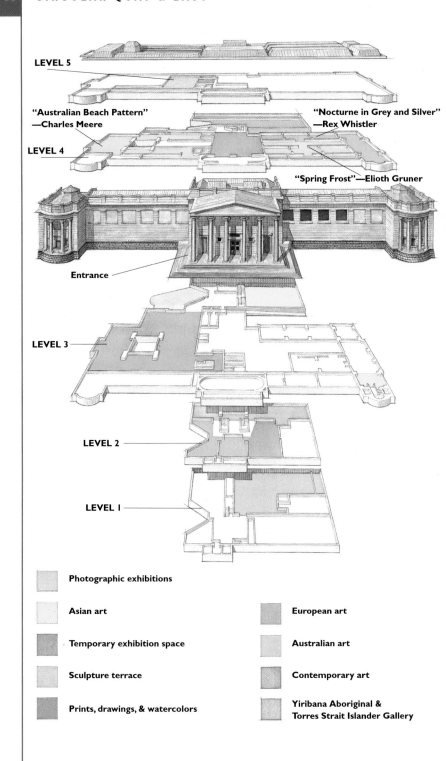

LEVEL 5

"Australian Beach Pattern"
—Charles Meere

"Nocturne in Grey and Silver"
—Rex Whistler

LEVEL 4

"Spring Frost"—Elioth Gruner

Entrance

LEVEL 3

LEVEL 2

LEVEL 1

- Photographic exhibitions
- Asian art
- Temporary exhibition space
- Sculpture terrace
- Prints, drawings, & watercolors
- European art
- Australian art
- Contemporary art
- Yiribana Aboriginal & Torres Strait Islander Gallery

LEVEL 3

Head down the escalators and you'll be among the Asian and Melanesian collections. The Asian collection, comprising art, sculpture, tapestries, and pottery, is well worth a visit. There are exquisite pieces from across Southeast Asia, China, and Japan. You'll find Indian sculptures dating from the 5th century and Japanese sculpture from the 12th century. As you walk round the gallery the objects get much older. The Tang tomb guardian figures are youthful 7th-century works, whereas the Han figures date from the second century. Don't miss the ceremonial vases from the Zhou dynasty (1000 B.C.–700 B.C.) and pottery disks from the Shang dynasty (2200 B.C.–1700 B.C.).

At this point you may be tempted by the café on this level with its harbor views and outdoor seating. For a full restaurant meal, go to level 5 where modern Australian cuisine is served.

LEVEL 2

Much of the exhibition space on this level is devoted to temporary exhibitions (usually of contemporary art). The more permanent areas concentrate on late 19th- and 20th-century British and European art. Examples of the gallery's collection of works by Bacon, Braque, Degas, Magritte, Picasso, Renoir, and others are usually on display. Exhibitions of prints, drawings, and watercolors are also held in this area. ■

"Spring Frost" by Elioth Gruner (1882–1939) won national recognition with a major award in 1919. The painting is commonly known as "The Cows."

A large Buddha figure by an unknown artist is sculpted in marble and stands just over six and a half feet tall (2 m).

Artists' views of Sydney Harbour

When the First Fleet sailed into Sydney Harbour, painters were on board ready to record one of the most momentous events in English history. They started a documentary process that has continued in Australian art for more than 200 years. Charles Gore, for example, recorded the fleet entering Botany Bay in 1788, and a watercolor by William Bradley, first lieutenant aboard the *Sirius*, shows the fleet entering Port Jackson. Other works from the same year show plans of the settlement by John Hunter and William Dawes.

You can see these and other representations of the harbor at the State Library of New South Wales (see p. 68) and Art Gallery of New South Wales (see pp. 56–59). If you tour through the galleries of 19th- and 20th-century art, you can trace the development of the city and the harbor through the eyes of some of Australia's best known artists.

In 1865, Eugène Von Guérard (1811–1901) painted "Sydney Heads," a luminous work whose setting (although considerably changed) is partly visible from the gallery itself. Two works from 1888 reveal a quite different view of the city; that of a busy working port. Charles Conder (1868–1909) painted "Departure of the Orient, Circular Quay," which shows the arrival of the steam age and the area where the Opera House is now located, while Tom Roberts (1856–1931) painted "Autumn Morning, Milsons Point," with the mist punctuated by the comings and goings of passenger ferries.

Heidelberg school

Near these two works are some of the best known paintings by artists of the Heidelberg school, a group of painters who had a major influence on Australian art (see pp. 39–40). The painting directly above the Tom Roberts is by Arthur Streeton; it depicts the countryside of Heidelberg. Another Streeton in the gallery, "Cremorne Pastoral," painted in 1895, reflects the school's interest in romanticizing and mythologizing the Australian landscape, but in a harborside context.

While walking from one room to the other, you can see both the changes in the harbor and in painting styles during the intervening years. A similar leap is made from the 19th to the 20th century. In the 20th-century gallery, the work of Roland Wakelin in "Down the Hill to Berry's Bay" (1916) and Grace Cossington Smith's muscular "The Bridge in Curve" (1928–29) show the strong influence of Impressionism. Cossington Smith's work, painted while the bridge was under construction, again captures the changing face of the harbor. From the same period, the work of Margaret Preston (1875–1963) shows the harbor as it is more often seen—fringed with the leaves of Moreton Bay figs or eucalyptuses, providing shadowy glimpses of water at dawn and dusk. The gallery also has several works by Lloyd Rees, one of the most eloquent and gifted of Australia's artists, including "City Skyline" (1935) and "Sydney Harbour" (1936), which show the harbor almost as French artist Paul Cézanne might have painted it. They provide a marked contrast with Rees's work from 1950, "The Harbour From McMahon's Point."

Also worth seeking out is Rees's "Yachts on Lane Cove River," which is more in keeping with his romantic vision of the harbor. Two other names that are closely linked with the harbor (but more often seen in temporary exhibitions) are Margaret Olley and Brett Whiteley. Olley's canvases luxuriate in color, the harbor providing a backdrop for her still lifes. Whiteley's interpretation of the harbor can be described in one word—blue. And what a blue. Typically, he paints the view from the window of his onetime studio/home in North Sydney, and it is well worth visiting his final studio in nearby Raper Street, Surry Hills (see p. 139). Among the works you'll find there is "Self Portrait In The Studio" (1976). Here, in terms of documenting Sydney Harbour, Whiteley carries on the tradition begun by the First Fleeters. In the top left-hand corner of the painting there is a glimpse of one of the harbor's latest additions, the Opera House. ∎

You can see Grace Cossington Smith's distinctive use of square brush strokes and radiant color in "The Bridge in Curve," depicting the construction of Sydney Harbour Bridge.

Eugène Von Guérard's "Sydney Heads," painted in 1865, shows a rural scene where Sydney's affluent suburbs now exist. Vaucluse House is center right.

Behind the facade
of the Australian
Museum is a mod-
ern building that
cleverly preserves
much of the orig-
inal structure—it's
almost a museum
within a museum.

Australian Museum

THE AUSTRALIAN MUSEUM HAS BEEN COLLECTING specimens of the natural and indigenous history of Australia since 1827. The first buildings were erected in the 1840s, although the present edifice on College Street wasn't completed until 1868. This was the first project to be undertaken in New South Wales by government architect James Barnet, although the original plan was for a much grander structure, one to rival that of the British Museum in London. It was to include an art gallery and library, but in fact these were built on Macquarie Street and Art Gallery Road, not as part of the museum as Barnet hoped.

Australian Museum

- Map p. 43
- 6 College St.
- 9320 6000
- www.austmus.gov.au
- $
- Museum Station

The museum has changed considerably since its inception when it largely consisted of rows of glass cases. These days it is much more stimulating and features many hands-on exhibits. The museum's major emphasis is on indigenous culture, ranging from spirituality and cultural heritage to themes of social justice (see p. 157).

Regular major exhibitions are staged, including dinosaurs, spiders, insects, and Egyptian antiquities, often presented with incredible giant-scale animatronic displays.

LEVEL G

The skeletons section here provides a fascinating look at the skeletal systems of a wide range of creatures, including humans. You can see exhibits of kangaroos and koalas, plus crocodiles, elephants, lions, giraffes, fish, snakes, and whales. A skeletal rider on a rearing horse is called the Bone Ranger, and a cycle machine with a skeleton shows how your bones move when you pedal.

In addition, there is a café and a comprehensive book and gift shop here selling Aboriginal publications and artifacts. Both café and shop can be visited without having to pay an entrance fee to the museum.

LEVEL 1

Above the skeletons are the **Planet of Minerals** and the **Chapman Mineral Collection.** This hall illuminates the vast wealth of minerals that have been found at numerous sites across Australia. Of particular interest are the reproductions of some of the enormous nuggets that have been found at Australian goldfields.

The Chapman Collection is the bequest of Albert Chapman (1912–1996), a local builder and mineral hobbyist, who built an impressive collection of over 800 pieces of the most beautiful crystals to be found anywhere in the world, then gave it to the Australian public.

LEVEL 2

Directly above the Planet of Minerals is the **Bird and Insect Hall,** with particular emphasis on the wide range of species to be found across Australia. Just outside the hall is **Search and Discover,** an area that allows you to scroll through the museum's computer databases, CD-ROMs, books, magazines, and many specimens that can be handled, looked at through microscopes, and generally experienced at close range. Access to the Internet is free.

Also on level 2 is the popular **More than Dinosaurs.** This includes an impressive, three-minute audiovisual display on the creation of life, and numerous fossils of some of the earliest lifeforms. Look out for examples of Australia's megafauna—giant kangaroos, giant wombats, and emus. Also on display is Eric, the opalized plesiosaur. When Eric was found he was in danger of being sold to overseas collectors, but a public appeal

raised enough money to keep him in Australia.

In the human evolution section, fossils and displays illustrate man's development. They show the progressive increase in the size of the brain, the development of the hand, early lifestyles, and some of our early predators.

The newest section on level 2 is **Biodiversity,** an extensive section looking at the incredibly rich range of life that exists in the many ecosystems of the Australian continent—deserts, reefs, rain forests, and more. Using videos, displays, and hands-on exhibits, the environment is presented in a stimulating and challenging format.

As if this isn't enough, level 2 has an exhibition hall that presents the country's culture, history, and centuries-old trading relationship with Indonesia.

LEVELS 3 & 4

Level 3 is devoted to the museum's research library, which is open to the public, and level 4 houses the Museum Society. ■

Visitors to the Australian Museum are treated to some impressive displays of indigenous artifacts.

A walk from Hyde Park to Circular Quay

This is one of Sydney's best walks, taking in the grand central boulevard of Hyde Park, the historic buildings of Macquarie Street, and the Art Gallery of New South Wales. Finally, the harbor esplanade winds through the Royal Botanic Gardens to Sydney Opera House. And it's all downhill.

From behind Museum Station in **Hyde Park,** walk to the 98-foot (30-m) art deco **Anzac War Memorial ❶,** erected in 1934 to commemorate those who died in World War I. Inside is a photographic exhibition of the war.

The Pool of Reflection next to the memorial is usually used as a birdbath by seagulls, Pacific or black ducks, ibis, and water hens. Hyde Park was the city's first public space and Australia's first recorded cricket matches were played here in 1804. The matches subsequently moved to The Domain (see pp. 54–55) when space in the park became restricted.

From the memorial, amble north along the park's central avenue and cross Park Street. On the right, a wisteria grove in the **Sandringham Memorial Garden ❷** provides a heady perfume in the summer months. The gardens were opened in 1954 by Queen Elizabeth II in memory of King George V and King George VI.

Return to the central avenue and continue northward to arrive at the **Archibald Fountain ❸,** which dates from 1932. J.F. Archibald founded the *Bulletin* magazine (Australia's version of *Time*) and established the Archibald Prize for portraiture in 1920. Just west of the fountain on the city (left) side is a giant outdoor chess set, generally in use every lunchtime during the week. The central avenue is lit up with fairy lights at night and visitors may spy possums scurrying across the lawns after dusk falls.

On College Street, which runs parallel to the central path on the east side of the park, is **St. Mary's Cathedral** (*Corner of College and Cathedral Sts., Tel 922 0400*). Free tours on Sundays at noon include the extraordinary mosaic floor of the cathedral's crypt. It took dedicated local artisans, the Melocco brothers, 16 years (1930–1946) to complete. They also created the floor of the Mitchell and Dixson Libraries foyer within the State Library of

N.S.W. (see p. 68), farther along Macquarie Street, and the State Theatre foyer. Also on College Street is the **Australian Museum** (see pp. 62–63).

At the northern end of the park's central avenue, enter Macquarie Street, with statues of Queen Victoria and her husband, Prince Albert, on the left and right respectively. Francis Greenway's **St. James Church** (1822) is on the left, and his **Hyde Park Barracks** (see p. 66) are on the right. **Sydney Mint** (see p. 68), next door to the barracks, now houses the offices of the Historic Houses Trust.

Next to Sydney Mint is the **Sydney Hospital ❹.** Outside is "Il Porcellino," a reproduction of the boar in Florence's market, Mercato Nuovo; it was donated to Sydney by a family of Italian surgeons who worked in the city. The bronze animal has a shiny nose that people rub for luck…well, it's worth a try.

The hospital itself has a beautiful central courtyard and fountain overlooked by the Nightingale Wing (1869), built to house Australia's first professional nurses.

Continue through the hospital courtyard into **The Domain,** or walk to the end of the block to visit the other Macquarie Street buildings (see pp. 66–68) and continue around the State Library of N.S.W. to the northern end of The Domain. Cross The Domain to the **Art Gallery of New South Wales** (see pp. 56–59) on the east side, then follow the path to the left over the Cahill Expressway into the **Royal Botanic Gardens** (see pp. 52–53).

Keep to the path to the right, overlooking the water, to reach the **Andrew (Boy) Charlton Pool ❺.** Charlton, a revered champion swimmer, was a gold medalist in the 1,500 meters race of the 1924 Paris Olympics.

From the pool the path leads northward to the water's edge to **Mrs. Macquarie's**

Chair **6**, a large seat carved out of the rock for the governor's wife, Elizabeth. Follow the path around the grand sweep of Farm Cove, exit through the gates of the botanic gardens, and carry on around the base of **Sydney Opera House 7** (see pp. 44–47).

Westward, at 1 Circular Quay East (*Tel 9247 2937*), you can get a plate of oysters and a glass of champagne or orange juice at the Sydney Cove Oyster Bar.

The walk concludes at the bus, train, ferry, and taxi terminus of Circular Quay. ■

⚏	Inside front cover C2
▶	Museum Station, Hyde Park
⟳	3 miles (5 km)
⏱	Allow 2 hours to half a day
▶	Circular Quay

NOT TO BE MISSED
- Anzac War Memorial
- St. Mary's Cathedral
- Sydney Hospital

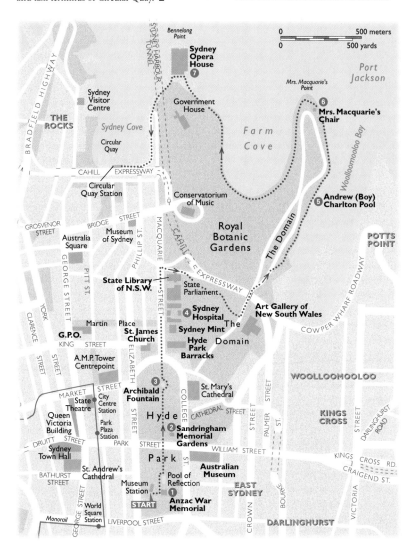

More places to visit around Circular Quay

HYDE PARK BARRACKS

A museum since 1979, the Hyde Park Barracks were built in 1819 to house the city's male convicts. Between 1848 and 1886, they became an immigration depot for single women, and the hammocks were replaced with iron beds. Destitute elderly women were cared for in the upper story. The barracks' surrounding buildings were variously used as the Government Printer, the Vaccine Institute, District Courts, and the headquarters of the N.S.W. Volunteer Rifles. From 1887 until 1979, they housed courtroom facilities and numerous government departments.

Today, you can see galleries devoted to Francis Greenway, who designed the buildings, and learn the history of the barracks. A display case with rats in it provides atmosphere, and members of the public can spend the night convict-style in a dormitory complete with hammock (*inquire of the staff*).
🅰 Map p. 43 ✉ Queens Sq., Macquarie St. ☎ 9223 8922 💲 $

MACQUARIE STREET

This is very much the "Establishment" street of Sydney, with Government House and the Conservatorium of Music (see p. 53) off to the east at the northern end, and government buildings, State Parliament House, the State Library of New South Wales, Sydney Hospital, and several other historic buildings at the southern end.

The second set of gates to the Royal Botanic Gardens, down Macquarie Street from the library, recall the Garden Palace, an imposing glass-and-timber building that rivaled the Queen Victoria Building when it was built in 1879. Dramatically, it burned down in 1882, three years after its completion.

Across the road from the gates are several noteworthy buildings. The **British Medical Association House** at Nos. 135–137 stands out. Built in 1929, it features griffins, shield-bearing lions, and knights guarding the top of the building. Next door, at No. 133, is **History House,** the home of the Royal Australian Historical Society. It is part of a row of grand terraced houses that used to grace Macquarie Street, now one of the few remaining Victorian terraces in the Central Business District. History House was completed in 1872 and is now used both as a functions and meetings center and a headquarters for the historical society. A reference library, which the public is welcome to use, includes records of convict transportation. Helpful staff is ready to assist and provide details of the society's program of lectures.

At the corner of Bridge and Macquarie Streets are two of the city's most impressive buildings. Take awhile to admire the statuary and stone carving on the former Colonial Secretary's Building, now the **Public Works Ministers Office.** Dating from the 1870s, it was designed by colonial architect James Barnet. The Museum of Sydney (see p. 49) is just behind.

On the opposite corner of Bridge Street from the works office building, the **Hotel Inter-Continental** (*117 Macquarie St., Tel 9230 0200*) rises above the facade of the former Treasury Building, completed in 1851 and designed by colonial architect Mortimer Lewis (1796–1879). Constructed on a slightly less imposing scale than the works office, it nevertheless incorporates some fine stonework on the front facade. Inside is a large atrium with a café, and of course the entrance to the hotel, which has splendid views of the Royal

"Il Porcellino," outside the Sydney Hospital on Macquarie Street, is a replica of the original in Florence—right down to the shiny nose.

Right: The courtyard within Sydney Hospital contains an art deco fountain (1907), incongruously sited against the classical revival style of the building.

Botanic Gardens and harbor. There is an interesting connection between this building and the birth of Australian viticulture (see p. 206). From the hotel, it is a short stroll downhill to Circular Quay.

RUM HOSPITAL

The buildings next door to the barracks, comprising **Sydney Mint, Sydney Hospital,** and the **State Parliament,** were originally all part of what was known as the Rum Hospital (built 1810–16). It was financed by Macquarie giving the builders a monopoly on the lucrative rum trade in the colony, a move that made the governor very unpopular. However, Macquarie silenced his critics when he revealed the government had ended up profiting on the deal to the tune of about U.S.$11,000.

Sydney Mint is now in the hands of the Historic Houses Trust, but in the 1850s it was used to process bullion from the

A typical 17th-century sailing vessel is illustrated in a marble and terrazzo mosaic on the floor of the Mitchell Library. The mosaic reproduces the original Tasman Map of 1644, also held in the library.

Australian goldfields.

Sydney Hospital next door is on the site of the central building of the Rum Hospital. The original building fell into disrepair and was demolished in 1879. A new hospital was built

in its place in the 1880s with features that include marble floors, a baroque staircase, and magnificent floral stained-glass windows.

The third of the Rum Hospital buildings is now the seat of the State Parliament. There are three tiers of Australian government: federal, state, and local.

The New South Wales State Parliament's lower chamber is known locally as the Bear Pit (visit when the honorable members' fur is flying to see why). The parliament is open to the public during the week, and free tours operate whenever the House isn't sitting; the public gallery is open when the parliament is sitting.

Pick up a free booklet on the House in the foyer and visit the photographic exhibition of works by prominent Australian photographers David Moore (1927–) and Max Dupain (1911–1992). A glass case displays the scissors used to open the Harbour Bridge in 1932 and the New Glebe Island Bridge in 1995.
Map p. 43   State Parliament House, Macquarie St.   9230 2111

STATE LIBRARY OF NEW SOUTH WALES

Although the State Library of New South Wales may not strike visitors immediately as the most enthralling of destinations, it contains a number of items of interest. The Mitchell Library, housed in the oldest part of the building (which dates from 1910, although the library has existed since 1826), has the country's greatest collection of Australiana. You can see items such as Captain Cook's diaries, 8 of the 10 known diaries written by First Fleeters, and numerous paintings dating from 1788. The general collection is housed in a new annex featuring changing displays that often include some of the library's rare treasures.

Worth a visit in itself is the foyer of the Mitchell Library, which has a stunning mosaic floor (1941) of marble and brass by Sydney's Melocco brothers. It presents a map of Dutch explorer Abel Tasman's voyages to *Terra Australis* (the "great south land") in 1642 and 1643. To see other impressive examples of their work, visit the crypt of **St. Mary's Cathedral** (see p. 64) and the **State Theatre foyer** (see p. 110).
Map p. 43   Macquarie St.   9273 1414; www.slnsw.gov.au ∎

The Rocks is Sydney's oldest suburb, taking its name from the rocky outcrop on which convict tents were first pitched in 1788. Today the area is a lively tourist enclave with plenty of shops, galleries, restaurants, and historic pubs.

The Rocks

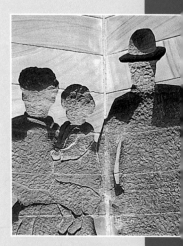

Detail from the "First Impressions" sculpture, Playfair Street

The Rocks

THE ROCKS WAS ONCE THE WORKING-CLASS AREA TO THE WEST OF CIRCULAR Quay. This is where convicts were originally quartered and where the first ramshackle houses were built. Much of the work of the port of Sydney was carried out here during the colony's early days, and this heritage is reflected in the number of warehouses and stores that reach around the waterfront beyond the imposing facades of the Museum of Contemporary Art and the Sydney Cove Overseas Passenger Terminal. Behind them, tiny cottages cluster together in narrow avenues, and there is a pub on nearly every street corner.

These days the area has been turned over almost entirely to tourism, with dozens of gift shops and eateries ranging from cheap and cheerful cafés to restaurants serving the finest fare. There are also several hotels, a few small museums, and the area is the base of the Sydney Theatre Company.

While most of the land between Sydney Cove and Darling Harbour is referred to as The Rocks, the western side of the promontory is known as Millers Point. Here the working-class origins of the area can still be seen. ■

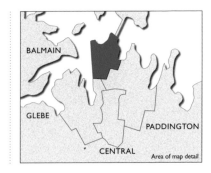

BALMAIN

GLEBE

PADDINGTON

CENTRAL

Area of map detail

Images of old and new: A reproduction of the *Bounty* is anchored in Campbells Cove. Modern high-rise buildings dwarf the historic Campbells Storehouses on the right.

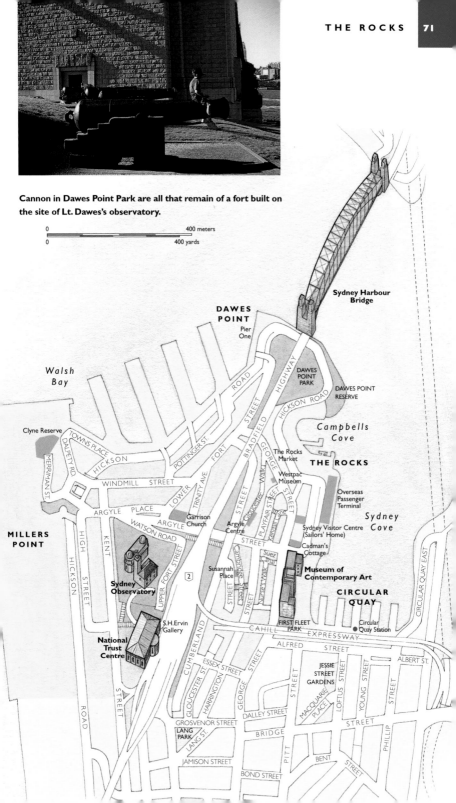

Cannon in Dawes Point Park are all that remain of a fort built on the site of Lt. Dawes's observatory.

0   400 meters
0   400 yards

Sydney Harbour
Bridge

DAWES
POINT

Pier
One

Walsh
Bay

DAWES
POINT
PARK

DAWES POINT
RESERVE

Clyne Reserve

TOWNS PLACE

DALPETY RD

HICKSON

MERRIMAN ST

ROAD

POTTINGER ST

FORT

STREET

BRADFIELD

HICKSON ROAD

HIGHWAY

GEORGE

Campbells
Cove

The Rocks
Market

THE ROCKS

WINDMILL STREET

LOWER

TRINITY AVE

STREET

CUMBERLAND WALK

PLAYFAIR STREET

Westpac
Museum

Overseas
Passenger
Terminal

Sydney
Cove

ARGYLE PLACE

Garrison
Church

WATSON ROAD

ARGYLE

UPPER FORT STREET

KENT

HIGH

STREET

Argyle
Centre

STREET

Cambridge

STREET

Susannah
Place

Suez
Canal

Nurses Walk

Harrington St

STREET

Sydney Visitor Centre
(Sailors' Home)

Cadman's
Cottage

Museum of
Contemporary Art

CIRCULAR QUAY EAST

MILLERS
POINT

2

Sydney
Observatory

S.H.Ervin
Gallery

National
Trust
Centre

CUMBERLAND ST

ESSEX STREET

GEORGE

STREET

Oasis

CIRCULAR
QUAY

FIRST FLEET
PARK

CAHILL EXPRESSWAY

Circular
Quay Station

Circular
Quay Station

ROAD

ALFRED

STREET

STREET

JESSIE
STREET
GARDENS

MACQUARIE

LOFTUS STREET

YOUNG STREET

ALBERT ST.

STREET

GLOUCESTER ST

HARRINGTON

GEORGE

DALLEY STREET

STREET

PLACE

PITT

BENT

STREET

PHILLIP

STREET

GROSVENOR STREET

LANG
PARK

LANG ST.

BRIDGE

STREET

JAMISON STREET

BOND STREET

The Museum of Contemporary Art constantly changes its exhibitions; items are taken from its own collection and touring shows.

Museum of Contemporary Art

THE MUSEUM OF CONTEMPORARY ART (MCA) IS HOUSED in the former Maritime Services Board building west of Circular Quay. Dating from the 1930s, it is a huge art deco edifice. The MCA as it exists today was established in 1989 by the University of Sydney— thanks to a bequest made by collector and artist John Wardell Power in 1939—and has been operating in the current building since 1991.

Museum of Contemporary Art

- Map p. 71
- 140 George St., The Rocks
- 9241 5892 (recorded information) www.mca.com.au
- $$
- Circular Quay Station
- Ferry: Circular Quay

The museum is Australia's only major institution dedicated to contemporary art, but because the amount of work it holds is so great (over 5,000 pieces), no one piece of the collection is ever on permanent display. So while the MCA has works by internationally known artists such as Pablo Picasso and Henry Moore, and local artists Brett Whiteley and Maria Kozic, it is a matter of luck as to whether you'll see the work of anyone in particular.

As the staff will explain, even the walls don't stay in the same places—they're constantly being shifted and shaped to accommodate the diverse range of work that appears in the gallery.

Ever since it opened, the MCA has been one of the most vibrant centers for the arts in Sydney.

In presenting contemporary art, which by its very nature tests the edges of what does and doesn't work in the public and artistic consciousness, it has created more than its fair share of headlines (and headaches). There is a reasonable expectation, therefore, that any visit will yield experiences that are stimulating, challenging, shocking, amusing, and exciting. Most of all, however, it will be enlightening and entertaining.

The MCA also houses a very popular café with wonderful views of the harbor, and a well-appointed gift shop. ∎

Foreshore

SINCE THE START OF THE COLONY OF SYDNEY IN 1788, THE stretch of shore on the western side of Circular Quay has been busy with the commercial activity of the city. These days it throngs with visitors, street musicians, and vendors, while its buildings present a mixture of styles spanning the entire history of Australia.

Cadman's Cottage

✉ 110 George St.

☎ 9247 5033

Sailors' Home (Sydney Visitor Centre)

✉ 106 George St.

☎ 9255 1788

Next to the MCA, on the foreshore, is **Cadman's Cottage.** Built in 1816 for John Cadman, a convict who had been transported to New South Wales for stealing a horse, this simple, two-story building is the oldest surviving house in the city. Cadman was eventually pardoned by Macquarie and went on to become the superintendent of government boats.

The cottage is now an information center for the New South Wales National Parks and Wildlife Service. It is also the reservations and departure point for a changing program of tours to several of the harbor's islands (see pp. 96–97) and the meeting place for special-interest walks around The Rocks area.

Just beside Cadman's Cottage is the **Sydney Visitor Centre,** occupying the **Sailors' Home.** It was originally built to provide visiting sailors with decent lodgings while they were in port. A guided walking tour of The Rocks leaves from the Sailors' Home several times a day, and inside you will find a wealth of information on tours, attractions, and places to stay in Sydney and beyond. The upper stories of the house present a comprehensive history of The Rocks.

Continuing on the foreshore, reach the Overseas Passenger Terminal and take the escalator to the top level for some great views across to the Opera House. There are various eateries in and around the terminal, which is also a major bus tour departure point; the tour office is at the southern end.

On the northern side of the terminal, past the tower of the ASN Company Building (1884), is Campbells Cove. The first wharves were built here in the early 1800s by a merchant, Robert Campbell, who also built the dockside warehouses that now house a collection

of restaurants, stores, and bars. Cruises of the harbor are conducted from a life-size model of the *Bounty* (used in the movie starring local boy Mel Gibson) moored in the cove.

The sweep of new buildings beyond Campbells Storehouses is the Park Hyatt Sydney. Stroll around the boardwalk at the front and continue on to Dawes Point (see p. 74), where Sydney Harbour Bridge (see pp. 86–89) vaults across to North Sydney at the narrowest point in the main harbor. ■

The Sailors' Home, next door to Cadman's Cottage, protected 19th-century sailors on shore leave from being lead astray in the notorious Rocks district.

The Rocks walk

A short stroll though The Rocks provides an excellent snapshot of the social, commercial, and maritime history of Sydney, plus some wonderful views of Sydney Opera House, Sydney Harbour Bridge, and the harbor. This is an extremely compact area jammed with historic buildings, shops, galleries, over 70 restaurants, and countless pubs. You'll find surprises around every corner and plenty of things that can turn an hour-long walk into a whole day's outing.

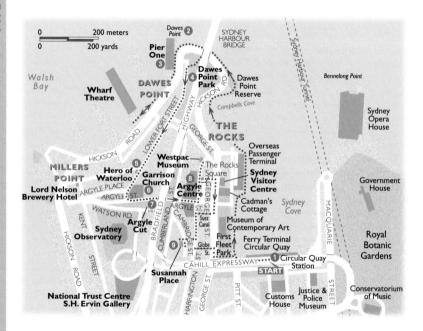

From **Circular Quay** ❶ (see pp. 48–51), follow the foreshore to the west then north to **Dawes Point** ❷. This was named after Lt. William Dawes, an officer of the First Fleet who established Australia's first observatory (initially for the purpose of observing Maskelyn's Comet), and a naval battery using cannon from the *Sirius* is here. Dawes fixed the exact position of Sydney in latitude and longitude with over 300 observations, and he was one of the first Europeans to record much of the language of the local Aborigine.

Just to the west of the Harbour Bridge is **Pier One** ❸, a collection of restaurants, bars, and stores with some impressive inner harbor views. This is the first of four finger wharves that were built in Walsh Bay in the 1920s. Some have been converted into prestige

- Inside front cover C5
- Circular Quay
- 1.5 miles (2.4 km)
- Allow 1.5 hours
- Circular Quay

NOT TO BE MISSED
- Dawes Point
- Pier One
- Lord Nelson Brewery Hotel
- Garrison Church
- The Rocks Market
- Susannah Place

Union bans in the 1960s protected much of The Rocks from high-rise development.

The southern pylon of the Harbour Bridge is open to the public and offers magnificent harbor views.

apartments, others are derelict. If you continue past Pier One, you'll find Pier 4/5 has been turned into the Sydney Theatre Company's **Wharf Theatre** (Pier 4, Hickson Rd., Walsh Bay, Tel 9250 1700, closed Sun.). There is a restaurant here, too, with more harbor views.

Backtrack to a path that leads up to **Dawes Point Park ④,** directly beneath the bridge, where a battery of cannon from the 1840s is all that remains of a fort built on the site of the first observatory. Cutting through the park is Lower Fort Street, with a row of Victorian terraces that dominated the

heights of The Rocks before the Harbour Bridge was built.

Farther along Lower Fort Street, the **Hero of Waterloo ⑤** (Tel 9252 4553) is one of the typical pubs of the area. Built in 1884, it is the city's second oldest hotel; the **Lord Nelson Brewery Hotel,** around the corner on Kent Street, in Millers Point, is the oldest, built in 1834 and licensed in 1842. Take a detour to stop in at the atmospheric bar and sample some of the many beers for which it is famous. From here, the **Sydney Observatory** (see pp. 78–79) and **S.H. Ervin Gallery** (see p. 79) lie straight ahead.

Back on Lower Fort Street, continue to the end and turn left onto Argyle Street. Well worth a visit is the **Garrison Church ⑥** (Holy Trinity Church), immediately on the left, with a fine stained-glass east window. The church was designed by Edmund Blacket (1817–1873) and built with stone quarried from the **Argyle Cut ⑦,** just down the hill on Argyle Street.

The cut was carved through solid rock by convicts in 1843 and completed by free labor in 1859; you can still see the marks of the chisels. At the bottom of the cut, stairs lead up to Cumberland Street and the start of the walk across the Harbour Bridge (see p. 90). Note, too, that at the top of the stairs is the **Glenmore Hotel,** whose rooftop beer garden has a great view across the Opera House to the harbor. If you want to end your walk at this point, continue east along Argyle Street into the heart of The Rocks, then walk down to the harbor to return to Circular Quay.

Alternatively, continue to walk along Argyle Street to reach the four-story **Argyle Centre** on your left. These converted warehouses were built in 1828 as a bond store; they now accommodate upscale stores and restaurants.

East of the center is Playfair Street, which leads to **The Rocks Square ⑧.** Here there is plenty of weekend entertainment and you can see the "First Impressions" sculpture, a sandstone monument to the convicts, soldiers, and free settlers of the early colony.

Beyond the square is the **Westpac Museum** (6–8 Playfair St., Tel 9251 1419), formerly the Bank of New South Wales, the colony's first bank, established in 1815. The building is the work of Ashley Alexander, who designed Dartmoor Prison in England.

Drop down from the square and you'll find yourself on Kendall Lane, near the stores and restaurants of The Rocks Centre. Stroll down farther still and you'll be on George Street, across the road from the **Sydney Visitor Centre** (see p. 73). If it's the weekend you'll have noticed, and probably been diverted by, **The Rocks Market,** which sets up stalls at the top of George Street. Here you'll find ceramics, original artworks, photographs, jewelry, handmade soaps, and plenty of food. You can't miss the Irish pubs that dot this stretch of George Street, either. Across the street from the pubs is the **Metcalf Bond Stores,** which houses several major galleries and boutiques.

George Street, the major street of The Rocks, was the first road to be built in the area. It replaced the track that ran from the western side of the Tank Stream (see p. 50) out to Lieutenant's Dawes's observatory and gun battery on Dawes Point (see p. 74). Originally known as Spring Row, George Street was renamed in 1810 to commemorate King George III and boasts some of the most important heritage buildings in Australia. These include Cadman's Cottage (see p. 73), the ASN Company Building, the Coachhouse (1853–1861), the former Police Station (1882), and the Mariner's Church (1856).

Just after crossing Argyle Street, keep an eye out for an alley heading off George Street to the right. Known as the **Suez Canal** because of the river of water that used to flow down it during heavy rain, this narrow lane is much as it was in the 1850s. The Rocks used to be full of such lanes, the haunt of gangs who preyed on the unwary, among them sailors who often found themselves kidnapped and sold to other ships.

The Suez Canal links through to Harrington Street. Halfway along the street is **Nurse's Walk,** another lane that looks much as it did in the 19th century, and which offers interesting shops in a quiet pedestrianized area. Harrington Street is a busy shopping and hotel area that contains **Reynolds Cottage,** a two-story house built in 1830 by Irish blacksmith William Reynolds; it is now a café.

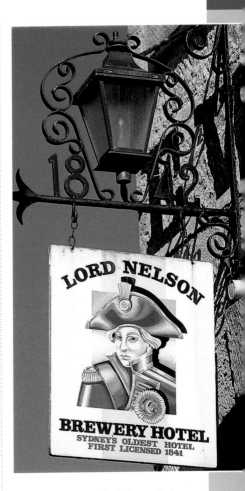

The old pubs of The Rocks have a lively atmosphere and specialize in microbrewed local beverages.

Just west of Harrington Street is **Susannah Place** ❾ (58–64 Gloucester St., Tel 9241 1893, closed Mon.–Fri., except Jan.), a row of four terraced houses and a corner store dating from 1844. The buildings now house a small museum of 19th-century inner-city life.

From Susannah Place turn right onto Harrington Street, then take a left to Globe Street, which will take you back to the main thoroughfare of George Street. Turn left into **First Fleet Park,** a good place to rest your weary legs before returning to Circular Quay. ■

The telescope domes on the top of the Sydney Observatory— note the time ball at the base of the weathervane.

Sydney Observatory

OBSERVATORY HILL, THE HIGHEST POINT IN THE SYDNEY area at 140 feet (43 m), was formerly known as Windmill Hill because the first windmill to be built in the colony in 1795 originally stood on the site. A few years later, in 1804, the construction of Fort Phillip was begun on the hill so the government would have somewhere to retreat in the event of an uprising.

Sydney Observatory

🅰 Map p. 71

✉ Watson Rd., Observatory Hill, Millers Point

☎ 9217 0485 www.phm.gov.au

💲 $$

🚌 Sydney Explorer bus or routes 431 & 433

As it turned out, four years after Fort Phillip was built, there actually was an uprising. However, the governor at the time, Capt. William Bligh, retreated not to the redoubt but under his bed and was placed under house arrest. Two of the fort's walls now form part of the observatory, which replaces the smaller one built on Dawes Point (see p. 74) in the early years of the colony.

During the last century Sydney Observatory was a prominent landmark, although it is now increasingly being enclosed by development. The surrounding park has an elegant band rotunda, with some harbor views, but the noise from the traffic on the Harbour Bridge detracts from the ambience.

Established in 1858 in Italian Renaissance-style buildings, the observatory took some of the first astronomical photographs of the southern sky, as part of an international project to produce the first complete atlas of the night sky. It operated until the 1980s, when

The time ball

In the 19th century, a vital function of the observatory was the daily dropping of the time ball. Located in the observatory tower, the ball was dropped at the stroke of 1 p.m. (cued by the observatory's highly reliable timepieces) to signal the firing of a cannon at Fort Denison. This allowed ships to check the accuracy of their chronometers, which were crucial for navigation. The firing of the gun was stopped during World War II after an attack on the harbor by a Japanese Midget submarine; several people were killed and Sydney's residents became fearful of gunfire. The practice of firing the gun daily was resumed in 1986, and the time ball is dropped if staff are available. So if you're in the vicinity at 1 p.m., set your watch. ∎

the bright lights of the city made use of the telescopes impractical. Sydney's rainfall is still measured on the site, however.

Along with telescopes, videos, and hands-on astronomical exhibits, the museum has information about the site's history and its contribution to astronomy.

You can also see displays on Aboriginal astronomy that depict the totally different constellations to those described in Western astronomy, plus the Dreamtime (see p. 153) stories related to them. How the stars are used to determine the seasons and when certain food supplies would be available is explained, too. Another attraction is the evening sessions, during which you study the night sky to view planets. These must be prebooked. ∎

National Trust Centre

National Trust Centre

✉ Observatory Hill, Millers Point

☎ 9258 0123

🕐 Closed Mon.

💲 $

🚌 Sydney Explorer bus or routes 431 & 433

The New South Wales headquarters of the National Trust of Australia is housed in Governor Macquarie's military hospital of 1815. Situated just behind the observatory, the building was used by the soldiers quartered in George Street until it moved to Victoria Barracks in Paddington in 1848 (see p. 136). The building, with its neoclassic facade added in 1871, operated as a school until 1974. The National Trust moved into the premises in 1975 and has information relating to the many significant buildings in Sydney and New South Wales.

Don't miss the **S.H. Ervin Gallery,** which occupies an annex of the military hospital, built in 1841, and operates on a similar, but much smaller scale to the Art Gallery of New South Wales (see pp. 56–59) or the MCA (see p. 72).

The gallery opened in 1978 and has been consistent in bringing interesting and easily digestible exhibitions for the public. In keeping with its relationship with the National Trust, its constantly changing exhibitions often have a historical theme relating to Australia's cultural heritage, both European and Aboriginal.

There are no permanent displays, but you'll find flyers outlining current and forthcoming exhibitions at the gallery and numerous tourist venues around the city.

The traditional tearooms on the premises provide refreshments. ∎

Workers' terraces on Millers Point, on the western side of The Rocks, preserve some of the area's history and are still used as affordable public housing.

More places to visit in The Rocks

GLOUCESTER WALK

One lane in The Rocks area not to miss is Gloucester Walk. From the northern end of George Street, climb westward across the top of a cliff that looks down into the gardens of the pubs and shops on George Street.

Along the way look for information boards that detail the earliest history of the area; it is known as Bunker's Hill, after a U.S. skipper, Capt. Eber Bunker (originally from Plymouth, Massachusetts), who was involved in the first whaling operations in New South Wales. The houses of Gloucester Walk, formerly Gloucester Street, were demolished after an outbreak of plague at the turn of the century.

In a short distance you will reach **Foundation Park,** with all that remains of some of the earliest houses in Australia. The sidewalk bears the numbers of the houses, and modern sculptures re-create some of the atmosphere of previous eras. From the park it is just a short walk to the small flight of steps that leads to the top of the Argyle Stairs.

Map p. 71

MILLERS POINT

On the western side of The Rocks is the quiet district of workers' cottages and warehouses, several of which have been converted into apartments or hotels, referred to as Millers Point.

From the Lord Nelson Brewery Hotel (see p. 76), cross Hickson Road to the elegant Palisade Hotel on Bettington Street. Continue northward on to Merriman Street, where you can look across to the west of the working port of Darling Harbour.

Note the large tower with an observation deck on top. This is the Port Operations Centre, known locally as "The Pill" because it controls all the berths in its vicinity. There is no public access.

Go to the northern end of Merriman Street to **Clyne Reserve,** which affords good views of the working port area. You'll see the fireboats of the Emergency Operations Unit moored below, finger wharves to the right, and the modern wharves of Darling Harbour to the left.

Map p. 71 ■

The jewel of the city is its spectacular harbor, where you can take a day cruise or rent a yacht to visit the many coves, bays, and islands, or catch the ferry to the beach resort of Manly.

Sydney Harbour

Detail of the steel structure of Sydney Harbour Bridge

Sydney Harbour

WHEN GOVERNOR PHILLIP FIRST ENTERED SYDNEY HARBOUR IN 1788, HE had no hesitation in describing it as one of the finest harbors in the world. And he wasn't exaggerating when he claimed "a thousand ships of the line could safely shelter in it/There'd be room to spare." The harbor was named Port Jackson by Captain Cook when he sailed past North Head and South Head in 1770, and it has been seducing visitors ever since. It is also a very safe waterway, with only one reef in the main harbor and deep water virtually everywhere else.

One of the main attractions is that, although surrounded by the most populous city in Australia, the harbor has managed to retain much of its natural beauty. Sydney Harbour National Park takes in many of the headlands and islands, and plenty of short walks snake through the harborside suburbs and bushland, with places to stop for a leisurely picnic.

The harbor, a drowned river valley covering 22 square miles (57 sq km) with 150 miles (240 km) of shoreline, comprises three main arms: North Harbour is the smallest, Middle Harbour reaches into the hilly terrain of the northern suburbs, and Port Jackson itself is navigable all the way to Parramatta, 15 miles (24 km) inland.

Options for exploring these waterways abound. You can walk around them, sail on them, take off and land on them in seaplanes, cross Harbour Bridge, or rent kayaks and paddle along some of the more sheltered parts. ■

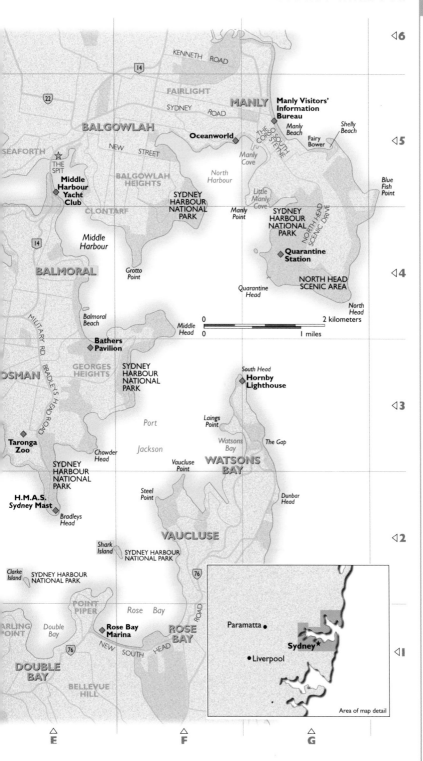

6

KENNETH ROAD

14

FAIRLIGHT

22

SYDNEY ROAD   MANLY   **Manly Visitors'
Information
Bureau**

Oceanworld   Manly
Beach   Shelly
Beach

BALGOWLAH   Fairy
Bower   5

SEAFORTH

NEW STREET   Manly
Cove

☆
THE
SPIT

**Middle
Harbour
Yacht
Club**   BALGOWLAH
HEIGHTS   North
Harbour   Blue
Fish
Point

CLONTARF   SYDNEY
HARBOUR
NATIONAL
PARK   Little
Manly
Cove

Manly
Point   SYDNEY
HARBOUR
NATIONAL
PARK

14

*Middle
Harbour*

BALMORAL   Grotto
Point   **Quarantine
Station**   NORTH HEAD SCENIC DRIVE   4

*Quarantine
Head*   NORTH HEAD
SCENIC AREA

MILITARY RD   Balmoral
Beach   North
Head

0   2 kilometers
Middle
Head   0   1 miles

**Bathers
Pavilion**   South Head   **Hornby
Lighthouse**

GEORGES
HEIGHTS   SYDNEY
HARBOUR
NATIONAL
PARK   3

OSMAN   *Port*   Laings
Point

BRADLEYS HEAD ROAD   Watsons
Bay   The Gap

**Taronga
Zoo**   *Jackson*   Chowder
Head   Vaucluse
Point   WATSONS
BAY

SYDNEY
HARBOUR
NATIONAL
PARK   Steel
Point   Dunbar
Head

**H.M.A.S.
Sydney Mast**   *Bradleys
Head*   VAUCLUSE   2

Shark
Island   SYDNEY HARBOUR
NATIONAL PARK

Clarke
Island   SYDNEY HARBOUR
NATIONAL PARK   76

POINT
PIPER   *Rose Bay*

ARLING
POINT   Double
Bay   **Rose Bay
Marina**   ROSE
BAY   HEAD ROAD   Paramatta •

76   NEW SOUTH   **Sydney** ★   1

DOUBLE
BAY   • Liverpool

BELLEVUE
HILL   Area of map detail

△   △   △
E   F   G

Cruises

YOU CAN'T SAY YOU'VE BEEN TO SYDNEY UNTIL YOU'VE taken a trip on its world famous harbor, even for the briefest of passages. And it should come as no surprise that there are a number of ways to do just that. So many, in fact, that it can be confusing. Take a moment to work out what you'd like to see—the classic journey from Circular Quay to Manly on a regular service, perhaps, a lunch or dinner cruise, a harbor lights cruise, or a short trip on a square rigger. Then it's bon voyage.

State Transit ferries operate from Circular Quay and service Manly, Kirribilli, Neutral Bay, Cremorne, Mosman and Taronga Zoo, Watsons Bay, and Rose Bay east of the bridge; Balmain, Darling Harbour, Hunter's Hill, and Parramatta to the west. The Manly trip is a must, but a run on the RiverCat to Parramatta (see pp. 188–89) takes in some of the idyllic harborside suburbs, wharf areas, and waterfront industries of the working port. It also passes the Olympic site at Homebush.

State Transit also operates three tourist cruises. The Morning River Cruise takes 2.5 hours and departs every day at 10 a.m. from Circular Quay. It takes in the main harbor and the Opera House to Shark Island, then passes under the Harbour Bridge and heads up the Parramatta and Lane Cove Rivers. The Afternoon Harbour Cruise takes 2.5 hours and departs at 1 p.m. Monday through Friday and 1:30 p.m. on weekends, passing the Opera House and main harbor sights before heading into Middle Harbour under the opening Spit Bridge. From Monday to Saturday at 8 p.m., the Evening Harbour Lights cruise (1.5 hours) shows you the illuminated Opera House, Fort Denison, Garden Island, and Darling Harbour.

Numerous other companies operate a wide selection of tours as well. The major tour operators are **Captain Cook Cruises, Vagabond Cruises,** and **Matilda Cruises.** Cruise details are available from booths at Circular Quay. All three companies offer cruises ranging from 1 to 2.5 hours with a choice of morning tea, lunch, or dinner, priced accordingly.

Captain Cook and Vagabond Cruises operate from Circular Quay; Matilda operates from Darling Harbour, near Sydney Aquarium.

Captain Cook also operates the Harbour Explorer, which runs every 2 hours and stops at The Rocks, the Opera House, Taronga Zoo, Darling Harbour, and Watsons Bay. Passengers can embark and disembark at their leisure from 9:30 a.m. to 3:30 p.m.

The National Parks and Wildlife Service also offers cruises and tours to several of the islands that are part of Sydney Harbour National Park. Reservations (*Tel 9247 5033*) and details are available at Cadman's Cottage in The Rocks (see p. 73).

Alternatives proliferate, with many companies offering specialized cruises. The paddle steamers of **Sydney Showboats** depart from Campbells Cove morning, noon, and night on jazz luncheon cruises, twilight cruises, dinner cruises, and sight-seeing cruises.

A reproduction of the *Bounty* leaves the same cove on similar cruises, but with a considerably more rustic vessel that provides plenty of photo opportunities. Make a reservation if you plan to take any of the weekend cruises.

On Sydney Harbour, ferries have right of way over sailboats.

The **Sydney Sundancers** are giant sailing catamarans offering lunch and dinner cruises. These cruisers stay on an even keel—ideal if your sea legs are not too good.

Sailing enthusiasts, and those who just want to get out onto the water and have a bit more control, are well catered for. There are many yacht, sailboat, and cruiser charter companies, with or without skippers. These include **Ausail** and **Eastsail,** which provide self-sailing or sailing with a skipper, and weekend flotilla sailing where a group of boats do the sights, restaurants, and waterways of the harbor together. Waking up on a yacht moored in a cove of Sydney Harbor could well be a highlight of your visit and, compared to the average room cost, such a cruise is quite competitively priced.

If a small catamaran, sailboat, or dinghy with outboard is more to your liking, try **Balmoral Boat Hire** at Middle Harbour. On the southside, try **Rose Bay Marina** or **Rose Bay Aquatic Hire.**

All of the above activities are ones you must pay for, but if you want to do some serious or not so serious racing, the Middle Harbour Yacht Club, Sydney Amateurs, and Cruising Yacht Club have race days on weekends and twilight races Wednesday and Thursday (usually on a less competitive level). Some clubs have crew lists and will charge a fee to include you, others will try to find you a boat if you just turn up—for example, Middle Harbour. Your accent can be a great passport to bending any rules, if you're polite, but remember that the quickest way to sour a day's sailing is to exaggerate your experience.

Finally, several interesting vessels conduct short cruises from the Australian National Maritime Museum (see pp. 128–29). ∎

CRUISE COMPANIES

State Transit
☎ 13 1500

Capt. Cook Cruises
☎ 9206 1111

Vagabond Cruises
☎ 9660 0388

Matilda Cruises
☎ 9264 7377

Sydney Showboats
☎ 9552 2722

Bounty
☎ 9247 1789

Sydney Sundancers
☎ 99371 0135

Ausail
☎ 9960 5511

Eastsail
☎ 9327 1166

Balmoral Boat Hire
☎ 9969 6006

Rose Bay Marina
☎ 9363 5930

Aquatic Hire
☎ 9371 7036

The view from atop Sydney Harbour Bridge, 439 feet (134 m) above the water; tours to the top of the arch are available.

Sydney Harbour Bridge

ALONG WITH THE OPERA HOUSE, THE SYDNEY HARBOUR Bridge is an instantly recognizable icon that says "Sydney." For 30 years it was the tallest structure in the city and even now dominates the harbor. It is one of the architectural and engineering wonders of Australia and, like the Opera House, you may find it has a surprise in store. When you see it for the first time, you'll discover that it's far grander than any photograph can convey.

Sydney Harbour Bridge

🅰 82 C2

💲 Bradfield Hwy. toll: $. Free to cyclists & pedestrians

Known locally as the "Coathanger," the bridge was designed by Dorman Long and Co. Ltd. of England to specifications of its chief engineer, Dr. John Bradfield (1867–1943). It carries eight lanes of traffic, two railroads, and two walkways—pedestrians are permitted on the eastern walkway and cyclists on the western walkway—on a deck that is 160 feet (134 m) wide.

Prior to the construction of the bridge, travel between North and South Sydney was by ferry or a 12.5-mile (20-km) road journey skirting the harbor. The decision to build the bridge was a welcome relief to the struggling ferries and its opening triggered a building boom on the north side of the harbor.

Bridge work commenced in 1923 when the city was enjoying prosperity, but was completed during the Depression in 1932. In these difficult years, the bridge became a symbol of hope for the future.

The opening ceremony in March 1932 was interrupted when

an anticommunist, Francis de Groot, rode forward on his horse and slashed the opening ribbon with a sword before it could be cut officially by the Labour premier, Jack Lang. After de Groot had been led away by the police, the ribbon was quickly rejoined and the official ceremony continued.

VITAL STATISTICS
The bridge weighs 51,965 tons (52,800 tonnes); when it was built it was the widest long-span bridge in the world (over 1,650 feet/502 m).

The bridge was originally designed to carry up to 6,000 cars an hour, but now tops 15,000 at peak times. Sixty years after the bridge's opening, the Sydney Harbour Tunnel was built to help cope with the increasing volume of traffic between north and south shores.

Of the 1,400 workers employed in the construction of the bridge, 16 were killed in accidents, mostly due to the absence of safety rails.

Today, maintaining the steel structure is an endless job: A single coat of paint requires 8,000 gallons (30,000 liters), and takes a team of bridge-painters around ten years to apply, at the end of which it's time to start again. ■

Below: At the bottom of the arches on the southern and northern shores, enormous bolts connect the bridge to its foundations.

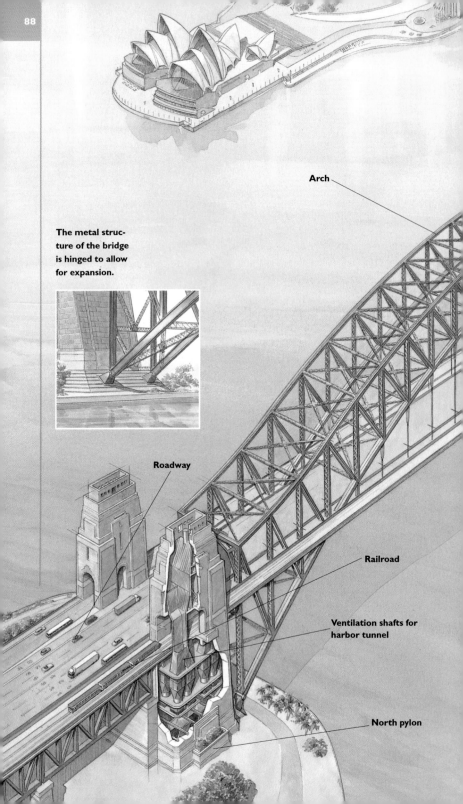

Arch

The metal struc-
ture of the bridge
is hinged to allow
for expansion.

Roadway

Railroad

Ventilation shafts for
harbor tunnel

North pylon

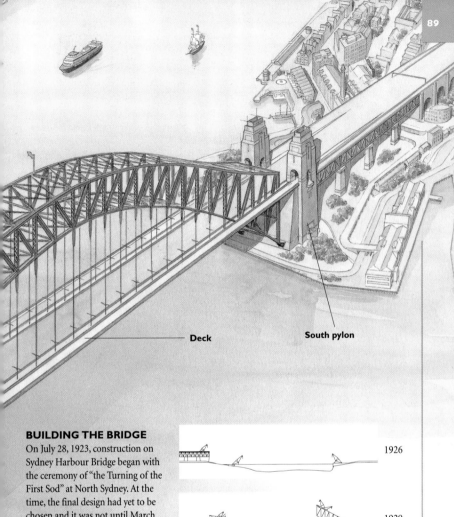

Deck

South pylon

BUILDING THE BRIDGE

On July 28, 1923, construction on Sydney Harbour Bridge began with the ceremony of "the Turning of the First Sod" at North Sydney. At the time, the final design had yet to be chosen and it was not until March 24, 1924, that the offer of Dorman Long and Co. Ltd. was accepted.

Once the foundations had been built, work on erecting the two halves of the arch, using creeper cranes, commenced in October 1928. Each half was firmly anchored by steel cables fixed in horseshoe-shaped tunnels dug into rock. By August 1930, the two half arches were ready to be joined, the gap between them just three and a half feet (1.07 m) apart.

Later that year, the deck was hung from the center outward, and by April 1931, both arch and deck were complete. ∎

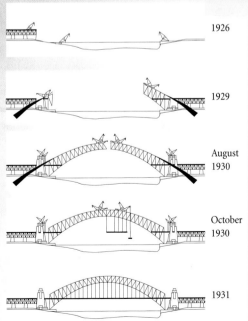

1926

1929

August 1930

October 1930

1931

Harbour Bridge walk

This short walk across the bridge from the city to Kirribilli and Milsons Point provides spectacular views of the harbor. If you want to make a longer route, combine it with The Rocks Walk (see pp. 74–77).

Silhouetted against the night sky, the bridge looms behind North Sydney Olympic Pool.

Start on the south side of the bridge at the entrance to the pedestrian walkway, located on the other side of the street from the Argyle Stairs that climb to the top of the Argyle Cut on Argyle Street (see p. 76).

As you move onto the bridge, one of the most wonderful views imaginable unfolds around you. Almost directly below are The Rocks, Circular Quay, and Sydney Cove. You have a bird's-eye view of the Opera House on Bennelong Point. Beyond it you'll see the sandstone structure of Fort Denison (see p. 97) rising straight out of the harbor. Behind that and to the right, the high-rise apartments of Darling Point stand on the water's edge, with Rose Bay and Vaucluse behind them. On the left are Kirribilli, Cremorne, and Mosman, with the bush-clad promontory of Bradleys Head.

The **Pylon Lookout** ❶ (*Tel 9247 3408*) on the city side of the bridge is well worth a visit (pedestrian access only). Not only are the views from the lookout itself—a 200-step climb—among the best in the city, but there are a display of photographs and information about the construction of the bridge in the **Harbour Bridge Museum** (*Tel 9247 3408*) in the base of the pylon.

If you have a good head for heights you can brave the three-hour tour to the top of the bridge arch with **BridgeClimb** (*5 Cumberland St., The Rocks, Tel 9252 0077; www.bridgeclimb.com*). Attached by a harness to a safety rail, which is used by bridge maintenance workers, you will be taken 440 feet (134 m) above the water by experienced guides. The views are fantastic.

Continuing to the far side of the bridge, descend the steps, and double back under the bridge to Milsons Point. From here, walk down the hill to the harbor and the **North Sydney Olympic Pool** ❷, a popular spot for a refreshing swim with spectacular views. Although it is no longer used for international

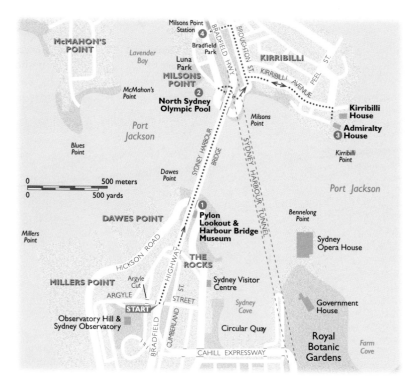

competition, more world records (86) have been set here than in any other pool in the world. This is due to the extra buoyancy, and therefore speed, afforded to swimmers by the saltwater.

You'll notice on the far side of the pool a large, laughing face over the entrance of **Luna Park.** Currently the amusements aren't operating due to problems with noise. After being established in the 1930s, it was the premier amusement park in the city until 1979 when a fire on a ride killed seven children and one adult. As a result the park was closed until the 1990s, but by that time the apartment development surrounding it meant that major attractions such as the roller coaster weren't permitted to operate because of noise and it was closed down again. You may see it illuminated at night, but its future is uncertain.

Walk back under the Harbour Bridge to **Bradfield Park,** where there is an unobstructed view across to the Opera House and city. When you head back up the hill, the road to the right, Kirribilli Avenue, winds around to

🗺	Inside front cover C5
▶	Entrance to pedestrian walkway, south side of bridge
↔	1.5 miles (2.4 km)
⏱	Allow 2 hours
▶	Milsons Point

NOT TO BE MISSED
- Pylon Lookout
- North Sydney Olympic Pool
- Bradfield Park

Kirribilli House (the Australian prime minister's Sydney pile) and **Admiralty House** ❸ (the governor general's Sydney residence). These are only open to the public on special occasions.

Retrace your steps along Kirribilli Avenue and up Broughton Street, where there are a number of cafés. Cross Broughton Street to **Milsons Point** ❹ and go under the bridge to the railway station. Alternatively, walk back across the bridge. ∎

Taronga Zoo

ONE OF THE QUICKEST AND EASIEST WAYS TO GET acquainted with the wildlife of Australia is to visit Taronga Zoo, the country's largest collection of native and exotic animals. As a bonus, it is superbly located on a hilltop position overlooking the city and the harbor (Taronga is Aboriginal for "water view").

From the ferry, the best option is to take the cable car or a bus up to the top entrance of the zoo and gradually make your way down. The cable car passes right over the hippos, so have your camera ready. Comprehensive guides to the zoo are available at the top and bottom entrances.

The zoo's enclosures have been significantly upgraded in recent years and most of the animals are kept in environments that are as similar to their natural habitats as possible. In one instance, this policy was so successful that keepers were surprised to discover an echidna had given birth in the privacy of her burrow. The first zoo staff knew of it was when visitors commented on how cute the baby echidna looked.

Nocturnal houses and low-light enclosures reduce the stress on sensitive creatures and allow visitors to observe the likes of possums and platypus.

Taronga has a strong reputation for wildlife conservation and is continually mounting new research projects and endangered species breeding programs.

Be sure to see the gorilla rain forest, the chimpanzee park, and the Sumatran tigers (the latter are one of the zoo's captive breeding successes). The koala enclosure features a walkway that winds up to the creatures in the treetops, and kangaroos, wombats, and other indigenous creatures are also on display.

Children can see and touch farm animals in the Discovery Farm; there is a seal show that is as educational as it is entertaining; and the zoo has one of the largest collections of marine life in the country. Looking through the glass wall of the seal enclosure is a particular treat.

You can also have your photograph taken with a koala, and there are zookeeper talks, several other animal shows and feedings throughout the day, plus numerous park and kiosk areas where you can have a picnic or buy lunch.

The zoo occasionally has night sessions, when many of the animals are more active. Special tours and guided tours can be arranged; contact the zoo for details. ■

The giraffe enclosure at Taronga Zoo, one of the most spectacular locations for a zoological garden anywhere in the world

The zoo's reptile enclosure houses such rare species as the endangered green and golden bell frog. The frogs have a natural habitat on the doorstep of Olympic Park, Homebush Bay.

Bradleys Head

If you have sufficient time, take the short walk south to Bradleys Head, not far from the zoo's lower entrance. From the ferry wharf at Mosman, walk about 200 yards (183 m) up the road to a path on the right, which leads through largely unspoiled bushland to the headland. Along the way there are good views back toward the city and several nice spots for a dip or picnic.

Now part of Sydney Harbour National Park, the headland was named after Lt. William Bradley, a cartographer with the First Fleet. You can find tiny pockets of rain forest in the valleys where colorful parrots fly free.

At the point, you will see several cannon dating from 1871—part of the harbor defenses built to protect the city from the perceived threat of the Russian fleet—and the mast from H.M.A.S. *Sydney*, a cruiser that participated in Australia's first naval engagement, sinking the German raider *Emden* in 1914.

Note the lighthouse, one of many that dot the harbor. These include the Wedding Cakes, visible offshore from the headland, which mark the east and west channels in the main harbor. The headland is a great spot to watch freighters putting out to sea, or the dashing 18-foot (5-m) skiffs (see pp. 94–95).

The National Parks and Wildlife Service *(Tel 9977 6522)* conducts bushfood tours of Bradleys Head on the first Saturday of each month; reservations essential.

Retrace your steps along the path you came on to return to the city by ferry or by bus. ■

Taronga Zoo

▲ 83 E3
✉ Bradleys Head Rd., Mosman
☎ 9969 2777
   www.zoo.nsw.gov.au
$ $$$
🚢 Taronga Zoo

ZOOLINK
From Circular Quay Station, or any railway station for that matter, pick up a travel and entry ticket that allows you to take the train or bus and then ferry across to the zoo at Mosman on the North Shore. Buying an all-in-one ticket is cheaper than buying tickets individually. ■

Eighteen-foot sailing skiffs

Sydneysiders never, ever, do anything by halves, and this also applies to the way they sail. As a recent world champion skiff sailor said of the 18-footers: "There used to be only two rules—the boat couldn't be more than 18 feet long; and you had to be at the start at 2:30 p.m." The width of the boat, the height of the mast, and the material used in the construction of the hull were entirely up to the crew.

The ultimate 18-footer can be seen in the Australian National Maritime Museum (see pp. 128–29). Called *Colour Bond,* it is 27 feet (8 m) across—thanks to the two enormous "wings" that extend on either side of the hull to give the boat stability—and the mast is 45 feet (14 m) high. Made of space-age carbon fiber, it cost in the region of $250,000. Since *Colour Bond* was built the rules have been changed to make the sport more affordable, although corporate sponsorship is still necessary to compete at the elite level.

Early days

The modern skiffs developed from the open workboats of the 19th century. In the 1890s the Sydney Flying Squadron was formed, and the first regular races were held with boats built and crewed by workers from the waterfront. The races were followed by large spectator fleets of chartered ferries, and the Sydney penchant for gambling found an outlet that was relatively safe from surprise raids by the police.

In the old days the boats used to sail one leg upwind and then one flying leg downwind. The huge sails made it very difficult to keep the boats upright on the upwind leg, which meant 16 or more "crew" were bundled aboard. These crews often consisted of beefy football (rugby league) players who were coerced into sailing during the off season and were seen wearing the "footy" sweaters that identified their club. On the return leg, however, this "ballast" was no longer needed, and in fact the excess weight stopped the boats skimming before the breeze.

Eighteen-foot skiff racing is a sailing class where the crew spend most of their time "overboard."

So what did the skippers do? They threw most of the crew overboard at the top mark, leaving them to cling to a buoy and wait to be picked up by a following ferry. These days, the rules state that you must finish a race with the same number of crew that you start with. There is no mention of it being the same crew, however.

In recent years there has been a nostalgic revival of the older-style boats, and crews wearing the sweaters of clubs from past eras can be seen sailing beautiful wooden boats. One of the boats of the 1940s, the cedar-built *Jean,* is on display at the maritime museum.

Watching the races

The modern sailing machines are a spectacular
sight as they scud across the water under their
brightly colored sails. Either follow the boats
from the shore, from a vantage point such as
Bradleys Head (see p. 93), or board one of the
charter ferries that convey passengers and
gamblers around the harbor to watch the races.

The Sydney Flying Squadron *(Tel 9955
8350)* conducts races from Milsons Point on
Saturdays; the Australian 18-Footer Club *(Tel
9363 2995)* races from Double Bay on Sundays.
Taking the ferry from these venues allows you
to watch the boats and crews up close. The SFS
has published a book, *Sydney's Flying Sailors*,
which is available from the club. ∎

Harbor islands

Shark Island was once used as a quarantine station for animals. It is now a popular site for picnics and corporate events.

SCATTERED THE LENGTH OF THE HARBOR, SYDNEY'S islands are great places to explore the different faces of a working port. Visit a fort one day, a shipyard the next, an idyllic picnic spot the day after that. Some of the islands are no longer recognizable as such, having been bridged to the mainland, and only their names betray their previous existence—Glebe Island, west of the city, and Garden Island to the east, for example.

Several of the islands form part of **Sydney Harbour National Park** (SHNP). The best known and most striking of these is **Fort Denison,** in the center of the main harbor. The First Fleeters named it Rock Island and banished particularly recalcitrant convicts to it with scarcely enough to eat, thus earning it the nickname "Pinchgut."

The island's golden yellow sandstone fort was built in the 1840s and '50s after two U.S. merchant vessels were discovered at anchor in the harbor one morning, having arrived undetected and unchallenged during the night. Work on the fort wasn't completed until 1857, when it was named after the governor in office, Sir William Denison. The fort has never had to fire a defensive shot, although it fires a gun every day at 1 p.m., originally on a cue from the time ball at the Sydney Observatory (see pp. 78–79).

Tours are conducted less regularly to **Goat Island,** west of the Harbour Bridge. The island was named by convicts because it was where goats, and later sheep, were kept. Like Rock Island, it was also where troublesome convicts sometimes found themselves. One of them, Charles "Bony" Anderson,

was chained to a sandstone ledge, the "Convict Couch," for two years.

The National Parks and Wildlife Service also administers three other islands: **Clarke** and **Shark Islands** east of the bridge, and **Rodd Island** tucked well into the harbor in Iron Cove. Clark Island was named after Lt. Ralph Clarke, who failed in an effort to grow corn, potatoes, and onions there in 1789. Shark Island is so named because its shape supposedly resembles a shark. Its location between Bradleys Head and Rose Bay means it has great views up to Manly and down to the city, the bridge, and the Opera House. Rodd Island has been popular for picnics since the early days of the colony; it has three Edwardian gazebos and a reception hall.

You can visit between 8 a.m. and sunset, although the islands are often reserved for private functions and numbers are restricted. Access is by private boat, although the National Parks and Wildlife Service sometimes runs tours.

During the school summer vacation, check to see if there are any special events being staged. At other times, water taxis or charter boats can provide access. ■

Fort Denison
🗺 82 D2

National Parks and Wildlife Service visitor information
✉ Cadman's Cottage, The Rocks
☎ 9247 5033

Dominating the approach to Sydney Cove, Fort Denison is also known as "Pinchgut" because convicts banished there on short rations had to tighten their belts.

Garden Island

Garden Island, at the end of Potts Point in the Kings Cross precinct, is part of Australia's major naval base. The **naval chapel** is open to the public for Mass on Sundays and is worth visiting for its historical memorabilia and impressive stained-glass windows. Next door to the chapel is a small **Naval Museum** (Tel 9359 2371, closed Fri.–Mon. & Wed.), which is full of interesting relics from visiting vessels dating back to

the First Fleet, including one of the Midget submarines that attacked Sydney in World War II.

Rock carvings of initials and the date "1788" were inscribed by mariners from the First Fleet who established vegetable gardens on the island (hence the name) in the year they arrived. Tours of the island are by appointment only, and it is best to call the museum before making a visit to the chapel or museum. ■

Manly

Manly is centered on a narrow stretch of land with the harbor on one side and its long surf beach on the other.

MANLY'S SLOGAN HAS LONG BEEN "SEVEN MILES FROM Sydney and a thousand miles from care." That just about sums up the shift that occurs when passengers disembark from the ferries or JetCats from Circular Quay with surfboards or towels tucked under their arms. The curious name came about because of the "manly" bearing of the Aborigines noted by Governor Phillip when he encountered them on a visit there.

A visit to Manly is a must do, not least because of the trip there. As the ferry approaches the heads you may spot dolphins, or little penguins from the colony near Manly Cove.

The obvious attraction of Manly is its beach, a short stroll from the ferry wharf through the pedestrian walkway called **The Corso**. This is a lively strip lined with fish-and-chip shops, restaurants, and cafés, bearing little resemblance to its namesake in Italy. On weekends there is open-air entertainment as well.

If a plunge in the high surf here isn't appealing, turn right at the beach for a short walk to the much calmer **Fairy Bower**, a small cove well protected by the headland opposite. Farther on, tucked under the headland, is **Shelly Beach,** one of the only two west-facing beaches on the east coast of Australia.

North Head, where sheer cliffs form a dramatic entrance to the harbor, has sweeping ocean and harbor views. It is accessible by foot, or there is a loop road. Buses (route 135) and short tours from Manly Wharf are available.

OCEANWORLD

A prime attraction in Manly is Oceanworld, just along the esplanade from the ferry wharf.

Take a seabed walk to see thousands of marine animals, including sharks, in the main tank. Species include grey nurse, wobegong, white-tipped reef, Port Jackson, and bronze whaler sharks. Trained divers feed the sharks Monday, Wednesday, and Friday at 11:30. There are stingrays, too.

Don't miss the exquisitely colored living coral reefs or touch pool (with guides) that provides hands-on experience of the local ecology, and shows of Australian and New Zealand fur seals.

Joining a dive course, either for beginners or advanced divers, is another option. ■

Manly
🅰 83 G5

Visitor information
✉ South Steyne
☎ 9977 1088

Oceanworld
✉ West Esplanade
☎ 9949 2644
www.oceanworldmanly.com/oceanworldmanly
💲 $$

Quarantine Station

Just above Spring Cove, on the way to North Head, you'll find the old Quarantine Station. Its attractive buildings belie a grim history, as this was where ships that could have been carrying epidemic diseases such as smallpox, Spanish influenza, and bubonic plague docked. On arrival, the passengers and crew were quarantined for several weeks.

The station opened in 1832 and continued operating until 1984, when it became part of Sydney Harbour National Park.

Tours (off North Head Scenic Drive, reservations essential, Tel 9977 6522, access by car or bus 135 from Manly Wharf) of the station are conducted daily. They take in the hospital, the mortuary, the disinfecting showers, and the accommodations.

Four nights a week (Wed.–Sun.), a very popular tour includes ghostly tales of the supposedly haunted buildings. Afterward, revive your spirits with tea and damper (a kind of cake or bread made of flour and water and baked in hot ashes).

The Quarantine Station Tour Unit operates a number of tours from the station to sites of interest around the harbor. These include the Manly Scenic Walkway (see pp. 100–101), bushfood tours to Bradleys Head, and tours to the forts and bunkers on Middle Head. Some trips are conducted regularly, others are run by arrangement only. Reservations are essential; phone as above. ■

A walk from The Spit to Manly

Known as the Manly Scenic Walkway, this popular stroll in the Sydney area can be joined at several points along the route. It explores beautiful scenery, offers great views, and passes several small coves and arms of the harbor. You'll find plenty of opportunities for safe swimming along the way and a choice of cafés at Manly's Corso or the wharf.

You can start the walk from either end, but the best option is to take the ferry to Manly and then catch a bus or taxi back to The Spit Bridge. Alternatively, buses from Wynyard in the city go to The Spit (*Tel 131 500 for timetable information*).

Start in the park at the northeastern (higher) end of **The Spit Bridge**. From here follow the path through to the harborside suburb of **Clontarf** and on to sandy **Clontarf Beach ❶**. There is a harbor pool here if you fancy a swim, plus a café/restaurant.

At the far end of the beach, follow the path into the bush once more, passing several small coves that are reasonably safe for swimming, though caution should be exercised.

Eventually you start to climb away from the water toward the heights of Dobroyd Head; a branch track, lined with colorful plants and flowers, runs down to the beautiful little lighthouse of **Grotto Point ❷**. Close by Grotto Point is secluded **Washaway Beach ❸**, which faces the harbor heads and open ocean.

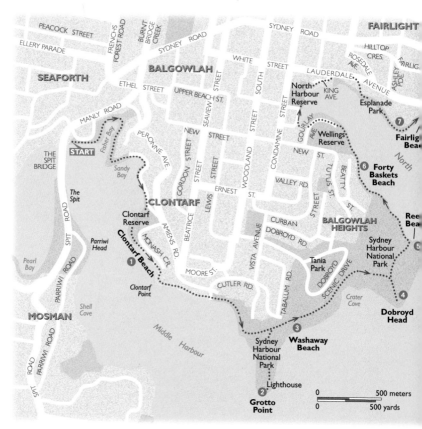

Up on **Dobroyd Head** ④, the view over the harbor to Manly is worth the long uphill haul. Far below, near the water's edge, you may be able to make out ramshackle huts that date from the Depression years and now form a small artists' enclave.

Follow the path away from the parking lot down to the end of the headland. From here wind your way back to the sheltered area of North Harbour and across the sands of **Reef Beach** ⑤, once a nude beach.

A short distance farther on is **Forty Baskets Beach** ⑥, a former fishing enclave with a harbor pool and some very exclusive real estate. The beach is so named because a catch made here of 40 baskets of fish was sent to a contingent of Sudanese troops being held at the Quarantine Station (see p. 99) in 1885. Just past Forty Baskets, a small marina sells drinks and ice cream.

Take time to explore the scenic North Harbour, where you can discover sheltered coves and idyllic beaches.

Follow the road up past the parking lot, turn right down a path that crosses a small bridge to reach the suburb of Balgowlah, then drop down to the park at the bottom. Cross the park, with the sand flats of North Harbour Reserve on the right. Continue up the other side to King Avenue. Follow it to Lauderdale Avenue and turn right. After a short distance, branch off to the right and pass the apartments and houses of Fairlight, with their marvelous views over North Harbour.

At **Fairlight Beach** ⑦ there is a harbor pool and another beach. Shortly after, Manly comes into view around a headland and you drop down to the aquarium complex of **Oceanworld** (see p. 99).

From there, the bright lights of civilization await at the ferry end of the esplanade. Here you can take a ferry back to the city or continue along The Corso to reach Manly Beach. ■

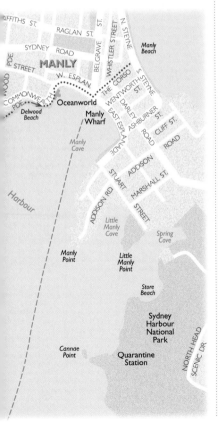

▲	83 E5
►	The Spit Bridge
↔	6 miles (10 km)
⏱	Allow 3–4 hours (don't forget to carry water)
►	Ferry Wharf

NOT TO BE MISSED
- Lighthouse on Grotto Point
- Washaway Beach
- Dobroyd Head
- Forty Baskets Beach

Shipwrecks

On a sparkling summer's day, when hundreds of boats flit across the surface of the water, the scene is idyllic. But while the harbor may be a safe haven today, several tales of disaster and woe are associated with it. One of the first vessels to visit the harbor, the First Fleet flagship *Sirius*, was wrecked off Norfolk Island in 1790. In 1834, 12 people died when the fully rigged *Edward Lombe* was wrecked on Middle Head, inside the harbor.

One of the blackest years in the city's maritime history was 1857. On the night of August 20, the crew of the clipper *Dunbar* mistook the lower cliffs of The Gap for the entrance to the harbor, and the ship foundered. James Johnson, the only crew member who survived (121 people died), was washed onto the rocks and clung to a ledge for 36 hours until he was rescued. Just two months later, the clipper *Catherine Adamson* was wrecked on inner North Head, with 21 fatalities.

The traumatic effect of these disasters was far reaching, and the following year the Hornby Lighthouse was constructed to more clearly mark the entrance to the harbor at the end of South Head.

In Watsons Bay, an anchor from the *Dunbar* lies at the front of Dunbar House, in the park that overlooks the ferry wharf. And in the cemetery of St. Stephen's Church in Newtown (see p. 163), you'll find a tomb marking the burial place of unidentified victims from both ships.

Harbor disasters

Tragedy has also occurred within the harbor itself. On November 3, 1927, the steamship *Tahiti,* running too fast as it rounded Bradleys Head, struck and sank the ferry *Greycliffe.* Among the 40 who drowned were many children on their way home from school.

In 1938, the small ferry *Rodney* was chartered to bid farewell to the visiting U.S. ship *Louisville.* Again off Bradleys Head, the overloaded ferry, listing on one side, capsized and 19 people were drowned.

Mystery surrounds the fate of one of the Midget submarines involved in the attack on Sydney on the night of May 31, 1942. One was sunk, one became entangled in antisubmarine nets, but a third disappeared without trace. It may have been sunk somewhere in the harbor, but it has never been located, despite extensive searches with metal detectors.

Another mysterious and well-known tragedy in the harbor involved the loss of just one life. One evening in the 1930s, an artist named Joe Lynch boarded a ferry with a group of friends; he was bound for a party on the North Shore, his greatcoat pockets laden with bottles of beer. Lynch was last seen sitting on the rail of the boat and presumably toppled overboard. Despite a wide search, no trace of him was ever found. The loss prompted his friend Kenneth Slessor to write the poem "Five Bells." In it, Slessor captured both the harbor's beauty and a poignant sense of mourning. The full text is in Slessor's *Selected Poems.* ∎

I looked out of my window in the dark
At waves with diamond quills and combs of light
That arched their mackerel-backs and smacked the sand
In the moon's drench, that straight enormous glaze,
And ships far off asleep, and Harbour-buoys
Tossing their fireballs wearily each to each,
And tried to hear your voice, but all I heard
Was a boat's whistle, and the scraping squeal
Of seabirds' voices far away, and bells,
Five bells. Five bells coldly ringing out.

Five Bells.
—Kenneth Slessor, "Five Bells" (1939), *Selected Poems*

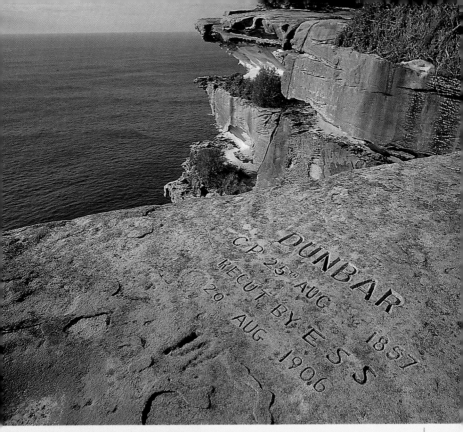

Above: A memorial to the *Dunbar* cut into the cliffs behind Watson's Bay
Left: The wreck of the *Dunbar* in 1857, artist unknown
Below: An anchor and cannon from the wreck of the First Fleet flagship *Sirius,* in Macquarie Place, near Circular Quay

On December 26, every vantage point on the shores and headlands of the harbor is crammed with spectators for the start of the Sydney to Hobart ocean yacht race.

More places to visit around Sydney Harbour

BALMORAL
One of the finest Inner Harbour beaches is Balmoral, in Middle Harbour. The area has been popular since a religious group in the 1920s became convinced it was going to be the site for the Second Coming of Jesus Christ. They were wrong, but the amphitheater they built on the site became an ideal entertainment venue.

There is a harbor pool and sailboat and dinghy rental nearby, plus one of Sydney's great waterside restaurants, the Bathers Pavilion (see p. 243).

83 E4 A ferry service runs to the beach in summer months. At other times take the ferry to Taronga Zoo (see pp. 92–93), then bus 238, or take bus 247 from Wynyard to Mosman, then bus 257 to Balmoral.

LAVENDER BAY
Lavender Bay is a small cove tucked under the office towers just downhill from North Sydney Station, at the end of Walker Street.

Access is also available by ferry, and there is a short harborside walk.

82 C2–C3

MARY MACKILLOP PLACE
At Mary MacKillop Place you can learn about Australia's only saint, Sister Mary MacKillop (1862–1909), through interactive displays. Her tomb is also here. She did a great deal for the poor in Australia and was beatified by Pope John Paul II in 1995.

To reach the museum, walk up the hill from North Sydney Station to Miller Street, then turn right. Two blocks later turn left onto Mount Street.

82 C3 ✉ 7 Mount St., North Sydney
☎ 9954 9900

NUTCOTE
Nutcote was once the home of children's author May Gibbs (1877–1969), whose characters were inspired by life in the Australian bush. Two "gumnut children," called Snugglepot and Cuddlepie, are the main heroes of her stories.

The easiest way to reach the house is from Kurraba Point Wharf. Turn left onto Kurraba Road, then turn left again and wind your way through to Wallaringa Avenue.

82 D3 ✉ 5 Wallaringa Ave., Neutral Bay
☎ 9953 4453 ⊕ Closed Mon.–Tues. ■

Scattered throughout the center of the city are several stunningly beautiful buildings, while to the south you'll find the delights of Chinatown and the lively Spanish Quarter.

City center & south

Window detail, Chinese Garden of Friendship

City center & south

THE COMMERCE OF THE CITY HAS ALWAYS BEEN SQUEEZED INTO THE
narrow strip of land known as the Central Business District (CBD), an area bordered
by Hyde Park on one side and Darling Harbour on the other. At times the focus of
business activity has been at the southern end; at others, nearer the harbor.

The result of this shifting is that the CBD has
different "centers" and reveals some opulent
buildings in areas that have become run down.
Recent prosperity and sprucing up in readiness
for the 2000 Olympics are changing the face of
the city once more. High-rise apartments are
springing up throughout the city, and new life
is being breathed back into the older areas.

These days, much of the city's finance sector
is found between Martin Place and Circular
Quay, while the shopping is between St. James
Station and the Town Hall. Between the Town
Hall and Central Station there are food and
entertainment venues. Down the hill from the
Town Hall you find movie theaters, Chinatown,
and the Spanish Quarter. The Capitol Theatre,
Her Majesty's Theatre, and the Entertainment

Centre account for the crowds grabbing a quick
bowl of noodles before heading to a show.

The central and southern part of the CBD
is the place to shop, spend a night out, or sight-
see, with some of the city's most interesting
buildings nestled beside huge towers offering
incredible panoramas of the city and beyond. ∎

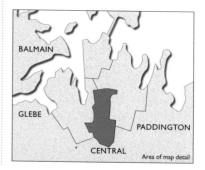

**The luxurious cosmetics hall
in David Jones department store**

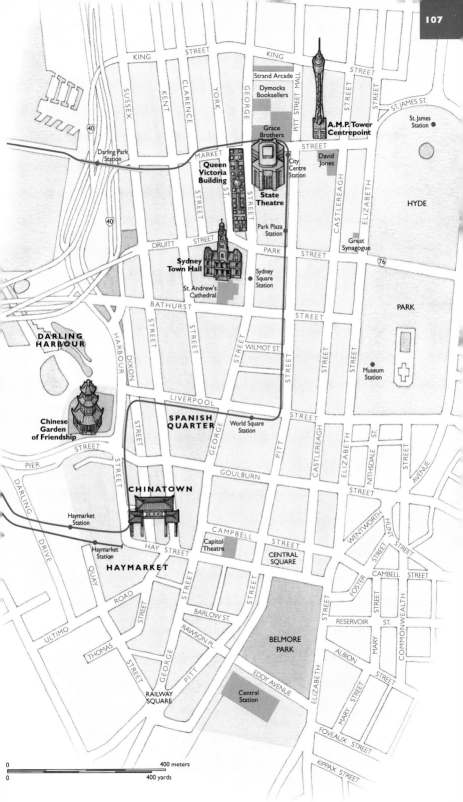

KING STREET

KING STREET

ST. JAMES ST.

Strand Arcade

Dymocks Booksellers

Grace Brothers

A.M.P. Tower Centrepoint

St. James Station

Queen Victoria Building

City Centre Station

David Jones

HYDE

State Theatre

MARKET ST

Park Plaza Station

PARK STREET

Great Synagogue

SUSSEX STREET

KENT STREET

CLARENCE STREET

YORK STREET

GEORGE STREET

PITT STREET MALL

ELIZABETH STREET

CASTLEREAGH STREET

Sydney Town Hall

DRUITT STREET

St. Andrew's Cathedral

Sydney Square Station

BATHURST STREET

PARK

DARLING HARBOUR

HARBOUR STREET

DIXON STREET

WILMOT ST.

Museum Station

LIVERPOOL STREET

Chinese Garden of Friendship

SPANISH QUARTER

World Square Station

PIER STREET

DARLING DRIVE

GEORGE STREET

PITT STREET

CASTLEREAGH STREET

ELIZABETH STREET

NITHSDALE ST.

AVENUE

GOULBURN STREET

CHINATOWN

Haymarket Station

HAY STREET

Capitol Theatre

CAMPBELL STREET

CENTRAL SQUARE

WENTWORTH STREET

HUNT STREET

Haymarket Station

HAYMARKET

QUAY STREET

ROAD

GEORGE STREET

PITT STREET

BARLOW ST.

RAWSON PL.

FOSTER STREET

CAMBELL STREET

COMMONWEALTH

ULTIMO

THOMAS STREET

BELMORE PARK

RESERVOIR ST.

ALBION STREET

MARY STREET

EDDY AVENUE

RAILWAY SQUARE

Central Station

ELIZABETH STREET

MARY STREET

FOVEAUX STREET

KIPPAX STREET

0   400 meters

0   400 yards

Centrepoint

ASK A TAXI DRIVER TO TAKE YOU TO THE A.M.P. TOWER AND he may look at you blankly. Ask him to take you to Centrepoint and you'll be at the corner of Pitt Street Mall and Market Street in a trice. At 1,000 feet (305 m) the tower is the tallest structure in Sydney. It rises above the Centrepoint Shopping Complex, a labyrinth of clothing, jewelry, food, and other outlets, and is the focal point of the main shopping area of the city.

A.M.P. Tower
Centrepoint
- Map p. 107
- 100 Market St.
- 9231 1000
- Observation deck: $$
- St. James Station

Built in 1981, the A.M.P. Tower comprises a central spike made up of 46 barrels stacked one above the other, with a golden turret on top that is anchored to the ground by 56 cables weighing 7 tons each. This top section weighs 2,000 tons, much of the weight being provided by more than 35,635 gallons (162,000 liters) of water. It acts as a counter-balance to any gust of wind, with the result that this "intelligent" building hardly sways at all, even in the strongest winds.

In the turret you will find an observation deck on level 4, two revolving restaurants—one on level 1 and one on level 2—and a coffee shop on level 3. In just 40 seconds, by way of the high-speed elevators, you leave the bustle and noise of the street far below and replace them with wonderful 360-degree views.

To the north is the harbor and in the far distance Pittwater (see pp. 178–80). To the east are the Pacific Ocean and miles of coastline.

To the south is Botany Bay, where the first settlement of Sydney was supposed to be based. And to the west, across Darling Harbour, the suburbs stretch to the feet of the Blue Mountains (see pp. 217–23).

CENTREPOINT SHOPPING

The area around Centrepoint is prime shopping territory, but the following are worth visiting for their aesthetic value alone. First of all is **Pitt Street Mall,** running off Market Street outside Centrepoint.

The pedestrianized section of the street features some excellent examples of Victorian architecture and is one of the city's busiest shopping precincts, open seven days a week. Pitt Street was named after the English prime minister William Pitt the "Younger" (1759–1806), who was responsible for the establishment of the colony of Sydney.

Halfway along the mall is the **Strand Arcade,** the most beautiful arcade in the city. It opened in 1892 and features much of the wrought-iron lacework, colored glass, and detailing typical of Victorian shopfronts. Badly damaged in a fire in 1976, it held such a place in the heart of the city and the shopkeepers that it was carefully restored to its original condition. At the George Street end of the Strand is **Dymocks Booksellers,** one of the biggest bookshops in Sydney.

On the corner of Pitt and Market Streets is **Grace Bros.** department store, refurbished in 1998 and now nearly as elegant as David Jones, on the other side of Centrepoint. **David Jones** describes itself as the "world's most beautiful store." It occupies two sides of Market Street at the Hyde Park end. Enter the left-hand store (as you face the park) at ground level to find gray marble, mirrors, huge sprays of flowers, and, at certain times, live piano music.

Across Market Street, go downstairs to discover the **David Jones Food Hall,** a food-lover's paradise. The oyster bar is especially good. ■

Opposite: The A.M.P. Tower Centrepoint is the most prominent landmark on the skyline and often serves as a backdrop for major firework displays.

State Theatre

State Theatre
- Map p. 107
- 49 Market St.
- 9320 9050

Sydney Film Festival
- 9660 3844
- 2 weeks in June
- St. James Station

The Grand Assembly Room in the State Theatre

ALONG MARKET STREET IS THE STATE THEATRE, A GRAND motion-picture palace from the silent movie era. When it was opened in 1929, the deputy premier declared that no words of his could do justice to the beauty of the interior. The theater is now a popular venue for drama, concerts, and the annual Sydney Film Festival held in June.

The aim of the theater's architect, Henry White, and the managing director of Union Theatres at the time, Stuart Doyle, was to bring many of the architectural styles of Europe (especially Gothic

and rococo) to the largely untraveled Sydney public. Particularly splendid is the domed Grand Assembly Room, with marble staircases sweeping up to a marble balcony. On the floor, a mosaic by the Melocco brothers (see p. 64) depicts St. George doing battle with the dragon, and there is another St. George scene over the doors in the entrance foyer. The foyer's bronze fan ceiling is modeled on Henry VIII's Chapel in Westminster Cathedral, London. Also note the dress circle foyer, which incorporates an art gallery with works by portrait painter Sir William Dobell (1899–1970), Thea Proctor (1879–1966), and others.

Inside the auditorium are busts of famous historical figures, and the stage is dressed by the Golden Arch—surmounted by the Crown of England—and flanked by Aboriginal maidens. The domed ceiling is made up of plaster octagons each containing a patterned snowflake.

The pièce de résistance, however, is the second largest cut-glass chandelier in the world (the largest is in the Hofburg Palace, in Vienna), with 321 lights and 17,363 pieces of glass.

Tours are occasionally available for groups of 15 or more, but you are welcome to join a group if one is booked (*Centrepoint Touring Company, Tel 8223 3854/3815*).

Alternatively, attend a show and have a night out and a good look around at the same time. ∎

Queen Victoria Building

Spectators watch the performing clock on the top level of the extraordinary Queen Victoria Building.

ANOTHER FINE EXAMPLE OF SYDNEY'S LATE 19TH-CENTURY architecture is the Queen Victoria Building (QVB), standing on Market Street at the corner of George Street. While the Town Hall was constructed in a period of prosperity, the QVB, built to commemorate Queen Victoria's Golden Jubilee, was completed in 1898, during a period of depression.

As a means of providing employment for unemployed craftsmen—especially stonemasons and stained-glass artists—it was a great success, and at the same time provided the city with a stunning building. The French fashion designer Pierre Cardin is reported to have called it the "most beautiful shopping center in the world."

Over the years the QVB has had many functions—it housed the city's produce markets in the 19th century, and was subsequently used as offices and the city library—and yet, unbelievably, in the 1950s the authorities considered tearing it down. Fortunately, it survived and in the 1980s, courtesy of a Malaysian company, underwent a massive restoration program and was converted into a shopping gallery.

Inside and out are breathtaking. Note the patterned tiled floors, polished woodwork, and elegant shopfronts. Also look for the Royal Clock which, on the hour, displays scenes from the lives of English kings and queens.

Particularly striking is the central glass dome, with beautiful stained-glass windows on either side, which creates a dramatic space between the multiple levels of stores. And what stores. There are nearly 200, including the city's and the world's biggest names. On the lowest level you'll find plenty of stylish cafés and eateries.

If you walk through to the far end of the QVB, a block along George Street, you'll come to the imposing statue of Queen Victoria herself, in the main forecourt of the building. And across Druitt Street you'll see yet another of Sydney's great Victorian buildings, the Sydney Town Hall (see p. 112). ■

Queen Victoria Building

🅰 Map p. 107
✉ George St.
☎ 9264 9209
🚉 Town Hall Station

Sydney Town Hall

⬛ Map p. 107

✉ Corner of George
& Druitt Sts.

☎ 9265 9007

Sydney Town Hall has been a social hub of the city since 1889. Its ornate exterior is rivaled only by its stunning interior.

IMMORTALITY
One of Sydney's most unusual sights lies between the Town Hall and St. Andrew's Cathedral (see p. 118). From Sydney Square, descend the steps to

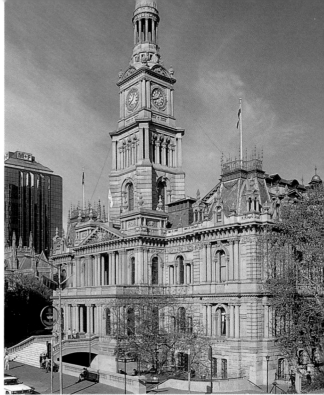

Sydney Town Hall

BUILT IN STAGES BETWEEN 1868 AND 1889 ON THE SITE OF the old Sydney Burial Ground, the Town Hall is another of the city's beautiful Victorian buildings. Its foundation stone was laid in 1868 by Prince Alfred, Queen Victoria's son.

a small courtyard. Here, on the ground in front of the fountain, you'll find the word "Eternity" cast in metal. What does it mean? For 30-odd years, reformed alcoholic Arthur Stace (1885–1967) chalked the word all over the city during the night. He had been helped by a Baptist preacher and in turn wanted people to think beyond the present. ∎

The interior is one of the finest examples of high Victorian decoration in Australia. Note particularly the vestibule, with its 1,952-piece crystal chandelier and stained-glass ceiling panels depicting the four elements and eight virtues.

The **Centennial Hall** was the home of the Sydney Symphony Orchestra until the company moved to the Opera House in the 1970s, but is still used for concerts and large public meetings. Constructed in 1890, the organ, with over 8,000 pipes, is one of the largest ever built. The ceiling of the hall—the largest pressed zinc

ceiling in Australia—is specially designed to withstand the vibrations it causes. Recitals are held on a regular basis, and there are free lunchtime concerts about once a month. Details of these and other events are available in the front foyer. Here you can also pick up a leaflet for a self-guided tour showing you where to find such curios as a marble sculpture of diva Dame Joan Sutherland's ear.

Meetings of the Sydney City Council are still held at the Town Hall, with the Lord Mayor usually presiding in ceremonial regalia. The public is welcome to attend. ∎

City south

THE ROOTS OF SYDNEY MAY BE FIRMLY SUNK INTO THE ground around Circular Quay, but as the city grew it spread south, away from the harbor. The southern end of the long finger of the CBD is where the locals generally gather to spend their free time.

On leaving the Town Hall, continue along George Street away from the harbor. If you are looking for movies, the multiplex cinemas on either side of the street should more than suffice. (Anyone who has just arrived in Australia will probably notice there is a time lag of a month or two in the release of movies.)

Farther down George Street, turn right onto Liverpool Street. This block is sometimes referred to as the **Spanish Quarter.** Among the dozen or so Spanish restaurants here is the Spanish Club, the focus of a small but very active Spanish community and a number of other Latin-American communities. There are dancing, food, and music, and visitors are very welcome.

A block farther down George Street from the Spanish Quarter is the more substantial **Chinatown** (see p. 116).

Continue to the bottom of the hill and you will come across tram tracks, the remnants of the city's once extensive tram system. Trams have begun to make their return in the form of Sydney Light Rail, ferrying passengers from Central Station to Darling Harbour and the Sydney Fish Market at Pyrmont.

Turn left and follow the tracks to reach the **Capitol Theatre** on Campbell Street. During the 1890s a market was held here, and later the site was used as an open-air theater and hippodrome.

In 1928 the existing theater was built by John Eberson with its beautiful interior, themed as a Florentine garden at night complete with shining stars reflecting the

southern sky, and drifting shadow clouds. The theater was faithfully restored to Eberson's original specifications in the mid-1990s and reopened to stage productions of the large musicals such as those imported from Broadway. It is worth seeing a show to appreciate the interior.

Continue following the tram tracks to reach **Belmore Park,** with its band rotunda and spreading Moreton Bay fig trees.

At the far end of the park is the grand Renaissance-style **Central Station,** built on the site of the Devonshire Street Cemetery in 1906. The arrival hall is the obvious must-see feature here, excepting the video destination screens. The original destination board is now in the **Transport Hall** of the **Powerhouse Museum** (see pp. 122–25). In the railway bar off the main hall is yet another Melocco brothers mosaic floor. ■

Polar bears and seals once performed in a tank that still exists beneath the seats of the Capitol Theatre.

Capitol Theatre

◩ Map p. 107

✉ 13 Campbell St.

☎ 9320 5000 (inquiries)

🕐 Box office closed Sun. Tours are conducted between show seasons.

A walk to the Chinese Garden of Friendship

This is a short, mostly downhill or level walk from Central Station through Chinatown to the Chinese Garden of Friendship and Darling Harbour. Walking time is only 30 minutes, but there are plenty of distractions. It is possible to cover most of the route from the comfort of the Sydney Light Rail system, hopping on and off as various sights attract your interest.

From Central Station, take the path that follows the tram tracks past **Belmore Park** ① and then turn left onto Hay Street. Having crossed George Street, enter Chinatown proper (see p. 116), with Sussex Street and the pedestrian walkway of Dixon Street to the right.

On the left is one of Sydney's institutions—**Paddy's Market** ② (*Corner of Thomas and Hay Sts., Haymarket, Tel 9325 6200, closed Mon.–Fri.*). The market has been here since the last century, only moving while the building that now towers over the site was under construction. It sells everything from leather jackets to ducks and puppies, from fruit and vegetables to watches and electrical goods. If you like shopping for bargains, this is the place to go.

After visiting the market, stroll north along Dixon Street, where there are lots of places to eat. At the top of the street, turn left and take the walkway across Harbour Street, then spiral down the path to the side of the **Sydney Entertainment Centre** ③ (*Harbour St., Haymarket, Tel 9320 4200*). This is the largest indoor complex in the city, seating up to 12,500. It is the venue for major international rock concerts, and the Sydney Kings basketball team also plays here.

Keeping the center on the left, follow Little Pier Street to the **Pumphouse Hotel** ④ (*17 Litle Pier St., Tel 9320 4200*). Originally, the building, dating from 1891, provided hydraulic pressure to operate the elevators of the city; it was then converted into a pub with brewing facilities and a

Looking for souvenirs at a stall in Paddy's Market. The market has operated for over a century and is a hive of activity on weekends.

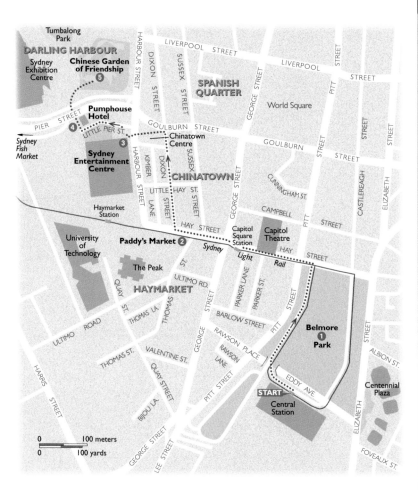

wide range of boutique beers, and is now a luxury hotel.

Just past the front of the Pumphouse Hotel you will come across the walkway that passes under Pier Street. If you look up you'll notice a long pipe running across the bottom of the road bridge that releases a curtain of water with unpredictable regularity. Kids love it and wait around in groups for the next soaking.

Just beyond the waterfall, Darling Harbour starts, although the **Chinese Garden of Friendship** ⑤ (see p. 117) marks the boundary of Chinatown. You can either end the walk here with traditional Chinese tea and cakes in the Tea House Courtyard, or continue by following the

🗺	Inside front cover C1
▶	Central Station
↔	1 mile (1.6 km)
🕐	Allow half a day
▶	Chinese Garden of Friendship

NOT TO BE MISSED
- Belmore Park
- Paddy's Market
- Sydney Entertainment Centre
- Chinese Garden of Friendship

Darling Harbour walk (see pp. 126–27), which ends at the Sydney Fish Market, an ideal place to stop for lunch. ∎

Kangaroos can be a hazard on Australian roads, but on Chinese New Year, dragons stop traffic.

Chinatown

SYDNEY CAN CLAIM TO HAVE HAD A CHINESE COMMUNITY ever since two Chinese cooks arrived with the First Fleet. Shortly after its foundation, the colony's trade with Hong Kong and other Asian centers saw rising numbers of Chinese people coming to Australia, which increased with the gold rushes from the 1850s onward.

NEW YEAR

In mid- to late January watch out for the dragons that dance up and down every street in Chinatown during the week-long Chinese New Year celebrations. Look, too, for shops with lettuces hung from the awnings as offerings to the dragons who in return will drive out evil spirits that are bad for business. ∎

Chinatown consists of a handful of streets around Dixon Street, although a stroll through the nearby suburbs of Surry Hills and Pyrmont will reveal many Chinese shops and houses. Here you can get a good meal, a massage, Chinese herbs and remedies, and plenty of the exotic flavor of Australia's Asian neighbors. The district also has a scattering of Japanese and other Asian restaurants.

Off Harbour Street, the pedestrian mall of Dixon Street and Sussex Street, food halls can be found on several stories of quite a few buildings. Specialties include "steamboat" (you broil food at your table) and "yum cha" (dozens of help-yourself trolleys are wheeled past your table). Note that opposite the Capitol Theatre (see p. 113) on Hay Street, Bohdi Restaurant has finger-lickin' vegetarian yum cha. If you're not sure how the ordering system in a place works, just ask.

At the bottom of Dixon Street, walk through to Thomas Street and the Burlington Centre, where there are several specialty shops. The main attraction, however, is the supermarket. This is well worth a visit for the sheer variety of weird and wonderful things on display, such as Chinese medicines, ducks' tongues, and sea urchins. ∎

Chinese Garden of Friendship

The Lenient Jade Pavilion, overlooking the Lotus Pond of the Chinese Garden of Friendship

DURING THE BICENTENNIAL CELEBRATION OF AUSTRALIA in 1988, marking 200 years of European settlement, Sydney and other Australian cities received numerous gifts from countries around the world. One of Sydney's presents was the Chinese Garden of Friendship, a gift from Guangdong Province in China.

The garden, the largest of its type outside China, is designed according to southern Chinese tradition. It combines pavilions, lakes, waterfalls, and winding paths with lush vegetation, cherry and lychee trees, and scented flowers, including many gardenias. The system of waterways is well stocked with fish, and shoals often congregate in the canal outside the entrance waiting to be fed (don't forget to take some bread with you).

A traditional two-story *gurr* (pavilion) on a high point of the garden sets the scene, but there are also many small rooms, gazebos, and walls that enhance the plants and rockeries. Notice, too, the elaborate wood carvings and statues that include lions, dragons, and chubby infants in repose. Traditional-style tearooms make the garden an ideal place to wind up at the end of a walk.

It doesn't take very long to walk around (the walled-in area covers only 2.5 acres/1 ha), but the intention of the design is to tempt the visitor to linger awhile, to sit and enjoy this oasis of peace in the midst of the bustling city. ■

Map p. 107
Corner of Pier & Harbour Sts., bet. Darling Harbour & Chinatown
9281 6863
$
Sydney Explorer bus, Sydney Light Rail from Central Station, Monorail

More places to visit in the city center

GREAT SYNAGOGUE

Amid all the commercial activity in the center of the city, two places of worship offer a respite from the shops and traffic. The first, the Great Synagogue, facing Hyde Park, was consecrated in 1878, although the history of Australian Judaism reaches back to a small number of Jews who arrived with the First Fleet. It was designed by Thomas Rowe in Byzantine style. Special features are the wrought-iron gate and railings, whose design is repeated in the wheel window above, and the decoration of the interior. Free tours, which include a film on Australian Judaism shown in the synagogue and a visit to a small museum (*entry via 166 Castlereagh St.*), are

St. Andrew's Cathedral, Australia's oldest, contains numerous memorials dating back to the First Fleet.

conducted on Tuesdays and Thursdays at noon. The tour is a great opportunity to see the interior of the synagogue. Look at the star-speckled ceiling in particular. The volunteer guides are very knowledgeable and willing to answer any number of questions.

Note that before and during World War II many Jews fled to Australia to escape persecution. Their story and more of the history of Australian Jews is told at the **Sydney Jewish Museum** (see p. 139).
 Map p. 107 187 Elizabeth St. 9267 2477; www.wej.com.au/greatsyn

ST. ANDREW'S CATHEDRAL

St. Andrew's Cathedral is the second refuge from the city's hustle and bustle. Situated alongside the Town Hall in Sydney Square, it is the oldest cathedral in Australia. Its foundation stone was laid in 1819 by Lachlan Macquarie, but construction was delayed by the fiscal rectitude of the governor's nemesis, Commissioner Bigge. The building was eventually consecrated in 1868.

Built in late Gothic style, it was designed by colonial architect Edmund Blacket (1817–1883). When he died, Blacket was buried in Blamain Cemetery, but after the cemetery was turned into a park, his ashes were reinterred under the cathedral's floor.

The cathedral's organ dates from 1866 (recitals are usually held twice a week) and there are a number of icons from Australian history within the building. Of some significance to Australians is a flag from Gallipoli, where, in 1915, thousands perished storming the Turkish ramparts and the newly independent country of Australia had its first baptism of fire. There is also a memorial to Samuel Marsden, the colony's first parson.

Other notable features in the cathedral include the original choir stalls that are carved in American oak, the Great Bible, dating from the 16th century, and a Union flag that was held by prisoners under the Japanese at Changi prison camp in Singapore. The marble floor in the side chapel came from St. Paul's Cathedral in London.
Map p. 107 Sydney Sq., George St. 9265 1661 ■

Museums, a casino, an aquarium, restaurants, shopping, live entertainment, parks, and gardens—there's something for everyone in this bustling tourist area.

Darling Harbour

Shellfish, Sydney Fish Market

Darling Harbour

THE DARLING HARBOUR AREA ENCOMPASSES BOTH THE OLDEST AND THE newest faces of Sydney: Old because it was where ships were unloaded from the early years of the 19th century onward; new because a large part of it was renovated and turned into a complex of stores, convention centers, exhibition halls, and entertainment facilities for the 1988 Bicentennial. Some of the old working port remains at the entrance to the harbor, but the rest of the area has been completely revamped.

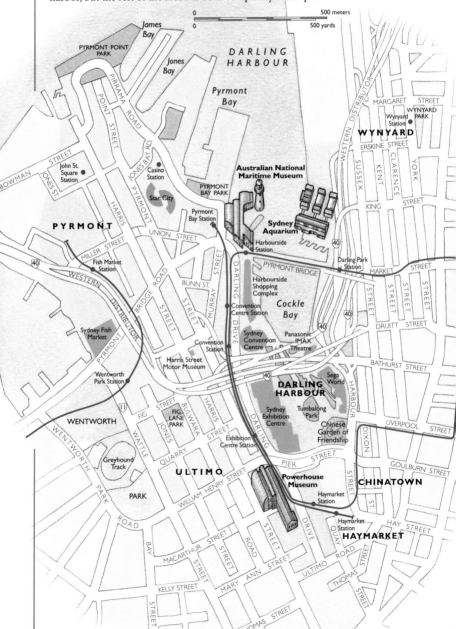

On all sides hotels and high-rise apartments are springing up. The precinct feels more like a theme park than any other part of Sydney—which may be a plus or a minus, depending on taste. But even if such amusements don't appeal, you will find some interesting and enjoyable alternatives.

Among the possibilities is the largest museum in the country, the Powerhouse, and the Australian National Maritime Museum, which

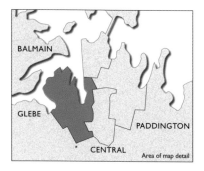

contains significant relics from Australian seafaring history. Pyrmont Bridge, the swing bridge spanning the center of Darling Harbour, is a beautiful piece of engineering, and one of the early Manly ferries, the *South Steyne*, now a floating restaurant, is permanently moored at the docks. A very pleasant walk around the waterfront areas brings you to the Sydney Fish Market—a great place for lunch. If you want to see the fish (and sharks) while they're still swimming, visit the nearby Sydney Aquarium.

Numerous other amusements include an IMAX theater, Sega World, and Star City, Sydney's casino. A variety of restaurants caters to nearly every taste and budget, and the shopping area is geared to visitors.

In addition, you can enjoy a full calendar of special events and free entertainment, staged in amphitheaters and on floating stages, year-round. Outdoor entertainment increases in the summer, and the place positively hums during the Christmas and January school vacations. ■

Pyrmont Bridge, which spans Cockle Bay, connects the city with Darling Harbour's shops and museums.

Powerhouse Museum

SO CALLED BECAUSE SINCE 1988 IT HAS OCCUPIED THE shell of the turn-of-the-century Ultimo Power Station, the Powerhouse Museum is the largest museum in the country. It houses a collection that was begun more than 120 years or so ago and now comprises 380,000 items (not all on display at once!). Despite its long history, the museum has a modern approach to the presentation of its material and the emphasis is on interactivity.

Powerhouse Museum

🅰 Map p. 120

✉ 500 Harris St., Ultimo

☎ 9217 0111
www.phm.gov.au

💲 $$

🚌 Sydney Explorer bus, Monorail, or Sydney Light Rail to Haymarket Station. Bus: 501 from Town Hall Station

Exhibits are displayed thematically on four levels (Levels 2–5), covering steam engines, flight and space exploration, decorative arts and design, and Australian social history. In addition, continually changing exhibitions take place throughout the museum based on its collections of porcelain, military memorabilia, furniture, clocks, relics of Sydney's history, music, and Aboriginal culture.

Orientation tours take place every 15 minutes Monday through Friday. In addition, there are two special interest tours a day (11:15 a.m. and 1:15 p.m.), as well as self-guided tours.

LEVEL 2 (COURTYARD LEVEL)

There are a number of fascinating exhibitions on this level, but you will find it particularly difficult to drag children away from the **Experimentations** section. This is a hands-on area where lights, levers, pulleys, knobs, and dials enable young and old to have a great deal of fun discovering the workings of such things as gravity, electricity, magnetism, heat, and light.

In **Chemical Attractions,** a special section of Experimentations, you can see and become involved in the processes that take place in the making of everyday items.

Perhaps the most spectacular section of the museum, though, is the **Transport Hall,** where

various forms of transport show how transportation has developed and changed our lives. The space section, for example, contains a space shuttle flight deck and a selection of satellites, Sputniks, and lunar landers. There are also pieces of equipment from China, Russia, and the United States.

The romance of rail travel is evoked by the original destinations board from the grand hall in **Central Station** (see p.113). Nearby is an entire switching room, and you can see some of the famous trains from Australia's history.

Another highlight of the transport area is the Bleriot monoplane suspended from the ceiling. It made the first flight from Sydney to Melbourne in 1914. Nearby is the plane used by the fledgling Qantas for its first commercial flight.

If you are interested in indigenous Australian music and dance, visit the exhibition opposite the courtyard called **Ngaramang Bayumi,** where a range of styles, from rock to ceremonial, are covered.

One of the smaller sections on this level features the numerous historically significant musical instruments that the museum holds.

Finally, for some refreshment, try the outdoor kiosk in the Grace Bros. Courtyard.

On a mezzanine level, **Little Wheels** looks at the history of transportation in miniature, with over 1,600 matchbox toys.

Opposite: The Transport Hall of the Powerhouse Museum features trains, planes, and automobiles, including a Catalina flying boat suspended from the ceiling.

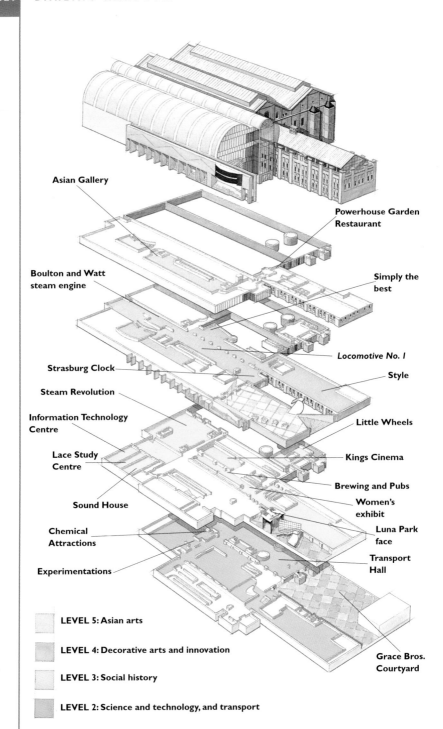

Asian Gallery

Powerhouse Garden
Restaurant

Boulton and Watt
steam engine

Simply the
best

Locomotive No. 1

Strasburg Clock

Style

Steam Revolution

Information Technology
Centre

Little Wheels

Lace Study
Centre

Kings Cinema

Brewing and Pubs

Sound House

Women's
exhibit

Chemical
Attractions

Luna Park
face

Transport
Hall

Experimentations

Grace Bros.
Courtyard

LEVEL 5: Asian arts

LEVEL 4: Decorative arts and innovation

LEVEL 3: Social history

LEVEL 2: Science and technology, and transport

LEVEL 3

This level is known as the **Theatres Level** because it contains several special-purpose venues for groups and school parties. The Kings Cinema, an art deco 1930s theater, shows nonstop news and feature films of the era.

Here, too, is an **Information Technology Centre,** where you can surf the Internet on weekends. A lacemaking study center and sound house (musical instruments and recording studios) also has public access at certain times on weekends.

Permanent exhibits include the **Steam Revolution,** which presents a variety of hands-on displays and historic engines that demonstrate the development of steam and the power available through air pressure.

Near the Kings Cinema you will find displays on significant elements in Australian culture, including the role of pharmaceuticals in Australian life; a look at the life and work of women in an Australian home; and an exhibition about the role that breweries have played in developing and promoting Australian cultural ideals.

LEVEL 4

Most of this level is devoted to temporary exhibitions, but there are three particular gems to seek out. The first two form part of the **Simply the best** exhibition, which features Australian items of outstanding design. Here you can see **Locomotive No. 1,** the first train to run in Australia, in 1863. It was built at Robert Stephenson's factory in Newcastle, England, in 1854, and brought to Sydney where it ran on the country's first railway line, from Redfern to Parramatta.

Just behind the train is the oldest rotative steam engine known to be in existence—the **Boulton and Watt steam engine.** It was

originally installed in a London brewery in 1785, where it ran for more than a hundred years.

Other railway items of interest are signals and signal boxes.

Near the glass elevator look for the **Strasburg Clock** (as Strasbourg was spelled when this one-sixth scale reproduction was built, between 1887 and 1889). It was modeled on the clock that has graced Strasbourg Cathedral, France, since 1354. Talks about the clock are given daily, as are demonstrations of its processions of figures.

In the **Style** section just opposite the clock, trace the changes and fashions in decorative arts.

While you're on this level, you might like to visit the museum's comprehensive gift shop.

LEVEL 5

Here the **Asian Gallery** houses changing exhibitions based on the museum's large collection of Asian cultural items.

The Powerhouse Garden Restaurant, which features artistic designs by prominent Australian artist Ken Done, is also on this level. ■

The forecourt of the Powerhouse features one of the large faces that adorned Sydney's Luna Park, which is no longer operating.

A walk to Sydney Fish Market

This is a nice level stroll through Darling Harbour and on to the Sydney Fish Market, passing several of the area's major attractions including the Sydney Aquarium and the Australian National Maritime Museum. Allow 1.5 hours for walking and the rest of the day for sight-seeing. A good idea is to arrive at the fish market for lunch. Note that this walk joins the Central Station to Chinese Garden of Friendship walk (see pp. 114–15).

Many of the points on this route are accessible from the Sydney Light Rail system.

Starting from the **Chinese Garden of Friendship** (see p. 117), walk through **Tumbalong Park ❶**, an open-air performance space. Keep to the right to pass the ornamental lake, **Sega World** (see p. 132), and **Panasonic IMAX Theatre** (see p. 132). Note the Wockpool restaurant—one of the city's best eateries—and Jordons Seafood Restaurant on the left facing the water.

Continue along the right-hand side of the bay, past Cockle Bay Wharf—a series of brand new shops and eateries—to **Sydney Aquarium ❷** (see pp. 130–31). Take the stairs or escalator to the deck of **Pyrmont Bridge ❸**. Opened in 1902, it was the first electrically operated swingspan bridge in the world and was powered by the Ultimo Power Station (see p. 122). The bridge is closed to traffic, though it still opens to allow tall-masted ships access to Darling Harbour. It opens only on demand, so you may or may not be lucky enough to catch it in operation.

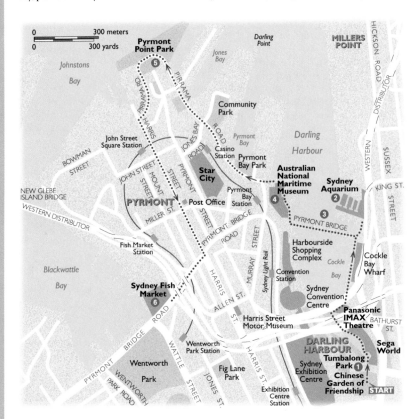

A shopkeeper at the Sydney Fish Market weighs out some "Balmain Bugs"—small crustaceans like lobster and just as tasty.

On the other side of the bridge, either descend to dock level on the left-hand side and be tempted by the stores, restaurants, and entertainments of the Harbourside Shopping Complex, or descend on the right-hand side to reach the **Australian National Maritime Museum** ④ (see pp. 128–29).

Walk along the harbor side of the museum and look over the museum's assortment of moored vessels for free. On the far side of the museum, Pyrmont Bay Park stretches past the front of **Star City** (see p. 132), the city's casino. Pirrama Road passes naval facilities and several finger wharves that were built between 1913 and 1933. Note the double-story roadway built out over the bay between parallel wharf sheds.

⚠ Inside front cover C2
▶ Chinese Garden of Friendship
↔ 3 miles (5 km)
⏱ Allow 1.5 hours
▶ Sydney Fish Market

NOT TO BE MISSED
- Sydney Aquarium
- Australian National Maritime Museum
- Pyrmont Point Park
- Sydney Fish Market

Just beyond the wharves is the little known **Pyrmont Point Park** ⑤. Opened in 1996, it features playgrounds, a waterfront promenade, and barbecues. Great views of the city, Sydney Harbour Bridge, and New Glebe Island Bridge (opened in 1995) can be enjoyed from here, too.

Follow the road around to Harris Street, passing several of the 1870s pubs and cottages that remain in the area. You'll find several cafés between John Street and Miller Street.

At the post office (circa 1895) on the corner of Miller Street, turn right and head down to the Fish Market Light Rail station. Alternatively, continue along Harris Street to Simon Johnson's Fine Foods, at No. 181. From there the **Sydney Fish Market** ⑥ (*corner of Bank St. and Pyrmont Bridge Rd., Tel 9660 1611*) beckons—just follow the signs.

Each weekday, the market auctions the previous night's catch in the early hours of the morning, finishing at about 8 a.m., and the fish is sold in the surrounding shops. Some of the shops will cook seafood platters for you; or you can try one of the open-air restaurants. A particular pleasure is to take your own picnic supplies out onto the docks and enjoy them while watching the yachts and cruisers coming and going.

Return to the city by Sydney Light Rail or walk straight up Pyrmont Bridge Road to Darling Harbour. ∎

Exhibits at the maritime museum include boats such as this small wooden sailing vessel, which is just visiting. It is moored in front of the permanently displayed big-gun frigate *Vampire*.

Australian National Maritime Museum

Australian National Maritime Museum

THE MUSEUM IS HOUSED AT THE WESTERN END OF Pyrmont Bridge in a distinctive building that resembles the spread of sail of a tall ship. Opened shortly after the Bicentennial (in 1991), its aim is to represent the relationship between Australians and the sea throughout the country's history. So, in one gallery you'll see dugout canoes built by Aborigines several thousand years ago, and in another high-tech 18-footers constructed from space-age materials. In between are many relics and treasures, including some of the earliest maps of Australia, navigational equipment, and presentations illustrating convict transportation and the arrival of the waves of immigrants to Australian shores.

One of the most popular and best known exhibits is *Australia II,* the 39-foot (12-m) yacht that won the America's Cup in 1983, thus ending the United States' 132-year winning streak. The boat is not in the water—it reaches from floor to ceiling of the main hall, its once secret, striking winged keel now exposed to all and sundry. Nearby, for those interested in 18-footers, are two examples of the craft from very different eras. One is a cedar-built racer from the 1940s; the other one of the ultimate racing machines from the 1970s (see p. 94).

On the lower level you can see the slowly rotating steam engine that was originally used in one of the car ferries that serviced North Sydney before the Harbour Bridge was built. Here, too, is the U.S.A. Gallery, housing both permanent and visiting exhibitions, yet another of the many presents that Australia was given to mark its Bicentennial.

Australian National Maritime Museum

Map p. 120

2 Murray St., Darling Harbour

9298 3777 or 1900 962 002 (recorded information)
www.anmm.gov.au

$$

Sydney Explorer bus, Monorail to Harbourside Station, or Sydney Light Rail to Pyrmont Bay Station

Darling Harbour

Funded by the United States, the gallery often mounts exhibitions that explore aspects of the relationship between the two countries. The ties go back to the 18th century, when the first foreign vessel to visit the fledgling colony in Sydney was a U.S. trading ship, the brig *Philadelphia,* which arrived in November 1792.

OUTDOOR EXHIBITS

Among several interesting vessels moored on the wharf outside, look for the *Krait,* a World War II commando boat that was used in daring raids in Southeast Asia; a racing cutter dating from 1888; and a Vietnamese fishing boat used by refugees fleeing to Australia after the Vietnam War (1975). Pearling luggers and Indonesian fishing boats are on display, and often visiting yachts are invited to moor at the museum because they have features of interest to visitors.

And, of course, there is the H.M.A.S. *Vampire,* one of the last big-gun destroyers (these days they're all guided missiles). Guided tours of the 1959 Royal Australian Navy ship, known as "The Bat," include presentations of naval actions.

On the water is the CL54 lighthouse ship *Carpentaria* (once used in the Gulf of Carpentaria) and on the dock the relocated Cape Bowling Green Lighthouse.

Right: Two of Australia's record-breaking vessels are displayed in the museum: *Australia II* **and the** *Spirit of Australia.* **The latter was the world's fastest boat when, in 1978, it reached a speed of 317 mph (511 kph).**

Note that the area between the museum and the water is open to the public, which means that, apart from *Vampire* and the onshore lighthouse, you can see the boats for free.

If all this exposure to things maritime has you itching to take to the water, join the introductory sailing school that operates from the wharf area. And on weekends, several of the local boating societies run short voyages aboard steam vessels and tugboats.

A café in front of the museum overlooks the waterfront, and the museum shop is well stocked with nautical gifts and books. ■

Captain Cook & the Hubble Telescope

One of the maritime museum's most interesting exhibits is what is thought to be the sternpost from Capt. James Cook's ship *Endeavour.* In the eyes of many Australians it is almost a holy relic, and while it reflects the close ties Australia has with England, it also has an interesting connection with the United States. Two engravings from the *Endeavour* were taken aboard the space shuttle *Endeavour* when it flew a mission to repair the Hubble Telescope. The connection is even more appropriate because one of Cook's tasks during his voyage was to observe the transit of Venus across the face of the sun—an astronomical activity akin to Hubble's. ■

Sydney Aquarium

Sydney Aquarium

- Map p. 120
- Aquarium Pier,
  Darling Harbour
- 9262 2300
  www.sydneyaquarium.
  com.au
- $$$
- Sydney Explorer bus,
  Town Hall Station,
  Monorail to Darling
  Park Station
- Darling Harbour

THE BUILDING HOUSING THE SYDNEY AQUARIUM (THE roof is adorned with a shark with jaws agape) on the city side of Pyrmont Bridge echoes the design of the Australian National Maritime Museum. One of the largest in the world, with a submarine walkway 158 yards (146 m) long, the aquarium features a diverse collection of aquatic life from a wide range of marine environments that extends from the tropics to Antarctic waters. There are more than 5,000 sea creatures and more than 50 specialized displays.

A tour of the aquarium starts with the freshwater fish of Australia and the first creature you'll see is the largest specimen, the murray cod.

Adjacent to the big cod is the platypus tank, which re-creates the animals' natural river habitat. Low-level lighting simulates dusk, the time when platypuses are naturally at their most active.

The freshwater section also features long-finned eels and numerous species of bass, perch, trout, minnow, and turtle. However, don't linger too long, because there is a huge amount to see ahead.

The mangrove section displays crabs, mudskippers, and fish of the intertidal zone, including huge barramundi, much prized by fishermen.

However, the aquarium's "barra" would snap most fishing lines.

And speaking of big, the aquarium also has a live estuarine crocodile from the Northern Territory. And saurians from the Top End of Australia—living "dinosaurs" that have survived virtually unchanged for around 65 million years—are two to three times the size of alligators in the Florida Everglades, measuring up to 23 feet (7 m) in length.

SHARKS & SEALS

The feature of the main tank is the sharks—gray nurse, Port Jackson, and shovelnose. Stingrays are on display, too.

Among the star attractions, however, are the seals. Kept in the separate **Seal Sanctuary,** they are

particularly mesmerizing for children, and the appeal is enhanced by the specially designed enclosure that encases visitors in glass so that the eastern fur seals can swim and glide around you in all three dimensions.

One of the aquarium's roles is its commitment to care for and rehabilitate any seals that are washed ashore along the New South Wales coast. Once the seals have fully recovered, they are released back into the wild.

Other facilities include the **touch pool,** where you can pick up the less harmful creatures of the deep and learn how they live.

CORAL REEF

The aquarium's latest project, and by far the most ambitious, is the Great Barrier Reef display, which occupies a new building behind the main complex. It is an attempt to produce and sustain a massive piece of tropical coral reef, complete with over 2,000 fish ranging from tiny, coral-dwelling species to tiger sharks. Several smaller tanks allow you to appreciate close-up the beautiful and delicate corals, anemones, and fish life of the reef, but the main tank is simply brilliant. Stocked with some of the most beautiful fish in the world, and the various sharks of the reef, the presentation includes floor-to-ceiling glass and grottoes where the smaller fish can keep out of the way of the predators.

And then you come to the huge glass tunnel. As you walk through, fish swim above and you can look straight down the length of the tank while white-tipped reef sharks, black-tipped reef sharks, and leopard sharks swim toward you; stingrays lie on the sand beneath and fish swim all around.

Near the exit is another glass wall and tiered seating to "sit at the bottom of the sea" and watch the fish swim by. ∎

BUDGET HARBOR

A Darling Harbour Superticket includes aquarium admission and a meal at the café, a Matilda Cruises Harbour Express Cruise, a Monorail ride, entry to the Chinese Garden of Friendship, and reduced admission to the Panasonic IMAX Theatre, the Powerhouse, and the mini-train that runs around Darling Harbour. The ticket is available from most of the above (*Tel 9262 2300 for details*). ∎

Darling Walk skirts a small pleasure lake with a water playground that can keep children amused (and wet) for hours.

More places to visit in Darling Harbour

HARRIS STREET MOTOR MUSEUM

This museum may not be large, but it houses an impressive collection of classic cars, commercial vehicles, and motorbikes. The exhibits—more than 150—date from the earliest years of the automobile to the present and give an account of the industry and the lives of the people involved in it during that time.

Map p. 120 320 Harris St., Pyrmont 9552 3375 Closed Mon.–Tues., except during school holidays Monorail to Convention Station

PANASONIC IMAX THEATRE

Located in the massive silver-colored building at the head of Darling Harbour, the IMAX theater boasts the largest screen in the world. Films about the scenic outdoors, featuring Africa, Antarctica, and the Himalaya, predominate.

Map p. 120 Southern Promenade, Darling Harbour 9281 3300 Monorail to Convention Station

SEGA WORLD

An indoor family theme park, Sega World aims to cater to a wide range of tastes with rides, attractions, and themes that are geared to the past, the present, and the future. Then there is a comprehensive range of the latest in electronic virtual reality games.

Map p. 120 1–25 Harbour St., Darling Harbour 9273 9273 Monorail to Convention Station

STAR CITY

Opened in 1997, Sydney's casino, Star City, was the city's first legal gaming house. It replaced many illegal establishments that had existed since the first years of the settlement. The casino is open 24 hours a day year-round, and has more than 200 gaming tables and 1,500 slot machines.

The complex also includes two theaters, 14 restaurants and bars, and a large hotel/apartment facility with harbor views, a pool, spas, saunas, a gymnasium, and a health club.

Map p. 120 80 Pyrmont St., Pyrmont 9777 9000 Free buses run to Star City from the city & Kings Cross all day every day. Sydney Light Rail & Monorail to Darling Harbour Ferry from Circular Quay on The Rocks side ■

Beach culture, elegant harborside living, artists' enclaves, the gay scene, and much more is compressed into the lively area between the city and the sea.

Eastern Suburbs

Bondi Beach lifeguard

Eastern Suburbs

COVERING THE AREA EAST OF THE CITY TO THE COAST, THE EASTERN Suburbs represents suburban, cosmopolitan, and cultural diversity. It is an incredible mix of the salubrious and the salacious—wealth, poverty, hedonism, and the highbrow. This is the most desirable precinct of Sydney, containing within its borders just about every lifestyle imaginable and every amenity of modern life.

Here you'll find major art galleries and museums, more restaurants and cafés than you could ever hope to try in one visit, and some of the most seriously rich harborfront living available. If you've made it here, you've probably made it everywhere, as the list of overseas property owners can attest—movie stars, business people, royalty.

Some of the most significant early houses in the country are found here, too, including Elizabeth Bay House and Vaucluse House, both beautifully preserved.

The Eastern Suburbs is also the center of Sydney's gay community, which is concentrated on the city end of Oxford Street and the surrounding area. The annual Sydney Gay & Lesbian Mardi Gras festival culminates in the Mardi Gras parade—one of the biggest street parades in the world with hundreds of spectacular floats watched by hundreds of thousands of people.

On the shores of the harbor, the various bays offer safe anchorage, restaurants, walks, and swimming. Beach life centers on Australia's most famous beach, Bondi. There can be no greater pleasure than a plunge into the Pacific Ocean breakers (always take care to swim between the flags), followed by an ice cream or fish and chips in one of the beach cafés. ■

Area of map detail

Picnickers enjoy the late afternoon sun under a Moreton Bay fig tree with large buttress roots at Nielsen Park, Vaucluse. In the background is Greycliffe House.

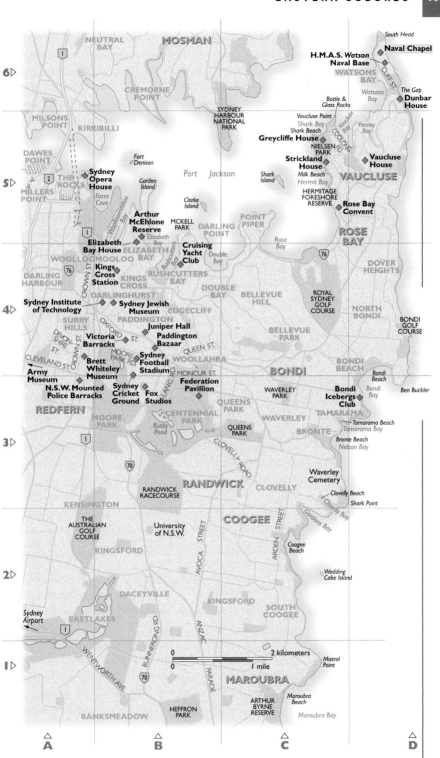

South Head

Naval Chapel

H.M.A.S. *Watson*
Naval Base

WATSONS
BAY

Watsons
Bay

The Gap
Dunbar
House

NEUTRAL
BAY

MOSMAN

CREMORNE
POINT

SYDNEY
HARBOUR
NATIONAL
PARK

Bottle &
Glass Rocks

Vaucluse Point
Shark Bay
Shark Beach

Parsley
Bay

Greycliffe House

NIELSEN
PARK

MILSONS
POINT

KIRRIBILLI

Fort
Denison

Port Jackson

Strickland
House

Shark
Island

Vaucluse
House

DAWES
POINT

MILLERS
POINT

THE
ROCKS

Sydney
Opera
House

Garden
Island

Farm
Cove

Clarke
Island

Milk Beach
Hermit Bay

HERMITAGE
FORESHORE
RESERVE

VAUCLUSE

Rose Bay
Convent

ROSE
BAY

Arthur
McEhlone
Reserve

MCKELL
PARK

DARLING
POINT

POINT
PIPER

Elizabeth
Bay

Rose
Bay

DOVER
HEIGHTS

Elizabeth
Bay House

ELIZABETH
BAY

Cruising
Yacht
Club

Double
Bay

WOOLLOOMOOLOO

DARLING
HARBOUR

Kings
Cross
Station

KINGS
CROSS

RUSHCUTTERS
BAY

DOUBLE
BAY

BELLEVUE
HILL

ROYAL
SYDNEY
GOLF
COURSE

NORTH
BONDI

BONDI
GOLF
COURSE

DARLINGHURST

Sydney Institute
of Technology

Sydney Jewish
Museum

EDGECLIFF

PADDINGTON

BELLEVUE
PARK

SURRY
HILLS

OXFORD ST.

Juniper Hall

Paddington
Bazaar

QUEEN ST.

WOOLLAHRA

BONDI
BEACH

Bondi
Beach

Ben Buckler

Victoria
Barracks

Sydney
Football
Stadium

MONCUR ST.

BONDI

Bondi
Bay

CLEVELAND ST.

Brett
Whiteley
Museum

MOORE
PARK RD.

Federation
Pavillion

WAVERLEY
PARK

Bondi
Icebergs
Club

Army
Museum

N.S.W. Mounted
Police Barracks

Sydney
Cricket
Ground

Fox
Studios

QUEENS
PARK

TAMARAMA

Tamarama Beach
Tamarama Bay

REDFERN

MOORE
PARK

Busby
Pond

CENTENNIAL
PARK

WAVERLEY

BRONTE

Bronte Beach
Nelson Bay

QUEENS
PARK

Waverley
Cemetery

CLOVELLY ROAD

RANDWICK

CLOVELLY

Clovelly Beach

Shark Point

KENSINGTON

RANDWICK
RACECOURSE

COOGEE

Gordons Bay
Clovelly Bay

THE
AUSTRALIAN
GOLF
COURSE

University
of N.S.W.

AVOCA STREET

ARDEN STREET

Coogee
Beach

KINGSFORD

Wedding
Cake Island

DACEYVILLE

KINGSFORD

SOUTH
COOGEE

Sydney
Airport

EASTLAKES

BUNNERONG RD.

ANZAC PARADE

WENTWORTH AVE.

0   2 kilometers

0   1 mile

Mistral
Point

MAROUBRA

BANKSMEADOW

HEFFRON
PARK

ARTHUR
BYRNE
RESERVE

Maroubra
Beach

Maroubra Bay

6

5

4

3

2

1

A   B   C   D

Paddington & Woollahra

ORIGINALLY A DOWN-AT-HEEL, WORKING-CLASS DISTRICT southeast of the city center, Paddington has become greatly gentrified since the 1970s. Young professionals, eager to live close to the center, started buying up the row houses in the area and renovating them with great sensitivity. This, together with subsequent guidelines from the local council, and recognition of the heritage value of Paddington, means the Victorian houses in the area are particularly well preserved. Today, residents can hardly change a lightbulb without complying with the appropriate code.

Cast-iron lacework is a feature of Paddington's well-preserved Victorian row houses.

From the shopping area in the middle section of Oxford Street, Paddington's main thoroughfare, deviate into the many side streets. Here you'll see beautiful houses with wrought-iron lace balconies, railings, arched windows, and window boxes spilling flowers.

Also on Oxford Street is **Victoria Barracks,** established in 1841, where Sydney's armed forces are stationed. The beautifully proportioned main building, which faces the parade ground, was built in the Georgian style by Lt. Col. George Barney of the

Royal Engineers and 150 convicts, including many French Canadians, transported after a rebellion in 1837–38. A changing-of-the-guard ceremony takes place at the barracks main gate on Thursdays at 10 a.m., followed by guided tours and band performances. You can also visit the **Army Museum** on the grounds of Victoria Park.

At 248 Oxford Street is **Juniper Hall.** Now owned by the National Trust, the hall is not currently open to the public. It is the oldest building east of the city, built in 1824 by Robert Cooper (a gin distiller, hence the hall's name) in colonial style. The stretch from here to Queen Street is full of cafés and boutiques.

On Saturdays, the **Paddington Bazaar** takes place on the grounds of the Paddington Village Uniting Church from 10 a.m. to 4 p.m. Clothes, trinkets, handicrafts, and food, among other things, are for sale. *(Note that parking is very difficult on weekends.)*

WOOLLAHRA

Just before reaching the large intersection of Oxford Street and Moore Park Road, Queen Street branches off east toward the suburb of Woollahra. Queen Street's grand terraces soon give way to a string of fine art and antique stores. Unlike the nascent Paddington, Woollahra has long been one of the redoubts of old Sydney money.

At the intersection of Moncur Street, in the Woollahra Hotel, you'll find one of the city's better known eateries, Bistro Moncur. Near the opposite corner is one of its best cafés, Zigolini's.

If instead of exploring Queen Street you continue to the intersection, you'll notice one of the entrances to **Centennial Park.** Reclaimed in 1888 from swampland that had been the source of the city's drinking water, the park has become the city's premier recreational area. You can rent horses from the old showground nearby, and cycle, jog, in-line skate, or walk during daylight hours. An extensive lake system attracts plenty of bird life and enthusiasts to watch it, and a fine café serves lunches and light meals *(Tel 9360 3355, reservations essential for weekend lunch)*. There is an in-line skate rental shop *(36 Oxford St., Tel 9380 6356)* near the intersection with Moore Park Road. Bicycles and in-line skates are also available for rent from several shops on Clovelly Road, Randwick *(Tel 9398 5027 or*

9399 3475). The park has ample parking (on some weekends, however, there are car-free days) and free barbecue facilities (bring some paper to clean off the grills).

Conveniently located between Centennial Park and the city are the Sydney Cricket Ground, the Sydney Football Stadium (a short taxi ride from the city, or buses are available from Central Station for sports events), and the old Showground. The latter is now a film lot for Fox Studios that includes an entertainment complex with movie theaters, arcades, and cafés. ■

Changing of the guard at Victoria Barracks, with one soldier in modern army uniform and another in a uniform worn circa 1840

Bohemian Sydney

FROM THE TIP OF GARDEN ISLAND, SOUTH THROUGH Woolloomooloo and Kings Cross, Darlinghurst and Surry Hills to Redfern, there is about as broad a cross section of life as you are likely to find anywhere. This is an area where artists, writers, and actors live and congregate, and where you'll find Sydney's gay community, educational establishments, and some great small museums.

Sydney Jewish Museum
- 135 B4
- ✉ 148 Darlinghurst Rd., Darlinghurst
- ☎ 9360 7999
- www.join.org.au/ sydjmus/index.html
- 🕐 Closed Sat.

Brett Whiteley Museum
- 135 A4
- ✉ 2 Raper St., Surry Hills
- ☎ 9225 1881. For visits on Thurs. & Fri.: 9225 1740 (Art Gallery of N.S.W.)
- 🕐 Closed Mon.–Wed.; Thurs. & Fri. by appt. only

Woolloomooloo (the "Loo" for short) was once one of the most disreputable and boisterous of Sydney's suburbs—full of sailors on leave, small-time criminals, prostitutes, and gangs. These days the area is a lot safer and more respectable, with public housing and gentrified apartments on the renovated finger wharf. The Tilbury Hotel features live jazz on Sunday afternoons.

Up the hill is **Kings Cross's** main thoroughfare, Macleay Street. There is a good choice of accommodations here, but the area in the immediate vicinity of the Kings Cross Station along to the El Alamein Fountain has become rather disreputable. Victoria Street, however, just behind the station, has a quite different atmosphere. This beautiful, wide, tree-lined street has numerous cheap hostels on its grand terraces, and several good-quality but affordable cafés and restaurants.

Darlinghurst, primarily an area of apartments, restaurants, and small art galleries, begins on the

south side of William Street. It boasts restaurant strips along Crown Street at its intersection with Stanley Street, Darlinghurst Road, Victoria Street, and Oxford Street.

The **Sydney Jewish Museum** can be found on the corner of Burton Street and Darlinghurst Road. Many European Jews who escaped the Holocaust have recorded their stories for the museum, and these now form part of a moving memorial to the history of Australian Jews reaching back to the First Fleet. Nearly half of the museum's 150 guides are Holocaust survivors, and the building is arranged around a Star of David.

Occupying the former jail of Darlinghurst, across from the museum, is the **Sydney Institute of Technology** (Forbes St., Tel 9339 8666). The buildings, designed by Francis Greenway, date back to the 1820s. A stroll through the grounds will bring you to Oxford Street and Taylor Square, the hub of the gay community.

South of Darlinghurst is **Surry Hills,** another former working-class suburb that has been renovated. It is a little quieter than nearby Darlinghurst, and the shops and restaurants along Crown Street have something of a village feel. One of the galleries worth visiting is the **Brett Whiteley Museum,** a block east of Crown Street.

Farther down Crown Street, just across Cleveland Street in East Redfern, is the **N.S.W. Mounted Police Barracks** (Tel 9319 2154). The barracks are not open to the public at specific times, but the staff is happy to welcome groups, preferably on Tuesdays or Thursdays, for tours and a visit to the small museum. ■

The interior of the Sydney Jewish Museum, showing one of the points of its Star of David design

PIE & PEAS

One of Sydney's most idiosyncratic icons, Harry's Café de Wheels, can be found on the waterfront at Woolloomooloo. The café started out as a pie cart, but someone stole the cart's wheels back in the 1950s, and the café has been stuck in this vicinity ever since. ■

Mardi Gras

Light shows, fireworks, thumping pop music, incredible costumes, colorful floats, thousands upon thousands of people: The sheer spectacle of the Gay & Lesbian Mardi Gras parade along Oxford Street and Flinders Street in Darlinghurst is one of the highlights of Sydney's annual calendar of events. Conducted every year in late February or early March, it celebrates something that many other cities and countries are still coming to terms with—their gay communities.

Early days
But it has not always been like this. In 1978, when the first march was organized, the climate was very different and the parade was marked by violence.

On June 24, events commemorating the ninth anniversary of the Stonewall uprising in New York, which also centered on gay and lesbian rights, were held in the city. When a parade began at Taylor Square, New South Wales police attempted to stop its progress. The marchers regrouped down the hill on William Street but were forced into Darlinghurst Road, where the police were waiting to set upon the marchers. Violence had been prevalent in the police force for years, but on this occasion TV cameras, photographers, and journalists were on hand.

The brutality gave credence to claims of intimidation that had been circulating for years. It also added to the increasing pressure for change, and the parade became both an annual event and a potent force on the political agenda. Numerous issues remain, but the parade held in 1998, the celebration of the 20th anniversary of the first march, provided a clear insight into how far Sydney has come.

As always, for many participants there are only two dress options—bare flesh or sequins. For others, however, the parade is still closely

Far left: Evening wear Mardi Gras style
Center: The well-drilled Marching Boys are
an annual feature of the parade.
Above: One of those outfits you might only
wear once a year

linked to its origins, so among the razzle-dazzle there are more subdued groups representing the different services and organizations found in all communities.

However, it is the showstopping element of the festival that draws the large crowds. Usually kicking off the proceedings every year are the Dykes on Bikes—bare-breasted lesbian women riding large motorcycles. One of the highlights of the parade is the Marching Boys, who perform elaborate routines along the mile-long (1.6-km) parade route.

Other groups specialize in biting satirical comment. For example, in the year that the female swimmers from China were accused of drug-taking at the Olympics, a group sporting red, one-piece swimming costumes, hairy chests, and beards entered the Mardi Gras parade as a Chinese women's swimming team.

Practical advice
There are a few tips worth noting for those intending to witness the parade spectacles. First, be prepared for some sights you may not

have seen before. Complete nudity isn't permitted, but many entrants get very close to it.

Second, bring some refreshments. There are food and drink outlets, but you may lose a good viewing position while you are trying to buy something.

Third, locate the portable toilet facilities and make sure you can get to and from them without getting lost.

Fourth, try and bring something safe to stand on so that you can see over people's heads. Afterward, be prepared for chaos on the roads and huge crowds trying to take public transportation. Most importantly, though, have a great time.

Details about the festival ☎ 9557 4332; www.mardigras.com.au ∎

Eastern Sydney beaches

Bondi Beach
🗺 135 D3–D4
🚌 Bus 380, 389, or L82 from the city; train to Bondi Junction Station then bus 380 or L82

Tamarama Beach
🗺 135 C3
🚌 Bus 361 from Bondi Junction Station

Bronte Beach
🗺 135 C3
🚌 Bus 378 from Bondi Junction Station

Clovelly Beach
🗺 135 C2–C3
🚌 Bus 339 from the city

Coogee Beach
🗺 135 C2
🚌 Bus 372, 373, 374, X74 from the city.
Note: All of the beaches to this point (except Clovelly) are serviced by the Bondi & Bay Explorer bus

Maroubra Beach
🗺 135 C1
🚌 Bus 395, 396, 377, X77 from the city

The sands of Bondi Beach looking north to the headland of Ben Buckler and some of the most sought-after real estate anywhere

SYDNEY HAS SOME OF THE MOST BEAUTIFUL BEACHES IN the world right on its doorstep. An office worker in the city can finish for the day and be in the waves half an hour later. From famous Bondi Beach to stylish Tamarama and family-oriented Clovelly and Coogee, this coast offers something for everyone.

BONDI BEACH

No beach in Australia is better known to overseas visitors by name than Bondi. To Australians, it is a symbol of the relaxed outdoor lifestyle that they cherish.

The Bondi Surf Bathers' Lifesaving Club, the first of its kind in the world, was formed here in 1906. At the south end of the beach, the Bondi Icebergs are a hardy bunch who swim throughout winter in baths at the southern end of the beach. Bondi is the most accessible beach from the city, a mere 5 miles (8 km) away, and being surrounded by apartments on all but the ocean side, it has been described as "Venice with a swell."

If you swim, do so between the pairs of flags placed at intervals along the beach and try to avoid taking any valuables to the beach. Note that there are protected swimming baths at both ends of the beach that are suitable for children.

Youth hostels abound here, and there are some good-quality hotels as well. Eateries on the whole are basic and cheap.

SOUTH OF BONDI

The first beach south from Bondi is **Tamarama Beach,** one of the smallest along this stretch of coast. The sand is often littered with beautiful people. There is a kiosk/café, and the beach has a surf patrol.

Winding around the next headland you descend to **Bronte Beach,** popular with surfers wanting to catch the strong current (a rip), known as the Bronte Express,

out to the back breakers. The beach is patrolled but tends to have fairly rough and unforgiving surf; if you want safer and more enjoyable waves, Bondi is usually a better option. There is a sheltered ocean pool, however, and plenty of picnic areas and cafés nearby.

Continue around the headland and through the Waverley Cemetery onto the paths and suburban streets leading to **Clovelly Beach.** Due to its sheltered position, this beach and its pool are ideal for families with children.

Farther on is **Gordon's Bay.** This is just a small unpatrolled patch of sand, but the area is popular for snorkeling, and there is an underwater "marine walk" for diving enthusiasts.

Next is **Coogee Beach,** one of the perennial favorites with families, as it is usually fairly sheltered from the ocean waves. There are ocean-fed pools as well.

Offshore is **Wedding Cake Island,** a rock named for its shape and white "icing" of guano. Back from the water is a shopping strip.

Maroubra Beach, 2.5 miles (4 km) farther south, is more suburban than the other beaches, but it offers an ocean pool and safe swimming. You'll find a café at the northern headland, and showers and a kiosk on the beach.

To explore the coast on foot, follow the walkway that starts from the southern end of Bondi Beach. Bus routes to the beaches along the way make it possible to catch a ride back to the city. ∎

A walk around South Head

This pleasant walk from Watsons Bay combines harbor and ocean views, including a great view of the entrance to Sydney Harbour. There are also several sites that have historical connections with the First Fleet, shipwrecks, and 19th- and 20th-century defenses such as cannon and antisubmarine stations.

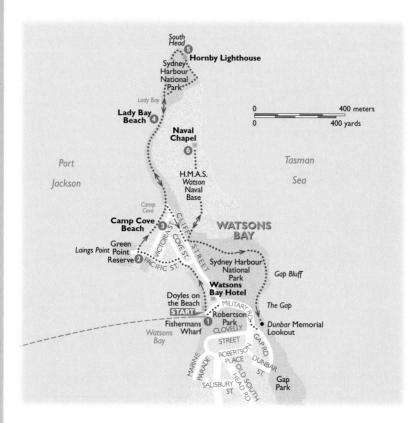

135 D6

Watsons Bay wharf

2 miles (3 km)

Allow 1.5–2 hours

Watsons Bay wharf

NOT TO BE MISSED

- Laings Point
- Camp Cove
- Hornby Lighthouse
- Naval Chapel

Start from **Fishermans Wharf ①** at Watsons Bay (*reached by ferry from Circular Quay, Bondi & Bay Explorer bus, or bus routes 324 and 325*) and take the promenade past the **Watsons Bay Hotel,** with its beer garden and outdoor bistro area, and Doyles On the Beach seafood restaurant (*see p. 250*), one of the city's institutions. Climb the stairs at the end of the promenade, then turn left and left again onto Pacific Street. At the end of Pacific Street you will come to a small headland, **Laings Point ②**. Here are the remains of World War II gun emplacements and the antitorpedo and submarine boom

Walk to the tip of the South Head peninsula for extensive views across the harbor to North Head and Middle Head.

that was stretched across the harbor during the war years.

Continue to the right, where there is a memorial to Governor Phillip. The small beach below is called **Camp Cove Beach** ❸; this is where Phillip first landed when he entered Sydney Harbour and spent his first night on Australian soil. At the other side of the sandy stretch of beach, ascend the stairs and you will shortly pass a gun that dates from 1872, part of the defenses built as fortification against a threat of invasion by Russia.

A little farther on is **Lady Bay Beach** ❹, currently the harbor's only designated nude bathing beach. The path passes discreetly above the beach, and just beyond the beach it breaks clear of the trees onto low headland heath, which Sydney Harbour National Park is regenerating to its original condition.

On the headland itself, one of the old lighthouse keeper's cottages is occupied by a caretaker who looks after the site; the other is undergoing restoration. These buildings

and the **Hornby Lighthouse** ❺, a little farther on, were built in 1858 after two tragic disasters the year before: the wrecks of the *Dunbar* and the *Catherine Adamson* (see pp. 102–103). You can also see World War II fortifications and gun emplacements on the headland.

Follow the path as it loops around the seaward side of the headland before rejoining the path from Lady Bay.

Back at Camp Cove, continue straight ahead down Cliff Street to the H.M.A.S. *Watson* Naval Base. A visit to the beautifully sited **Naval Chapel** ❻ (see p. 148) is well worthwhile. The short road to the right leads past a function center of Sydney Harbour National Park.

On the far side of the center, a small path cuts straight across to The Gap, where the *Dunbar* came to grief. There are several paths around the cliff tops here, and it's just a short stroll west along Military Road to the bus stop and the wharf on Watsons Bay. ∎

The Bays

ONE OF THE FEATURES OF THE EASTERN SUBURBS THAT gives the area much of its character is the succession of bays and headlands that stretches from Garden Island eastward along the harbor to South Head. The bays boast some of the most expensive real estate in the world, with lavish waterfront houses, delightful parks, and historic estates dating from the 19th century.

Heading east from the city, the first bay you'll reach is **Elizabeth Bay,** just down the hill from Kings Cross railway station. A pleasant place for a picnic, and a pocket of some of the most expensive real estate in the city, one of its prime assets is **Elizabeth Bay House,** on Onslow Avenue. Completed in 1839 for the colonial secretary of New South Wales, Alexander Macleay, its showpiece feature is the oval main saloon with a cantilevered stone staircase and soaring, domed ceiling. The views from the upper windows across Sydney Harbour to the heads are alone worth the price of admission.

After your visit, if you are waiting for a Sydney Explorer bus, check out the the tiny **Arthur McElhone Reserve,** just behind the bus stop, to pass the time. This small public garden was established in 1952 and named after Sydney council alderman Arthur McElhone, who represented the local ward for 44 years.

The next bay eastward is **Rushcutters Bay,** where the Cruising Yacht Club of Australia is based. The club, at the head of the bay, is responsible for the Sydney end of the Sydney to Hobart Yacht Race. In the days prior to the start of the race, on December 26, the whole area takes on a carnival atmosphere as the boats begin to assemble.

The very expensive piece of real estate that forms the next headland is **Darling Point,** where there is a delightful little picnic and scenic spot, **McKell Park,** the site of a former hospital.

On the other side of Darling Point is **Double Bay.** There are three things of particular note here—exclusive shopping, exclusive hotels, and the elite of Sydney Harbour skiff racing (see pp. 94–95). Double Bay boasts some of the best cafés, restaurants, clothing boutiques, and jewelers in the city; the Ritz-Carlton Hotel is where prime ministers and presidents usually stay; and the 18-foot skiffs sail from the club on the waterfront.

Beyond the next exclusive headland, Point Piper, is **Rose Bay.** From here you can take a seaplane ride (*Tel 9388 1978*), either on a joy ride, or up to **Pittwater** (see pp. 178–80) and beyond. The impressive building on the hill is the **Rose Bay Convent.** You can walk around the headland to Watsons Bay from Rose Bay, although you should allow about half a day to do this.

If you get off the bus (*Bondi & Bay Explorer bus or route 325*) at Tivoli Avenue and follow it down to the end of Bayview Hill Road, you reach the **Hermitage Foreshore Reserve.** A short walk through the reserve passes tiny Hermit Bay and Milk Beach (below Strickland House, a former convalescent hospital) and continues around to Shark Bay and Nielsen Park (*also accessible by route 325*). Just back from the water at Nielsen Park is

Elizabeth Bay House

🅰 135 B5

✉ 7 Onslow Ave., Elizabeth Bay

☎ 9356 3022

www.hht.nsw.gov.au

🕐 Closed Mon.

💲 The house is part of the Historic Houses Trust Ticket Through Time

🚌 Bondi & Bay Explorer bus

Greycliffe House, built in 1852 and now an office for the National Parks and Wildlife Service. **Shark Beach** is netted and safe for swimming, and Nielsen Park Kiosk is a popular restaurant.

Beyond Shark Bay is **Vaucluse Point** and the Bottle and Glass Rocks. This is a great spot to watch yachts sweeping down the harbor under spinnaker on a summer's afternoon.

Continue along Coolong Road to **Vaucluse Bay** and **Vaucluse House** (see p. 148). Cut across Boambillee Avenue and Fitzwilliam Road to the inlet of **Parsley Bay,** where a large grassy area attracts weekend picnickers in droves.

The major tourist mecca, however, is **Watsons Bay** (*Map 135 D6*), tucked into the western side of the peninsula as it narrows toward South Head. Formerly a military base and fishing village, the suburb has a small town atmosphere, and you'll find swimming pools, picnic spots, restaurants, and walks. On weekends, it is very popular (and often easier to visit by ferry or bus than by car). As you face the shore, note Dunbar House. ■

Seen from above, the harbor shore-line is character-ized by a series of bays interspersed with small islands.

Antiques dating from the time the building was first occupied decorate the interior of Vaucluse House.

More places to visit in the Eastern Suburbs

NAVAL CHAPEL

Built in 1961 as a memorial to the naval personnel who lost their lives in the service of the country, the chapel is one of the most beautiful in Sydney. A wall of glass rises behind the altar, giving spectacular views out to the Pacific Ocean, past the imposing precipice of North Head. If you climb up to the organ loft by the spiral stairs to the right, you can see back across Sydney Harbour to the city.

The chapel itself has several interesting features, including the altar, which was constructed with stone from cathedrals and churches in Jerusalem, Washington, London, Cape Town, and other cities.

On the left of the chapel two carved stone heads from Southwell Minster in London, dating from A.D. 630, support the credence table (where the elements of the Eucharist are held before they are consecrated); the lectern is a New Zealand bird, a kea, carved in wood at the Auckland Naval Dockyard; and the chapel font is an inverted ship's bell.

Weddings are frequently held here, and a Catholic service is held at 9:00 a.m. on Sundays. 🅜 135 D6 ✉ Access to the Naval Chapel is via the H.M.A.S. *Watson,* entered from Cliff St. 🕒 Open daylight hours

VAUCLUSE HOUSE

Vaucluse House, between Watsons Bay and Nielsen Park, was built in the 1830s (around an earlier house of 1803) for the explorer and political figure William Charles Wentworth (1793–1872) and his family. Wentworth was one of the party that found a route across the Blue Mountains (see pp. 217–23).

The house, a well-preserved example of colonial architecture with grand halls and wide balconies, is lavishly furnished with period items. Formal gardens and parkland make up the grounds, which reach down to the harbor. The well-known tearooms serve refreshments. 🅜 135 D5 ✉ Wentworth Rd., Vaucluse ☎ 9388 7922; www.hht.nsw.gov.au 🕒 Closed Mon. 💲 $ 🚌 Bus 325 from Circular Quay or Bondi & Bay Explorer bus ∎

In and around the city are thousands of relics left by the Aborigines, the original inhabitants of Australia. For visitors to Sydney who want to experience indigenous culture and art, the choice of galleries and cultural centers is wide.

Indigenous Sydney

Aboriginal design, Darling Harbour

Indigenous Sydney

ALTOGETHER, THE SYDNEY REGION HAS SOME 1,200 KNOWN SITES WHERE rock engravings, cave paintings, and remains of campsites can be seen, or where Aboriginal ceremonies were held. Sydney's indigenous heritage is one of the richest of any city in the world, and research has shown that as many as 70 percent of visitors to Australia hope to experience this heritage in some form. Many people at the sites described on the following pages will help to take you a step beyond the usual tourist presentations.

The Aboriginal people of Australia have had it hard since the Europeans arrived in 1788, falling victim to disease, massacres, the state-sanctioned separation of children from their parents, and exile to mission stations. For most, the traditional way of life has been overwhelmed, and Aboriginal people have struggled to find a place in the modern world—a situation not helped by the apathy or discrimination of the European settlers. The consequences of unemployment, lack of education, and poor health standards are still widespread.

The good news is that Australia is actively engaged in a process of reconciliation that has placed the delivery of improved health, economic opportunities, and cultural respect and recognition high on the national agenda. There is a very, very long way to go, but some benefits are already beginning to be felt. Perhaps the most significant development is pride; where once some people kept their Aboriginal heritage secret, they are now embracing it.

Visitors can learn something about this culture by visiting gallery and museum exhibitions and cultural centers, attending music and dance performances, shopping for indigenous art and artifacts, or joining tours to significant sites led by Aboriginal guides. ■

Aboriginal sites

ALL THE NATIONAL PARKS AROUND SYDNEY HAVE significant Aboriginal sites that include carvings, paintings, and middens (campsites where people gathered to eat oysters, mussels, and other shellfish). Many of these sites are carefully protected, but there is still much to be seen.

At **Ku-ring-gai Chase National Park** (*Map 175 D4, Visitor information, Tel 9457 1049; see pp. 176–77*) north of the city, three trails—the Basin Track, the Red Hand/Resolute Picnic Area Track, and the Echidna Site—on the road to West Head lead to significant sites. Dreamtime figures, animals, people, weapons, and tools are portrayed. Other sites can be found on the Elvina Track at West Head and the Bobbin Head Track.

One of the most accessible rock carving sites is in the **Royal National Park** (*Map 187 D2, Visitor information, Tel 9542 0648; see pp. 195–97*), on Port Hacking Point near the tiny township of

Bundeena. Take the ferry from Cronulla, then walk along Loftus Street and Jibbon Beach to the point. This is the start of the coast walk to the southern end of the park.

You can explore a number of sites in **Sydney Harbour National Park.** The Tour Unit at the Quarantine Station (see p. 99) conducts a two-hour bushfood tour on the first Saturday of each month at Bradleys Head. You visit an Aboriginal midden and sample wattleseed biscuits, bush tomatoes, and lemon myrtle. Bush remedies and tools are demonstrated, too. The unit also conducts four-hour tours of the Manly Scenic Walkway, passing several Aboriginal engravings. ■

Quarantine Station Tour Unit
☎ 9977 6522
🕐 Tour at 10:30 a.m., reservations are essential

Early morning and late afternoon, when the sun is low, are ideal times to see rock carvings at the naturally occurring outcrops around the city.

Opposite: Young Aborigines take part in a land-rights demonstration.

Indigenous tours, such as this one to Ku-ring-gai Chase National Park, offer a very different way of looking at Sydney, with trips on land and around the harbor.

Tours to Aboriginal sites

A NUMBER OF EXTENDED TOURS TO INDIGENOUS SITES depart from Sydney. Some, such as Austral Bush Tours, include four-day trips that are educational and ecological, with an emphasis on wildlife; Aboriginal culture, including visits to tribal elders; and bush activities. Sydney Aboriginal Discoveries, which is Aborigine owned and operated, offers tours in the city, around the harbor, and to the national parks. Trips range in length from two hours to overnight, and cover culture, rock art, bushfoods, and medicines.

Austral Bush Tours
✉ 40 Dunns Rd., Maraylya
☎ 9633 2136
www.hawknet.com.au/~austral
$ $$$$$

Sydney Aboriginal Discoveries
✉ Dallas's Restaurant, 7 Stanley St., East Sydney
☎ 9368 7684
$ $$$$$

Cultural tours operated by Sydney Aboriginal Discoveries include harbor cruises that leave several times a month from the Man o' War steps near the Opera House. The two-hour tour led by Aboriginal guides explains the significance of landmarks such as the Opera House and Darling Harbour, through Dreamtime stories.

At Nielsen Park in the Eastern Suburbs, during a two-hour bush-walk along the foreshore your guide explains the landscape, the history of the area, the coastal marine environment, bushfood, and medicine sources. Social and cultural systems of Sydney's original inhabitants are discussed, too.

For the more adventurous, the company organizes 24-hour overnight camps, based at Wattamolla Beach in the Royal National Park. Aboriginal guides explain bush survival skills, the different uses of fresh- and saltwater

ecosystems, and fish farming. In the evening Dreamtime storytelling takes place around the campfire, and talks interpret the stars and constellations according to Aboriginal thinking. Time is made, too, for relaxing and activities such as swimming. Meals consist of traditional foods. Camping equipment can be provided.

With the exception of the Harbour Cruise, which takes between 50 and 120 people, group sizes are kept between 10 and 25. All tours and cruises operate on demand only. ■

Dreamtime

One of the most frequently used expressions you'll encounter in association with Aboriginal culture is "Dreamtime." But what does it mean? In essence, it is a simple term used to describe a remarkably complex set of stories and beliefs. These provide a detailed description of the creation of the world and many of its features, plus the Aborigines' relationship to the land, their responsibilities to it, and the code of conduct by which they live. For example, a particular feature of the landscape will mark where someone was punished, perhaps for breaking the tribal law. Other Dreamtime stories relate to journeys made by mythical creatures across the bare landscape and the features they made along the way. In other words, a Dreamtime story can also be a "map." So what happens if a new feature is made? Easy. A Dreamtime story is created to include it. ■

REEF DREAMING

At night, Darling Harbour provides the setting for a water, laser, and film show based on an Aboriginal Dreamtime story, Reef Dreaming. Motion picture and laser images are projected onto a giant screen created by spraying water 80 feet (24 m) high. Figures from the Dreaming rise out of the harbor during the narrative. (*Screenings: Wed.– Sun. 7:10 p.m. and 8:10 p.m. April–Oct.; 8:10 p.m. and 9:10 p.m. Nov.–March*). ■

Aboriginal art

From one side of Australia to another, Aboriginal people have been creating art for thousands of years. It ranges from the purely decorative to the deeply significant, going to the heart of the country's culture.

Traditionally, Aboriginal art adorned a wide variety of surfaces—the human body, rock, and bark, for example. Designs were also drawn on the ground and on everyday items. Some designs and images had great ceremonial significance, others were simply decoration for spears, boomerangs, clap sticks, didgeridoos, and domestic objects. Clays, dyes from certain roots, charcoal, and animal blood were used. In the northern areas, figures were carved in wood; some were quite large and planted in the ground like totems.

A great deal of Aboriginal art is closely linked with ritual and mythology. It also expresses the way the world is formed and how it functions. The landscape, together with water and food sources, is a common theme. In some areas, rock art was used to warn of danger. For example, a dangerous looking spirit figure painted on rocks indicated barren land ahead.

Different styles
The northern areas of Australia, where resources were more plentiful, tend to have more developed painting styles: X-ray painting; an "elegant" style, with elongated figures and crosshatching; and contact art (reflecting encounters with Macassar traders and Europeans). On Bathurst and Melville, islands just north of Darwin, huge slabs of bark are painted. Since the availability of metal axes and the lure of big art prizes, the scale of these works has increased dramatically.

Central Australia is another major center for painting, with the dot style predominating. Until recently, there were few examples of this painting in existence because of the non-durable nature of the surfaces that were used. However, with the increasing demand for Aboriginal art and the ready availability of more lasting modern materials, the style is being revived.

The first Aboriginal artists to paint in the European tradition came from this area. Members of the Hermannsburg school, based in a settlement 150 miles (240 km) west of Alice Springs and led by Albert Namatjira (1902–1959), mainly painted landscapes in oils and watercolors. And yet they retained the principal concerns of Aboriginal people. If you look closely, most of their paintings are full of Dreamtime (see p. 153) images: Faces and figures can be found everywhere—in the rocks, the trees, the hills.

Telling a story
Most pieces of Aboriginal art either represent the land to which the artist is attached, or tell a story relating to it; sometimes a painting will do both. A work may show how the land was formed, or indicate when to expect certain food sources to become available. In central Australia, because water holes are vitally important, it is common to represent the trails between them with dotted lines. A creature's tracks are frequently presented, too, particularly if it can be eaten.

Paintings may also be "layered," with representations of the same area in times of drought and rain, or when different plants are producing food, overlapping one another. Many Westerners want to know the story of a painting, but often there just isn't one, or the artist is forbidden by tribal law to explain it.

The power of Aboriginal art is reflected in the demand for it around the world. Collectors flock to exhibitions, and auctions are conducted by satellite video link, with works in central Australian deserts being shown on screen to buyers in major galleries.

There are many places to buy Aboriginal art in Sydney, with the choice ranging across a broad spectrum of styles and prices. Most reputable dealers provide information on the artists and their cultural origins. If you are considering a major purchase, it is worth visiting the Art Gallery of New South Wales (see pp. 56–59) to get a good grounding in Aboriginal art beforehand. Shops here and at the Australian Museum (see pp. 62–63) have good selections of books on Aboriginal art. ■

Sydney has some caves with paintings (such as **Red Hand Cave** at **Ku-ring-gai**), but most are not accessible to the public. This rich art site is near **Mount Borradaile, Northern Territory.**

Desert art such as this from central Australia is often characterized by a dot style that either tells a story or depicts an area of land.

The dot painting seen on many didgeridoos is purely decorative. In fact, the best sounding didgeridoos are usually left bare.

Cultural centers

An Aborigine in traditional dress sells crafts at one of the city's cultural centers.

THE ONLY SOLELY ABORIGINE OWNED AND OPERATED center in Sydney is Gavala, in the Harbourside Shopping Complex (see p. 127) at Darling Harbour. Established in 1995 to provide first-hand experiences of Aboriginal culture, the center has an education and lecture program—presented by qualified Aborigines—that introduces visitors to indigenous art, dance, crafts, and music.

Gavala Gallery
- Map p. 120
- Harbourside Shop 32
- 9212 7232

Boomalli Aboriginal Artists Co-operative
- Map p. 71 & 161 E3
- 18 Hickson Rd., The Rocks, & 191 Parramatta Rd.
- 9698 2047
- Closed Sun.–Mon.

The **Gavala Gallery** provides explanations of tools and artifacts, and visitors are generally encouraged to participate, especially in activities such as didgeridoo playing and boomerang painting (you get to keep your efforts). You can also listen to Dreamtime (see p. 153) stories. Packages can be tailored for groups of 10 to 20 that include a variety of activities such as tastings of bushfoods.

The gallery also offers you the opportunity to buy traditional and contemporary art by Aboriginal artists from all over Australia. Authentication of work includes photographs and written information on the artist, and artists-in-residence are happy to discuss their work, along with its history and their artistic technique.

The **Boomalli Aboriginal Artists Co-operative** has constantly changing exhibition space in Annandale and an Aboriginal cultural center in The Rocks. Most of the works tend to be contemporary, although many reflect Aboriginal culture.

MAJOR EXHIBITS

All of Sydney's major galleries and museums have Aboriginal sections. Two in particular—the Art Gallery of New South Wales and the Australian Museum—have substantial collections.

Art Gallery of New South Wales

The Art Gallery of New South Wales's indigenous exhibition, Yiribana, located on the lower ground floor of the museum (*Map p. 43*; see pp. 56–59), is one of Australia's most extensive collections of Aboriginal and Torres Strait Islander art and culture. It reflects the fundamental connection between Aboriginal art and the land and includes items collected in the 1930s and '40s. A special outdoor section has a display of northern Australian totemlike post figures, complete with sandy ground and native plants.

Contemporary works reflect the Aborigines' emerging sense of cultural pride, often mixed with a sense of humor. Notable are the works of Emily Kame Kngwarreye (circa 1916–1996), deeply personal expressions of central Australia, her homeland. Lin Onus (1948–1996) depicts the meeting of Aboriginal and European culture with gentle humor in his sculpture "Fruit Bats."

Australian Museum

In the Indigenous Australians Gallery of the Australian Museum (*Map p. 43*; see pp. 62–63), artifacts from the past illuminate spirituality and cultural heritage, while contemporary materials explain current social justice issues. A wide variety of tools and weapons from different tribal groups across the country are presented, as are types of shelters, bushfoods, and cooking methods.

The struggle of Aboriginal people for recognition of their very existence and for land rights is presented in picture and video.

Other galleries & museums

Aboriginal canoes that are thousands of years old can be seen at the **Australian National Maritime Museum** (*Map p. 120*; see pp.

128–29). Exhibits at the **Sydney Observatory** (*Map p. 71*; see pp. 78–79) show how Aborigines used the night sky to determine the seasons and predict when various foods would be available. The **Powerhouse Museum** (*Map p. 120*; see pp. 122–25) mounts regular exhibitions on specific areas of art and culture.

Newly opened, the **Djamu Gallery** (*Customs House, Circular Quay, Tel 9320 6393*) has Aboriginal and Pacific artworks and cultural materials, and gives performances. The **Museum of Sydney** (*Map p. 43*; see p. 49) has a section on Aboriginal culture and Aboriginal totems outside its entrance. ■

David Malangi's bark painting entitled "Two blue-tongued lizards" (1983) can be seen at the Art Gallery of New South Wales.

More places to visit

Aboriginal art is not restricted to canvases. You can see this decorated shield at an outlet in The Rocks.

ART

Many galleries around the city specialize in Aboriginal art. **Jinta Desert Art** (*154–156 Clarence St., Tel 9290 3639*) concentrates on central Australian artists, both traditional and contemporary. **Utopia Art Sydney** (*Top floor, 50 Parramatta Rd., Stanmore, Tel 9550 4609*) specializes in the work of artists—especially Emily Kame Kngwarreye—from the Utopia community of central Australia.

The **Aboriginal & Tribal Art Centre** (*117 George St., The Rocks, Tel 9247 9625*), conveniently located in one of the major visitor precincts, has a comprehensive collection of Aboriginal art from the central Australian region, including sculptures, bark paintings, and contemporary works on canvas.

Other stores specializing in Aboriginal art are **Bulurru Art** (*Nurses Walk, The Rocks, Tel 9247 1436*), and **Balarinji Australia** (*International Airport Terminal, Tel 9252 0047*), whose designs also adorn two Qantas 747s.

Major auction houses conduct regular sales of Aboriginal art. Get details from Christie's (*Tel 9326 1422*), Lawsons (*Tel 9241 3411*), and Sotheby's (*Tel 9362 1000*).

DANCE

One of the premier Aboriginal dance groups in Australia, the **Aboriginal Islander Dance Theatre** (*Tel 9252 0199*) frequently tours overseas, with great popularity. When the group is in Sydney performances are conducted at various venues.

Another highly regarded group is **Bangarra Dance Theatre** (*Tel 9251 5333*), which has a busy touring schedule, but also currently conducts an annual season in Sydney in November. **Aboriginal Dance Theatre** (*Tel 9699 2171/9172*) also performs at various locations in Sydney.

LA PEROUSE MUSEUM

One of the Aboriginal communities that has been exposed to European settlement the longest is La Perouse community; it witnessed the arrival of Captain Cook and the First Fleet in Botany Bay. La Perouse Museum (see p. 190) has been refurbished and on Sundays conducts boomerang-throwing demonstrations, and boomerangs and other artifacts are on sale. To liven things up, there is a snake show, too.

🗺 187 E4 ✉ Cable Station, Anzac Parade, La Perouse ☎ 9311 3379 ∎

S prinkled across the vast suburbs stretching to the west of Sydney are many different aspects of the city—the site of the 2000 Olympics, elegant shopping areas, and lively expressions of a range of immigrant cultures.

Western Suburbs

Mural on Main Street, Cabramatta

Western Suburbs

CONSIDERING SYDNEY'S SIZE (OVER 5,000 SQUARE MILES/13,000 SQ. KM), IT IS not surprising that it should have a number of "centers" beyond the main business district. These days there are many localities that are both communities in their own right and attract large numbers of visitors. Don't miss the historic buildings of Parramatta, the boutiques of elegant Mosman, the gentrified workers' suburbs of Balmain, and the ethnic diversity of Cabramatta and Campsie.

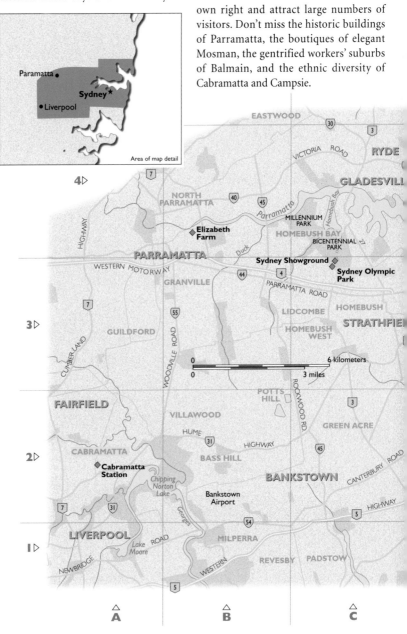

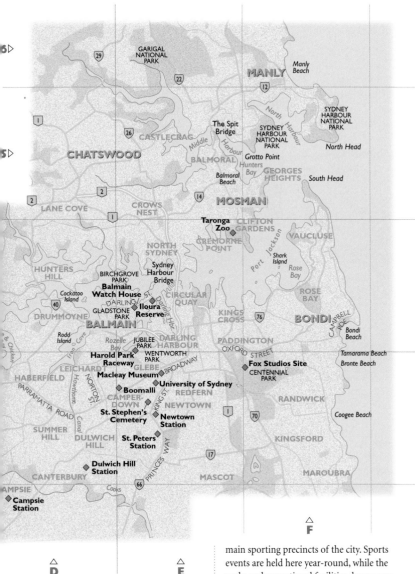

Balmain and Parramatta offer some of the oldest buildings in the city, along with picnicking, walking, and boating. Some precincts are just a cluster of shops, but contain particular gems—especially foods such as sausages, breads, or pastries—that attract people from miles around.

And then, of course, there is the main Olympic site at Homebush Bay, one of the main sporting precincts of the city. Sports events are held here year-round, while the parks and recreational facilities draw many visitors in search of fresh air or exercise.

In a sense, this section is a kaleidoscope of places and things to see and do. Whether it is a tour of some of Australia's oldest and most historic buildings, a visit to a famous sporting venue, a stroll through an exclusive shopping precinct, or a relaxed coffee in a café full of Sydneysiders, there are many places where you can get a feel for the Sydney that the locals enjoy. ■

Inner west

RIGHT ACROSS SYDNEY THERE ARE SEVERAL AREAS WHERE the locals congregate in droves. Many are mentioned elsewhere in the book—Darlinghurst, Kings Cross, Manly, Bondi, Paddington, and others—but several more are worth visiting, too. The following districts lie south and west of the city center.

NEWTOWN

Newtown (*Map 161 E3*) revolves around **King Street,** one of the longest food and shopping streets in the city. It reaches from the University of Sydney to Newtown Station and then continues on to St. Peters Station. The precinct is an enclave for students and a kaleidoscope of people leading "alternative" lifestyles, the prime activity being to sit in the cafés and watch the human menagerie pass by— punks, hippies, Gothics, students, musicians, artists. Thai restaurants of a consistently good standard dominate, but plenty of other cultures are represented as well.

Northeast of Newtown is the **University of Sydney,** Australia's oldest university. It dates from the 1850s and has many fine buildings designed by colonial architect Edmund Blacket. Don't miss the quadrangle, the beautiful Great Hall, and the clock tower (*Tours conducted by volunteers Tues.–Thurs. at 10:30 a.m., Tel 9351 4002*).

Also worth visiting and part of most tours is the **Macleay**

Macleay Museum
161 E3
Science Rd., University of Sydney
9351 2274

Museum, off Science Road on the Glebe side of the university campus. It was first established by the Macleay family, who built the **Elizabeth Bay House** (see p. 146). The museum's eclectic, if sometimes macabre, collection features zoological specimens, bark paintings, Aboriginal artifacts, and early photographs of Sydney.

Alexander Macleay, colonial secretary and father of the family, is buried in **St. Stephen's Cemetery** (1849) on Church Street, in the heart of Newtown.

The Macleay tomb stands at the back left-hand corner of the cemetery. As you face the grave, a short way along the wall to the left is the mass tomb containing all the unidentified bodies from the wrecks of the *Dunbar* and the *Catherine Adamson,* which between them took 143 lives in 1857 (see p. 102). You'll find more graves of *Dunbar* victims back toward the church on this side, and the grave of Napoleon Bonaparte's harpist, Robert Boscha.

Access is by rail to Newtown Station (as you leave the station most of the action is along the street to the right, but there is plenty to eat and buy if you go left) and bus routes 422, 423, 426, 428, L23, and L28 run from the city.

GLEBE

Much of this suburb (*Map 161 E3*), more properly called The Glebe, north of the University of Sydney was originally owned by the Anglican Church. By the 1820s, however, most of it had been sold, and handsome Victorian houses sprang up in the following years. Look for the deep verandas and detailed wrought-iron work.

Set by the harbor just across the water from the Sydney Fish Market near Darling Harbour, the area features several pleasant waterside

parks. It largely consists of workers' cottages dating from the last century with a scattering of grand Victorian terraces.

The suburb's main thoroughfare, **Glebe Point Road,** stretches from Broadway, one of the main routes into the city from the west, over to Jubilee Park at Rozelle Bay. For most of its length, Glebe Point Road is a "food" street, lined with restaurants interspersed with a few hairdressers, gift shops, and bookstores. Gleebooks (*Tel 9660 2333*) at No. 49 is one of the best bookstores in town. Readings by local and overseas writers are held here regularly.

Very popular markets take place at the Glebe Public School every Saturday, and you'll find an independent cinema, **The Valhalla** (*Tel 9660 8050*), at 166 Glebe Point Road, and a

---

GREAT EXPECTATIONS

One of the graves in St. Stephen's Cemetery is that of Eliza Donnithorne. Jilted by her fiancé on her wedding day in 1854, Eliza kept her table set for her wedding feast for the next 30 years, often wore her wedding dress, and sometimes left the front door of her house ajar in the hope that her beloved would return. Her story is thought to be a possible source for Miss Havisham in Charles Dickens's *Great Expectations.* ∎

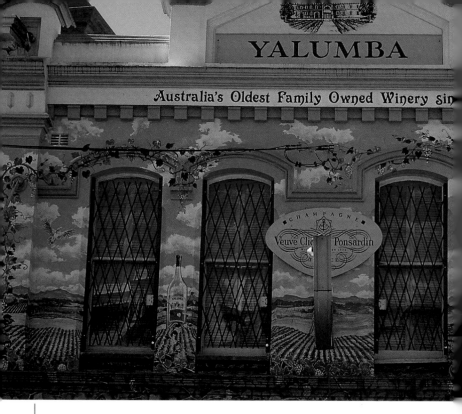

YALUMBA

Australia's Oldest Family Owned Winery sin[...]

CHAMPAGNE
Veuve Cli[...] Ponsardin

Balmain, tucked away on its own peninsula in Sydney Harbour, retains a village feel. A shop facade looks like something out of Tuscany.

youth hostel (*Tel 9692 8418*) at No. 262. Elsewhere in the suburb is a dog track (Wentworth Park) and a harness racing track (Harold Park Paceway).

Glebe is a short taxi ride from the city, or bus routes 431, 432, 433, and 434 depart from the city.

LEICHHARDT

To get a sense of the multicultural flavor of Sydney, try Leichhardt (*Map 161 D4–E4*), a precinct west of Glebe. The area was named after a German explorer who disappeared in the northern regions of Australia in 1848, and who was the inspiration for Nobel Prize-winning author Patrick White's book *Voss,* which is partly set in Sydney.

During the 19th century, Leichhardt was often visited by whalers who used to row up Hawthorne Canal to the pubs here and in nearby Summer Hill.

Leichhardt is the so-called Italian Quarter of Sydney, with a string of Italian restaurants and cafés along two main restaurant strips, **Norton Street** and, intersecting at Norton Street's southern end, **Marion Street.** Access is by car or bus routes 436 and 438 from the city.

BALMAIN

Another of the former working-class suburbs of Sydney, Balmain (*Map 161 D4–E4*), north of Leichhardt, occupies the peninsula between Iron Cove and Darling Harbour. Its abundance of once affordable waterfront property has made this one of the most sought-after districts in the city. Today, most of the working-class cottages and row houses have been renovated, and the lifestyle here rivals that of the affluent Eastern Suburbs (see pp. 133–48).

This is a suburb of successful artists, actors, and business people, but it still has pockets of its original working-class roots. Numerous boutique pubs are dotted around the peninsula and lively cafés, bookshops, bakeries, and antique shops line **Darling Street,** which runs the length of the peninsula.

Every Saturday a market is held on the grounds of St. Andrew's Church, on the other side of Gladstone Park.

Down the hill from St. Andrew's, the **Balmain Watch House** (*179 Darling St., Tel 9818 4954, closed Fri.–Sun., except by appt.*) dates from 1854 and was designed by Edmund Blacket. The simple, elegant building is now the headquarters of the Balmain Association, which aims to preserve local buildings, their history, and atmosphere. Art exhibitions are held here on many weekends, and you can join guided walks.

Two lovely parks for picnics can be reached by ferry from Circular Quay—**Birchgrove Park** and Balmain East's **Iloura Reserve.** A smaller park, near Birchgrove Park at the end of Long Nose Point, is also accessible by ferry to Louisa Street Wharf, Birchgrove.

Apart from its physical heritage, this suburb has also contributed major figures to the national and world stage. Dr. H.V. Evatt, one of the founders of the United Nations and president of the U.N. General Assembly (1948–49), was the local member in the state and federal parliaments. A prime minister, Billy Hughes, had been a shopkeeper in Balmain, and Olympic gold medal swimmer Dawn Fraser is also identified as a local.

Access to Balmain is by bus 433 or 434, or ferry from Circular Quay to Darling Street Wharf. ■

The Balmain Courthouse on Darling Street used to dispense quick justice in what was once a rough-and-tumble working-class suburb.

Homebush Bay Olympic site

THE OLYMPIC PARK AT HOMEBUSH BAY, THE MAIN VENUE of the 2000 Olympic Games, is the sports and recreation hub of the entire city. The site at Homebush Bay includes the Millennium Park, a vast recreation area and natural habitat for numerous birds and animals, the Sydney Showground, the main Olympic Stadium, and Sydney International Aquatic Centre.

Homebush Bay
160 C3–C4
See pp. 170–71

Visitor information
9735 4800

Olympic Stadium
Olympic Blvd.,
Homebush Bay
9752 3666

MILLENNIUM PARK

At 1,086 acres (439 ha), Millennium Park is the largest park in Sydney and incorporates the 250-acre (101-ha) Bicentennial Park, opened in 1988.

Within the park are the wetlands and mangroves of Homebush Bay, the former quarry for the State Brickworks (since identified as a breeding ground for the green and golden bell frog), and remnant eucalyptus forest and regenerated casuarina pine forests, both of which are breeding grounds for parrots and some of the 140 other species of birds found around the Homebush Bay site.

HOMEBUSH EASTER SHOW SITE

Each year, in the first two weeks of April, the **Royal Easter Show** (*Tel 9704 1000*) is held at the

Sydney Showground. Here you can enjoy rides in sideshow alley, and see displays and exhibitions of New South Wales's best produce and livestock. The Royal Easter Show moved here in 1998 from its traditional home near the city to make way for the Fox Studio and Entertainment complex.

OLYMPIC STADIUM

The main Olympic Stadium is the focal point of the site. Completed in 1999, it is designed to seat 110,000 spectators. Track and field events, the finish of the marathon, the football (soccer) final, the opening and closing ceremonies of the games, and the Paralympics will all be held here.

After the games, the building will be converted into an 80,000-seat stadium for sporting events such as Australian Rules Football, soccer, and Rugby League and Rugby Union international matches.

SYDNEY INTERNATIONAL AQUATIC CENTRE

Equally adaptable is the Sydney International Aquatic Centre, built in 1994. Currently it can seat about 5,000 people, but during the games the capacity will expand to accommodate 15,000. The center was a success from the moment it opened its doors and has nearly three million visitors a year.

Facilities include the international competition-standard pool; leisure, training, and diving pools within a temperature-controlled building; and landscaped gardens. In addition, there are child-care facilities, a gymnasium, a restaurant, shops, water slides, and

In the run-up to the XXVII Olympiad, events such as this laser show are held in the Olympic Stadium.

Sydney International Aquatic Centre

✉ Olympic Blvd., Homebush Bay

☎ 9752 3666

🕐 Tours are conducted Mon.–Fri. at 10 a.m., noon, & 2 p.m., & on weekends at noon & 2 p.m.

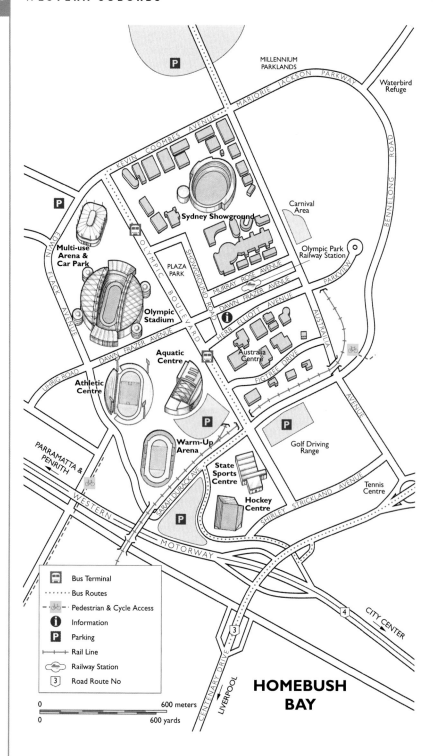

MILLENNIUM PARKLANDS

Waterbird Refuge

Carnival Area

Sydney Showground

Olympic Park Railway Station

Multi-use Arena & Car Park

PLAZA PARK

Olympic Stadium

Aquatic Centre

Athletic Centre

Australia Centre

Warm-Up Arena

Golf Driving Range

State Sports Centre

Hockey Centre

Tennis Centre

PARRAMATTA & PENRITH

MOTORWAY

CITY CENTER

Bus Terminal
Bus Routes
Pedestrian & Cycle Access
Information
Parking
Rail Line
Railway Station
Road Route No

0 — 600 meters

0 — 600 yards

HOMEBUSH BAY

fountains. The center is also the base for the swimmers of the New South Wales Institute of Sport.

OTHER FACILITIES

Other facilities in the Olympic Park at Homebush Bay include an archery site, a baseball field, a golf driving range, a hockey center, a tennis center, the Sydney Indoor Sports Centre, an athletics center and training facilities, and the State Sports Centre.

Strangely, there is virtually nowhere to park your car; visitors are strongly encouraged to use public transportation as much as possible. The site is extremely well served in this respect with a ferry stop on the Circular Quay-to-Parramatta RiverCat run and the Olympic Park Station beside the Sydney Showground site (which is less than half a mile/1 km from the Olympic Stadium), plus regular bus services. ■

The Sydney International Aquatic Centre maximizes use of natural light and ventilation for energy efficiency and comfort.

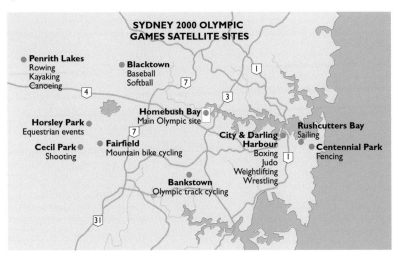

SYDNEY 2000 OLYMPIC GAMES SATELLITE SITES

Penrith Lakes
Rowing
Kayaking
Canoeing

Blacktown
Baseball
Softball

Horsley Park
Equestrian events

Homebush Bay
Main Olympic site

City & Darling Harbour
Boxing
Judo
Weightlifting
Wrestling

Rushcutters Bay
Sailing

Cecil Park
Shooting

Fairfield
Mountain bike cycling

Centennial Park
Fencing

Bankstown
Olympic track cycling

Olympic survival guide

The majority of events for the 2000 Olympics, held from September 15 to October 1, 2000, will take place within the suburb of Homebush Bay. The other major venue is Darling Harbour. Additional events will be held at special locations in the city.

Events at Homebush Bay

Archery, track events, badminton, baseball, basketball, diving, fencing, football finals (preliminaries will be held at the Sydney Football Stadium and in other Australian cities), gymnastics, handball, hockey, swimming, table tennis, tae kwon do, tennis, and volleyball. ⊞ Access by bus and rail ⊞ During the Olympics, the ferry service to Homebush will be used by Olympic officials only.

Boxing, judo, weightlifting, & wrestling

✉ Darling Harbour ⊞ Ferry, Sydney Light Rail, bus, or Monorail from the city

Canoeing, kayaking, & rowing

✉ Sydney International Regatta Centre, Penrith Lakes ⊞ Train to Penrith then bus

Olympic track cycling

✉ Bankstown Velodrome ⊞ Train to Bankstown then bus

Equestrian events

✉ Olympic Equestrian Centre, Horsley Park ⊞ Bus or rail. Also park in city & ride bus

Fencing

✉ Hordern Pavilion, Centennial Parklands ⊞ Bus

Shooting

✉ Sydney International Shooting Centre, Cecil Park ⊞ Train to Liverpool or Fairfield then bus

Softball

✉ Rooty Hill, Blacktown ⊞ Train to Blacktown then bus

Beach volleyball

✉ Bondi Beach ⊞ Train to Bondi Junction then bus

Yachting

✉ Sydney Harbour and offshore ⊞ Public transportation only to harborside vantage points; car or public transportation to coastal vantage points

Other events

Modern pentathlon, triathlon, road cycling, mountain biking, and the marathon will be conducted at venues around the city, including some of those mentioned above.

Transportation & tours

Huge numbers of people and vehicles trying to move around the city during the Olympics will inevitably cause a certain amount of chaos. See rail and bus details for events listed above; call the Infoline (*Tel 13 1500*) for timetables. Prior to the Olympics, ferry and bus tours to the site are being run from Circular Quay (*several tours daily, Tel 9207 3170*). An Explorer bus service loops continually through the Homebush Bay complex (*daily, 9:30 a.m.–3:30 p.m.*), stopping at ten locations. One ticket is valid all day and allows you to hop on and off at will.

Accommodations

More than 35,000 hotel rooms will be available during the Olympics. You can choose from motels, recreation centers, backpacker lodges, caravan parks, rented houses, and hospitality programs in regional areas. Reservations and information should be made in advance with travel agents. Two private home rental programs have been established. Homestay offers vacant furnished homes and apartments; Homehost offers bed-and-breakfast-style accommodations. A local real estate chain is managing both programs— Ray White Real Estate (*GPO Box 5200, Sydney NSW 2001, Tel 61 2 9262 3700, fax 61 2 9262 3737; www.raywhite.net*).

Tickets

Obtaining tickets to Olympic events is likely to be difficult. While some tickets will be available through the Olympic committees of participating nations, it is unlikely you will come by tickets for the opening and closing ceremonies or major finals. Swimming, one of Australia's strongest sports, is particularly popular. However, tickets to many of the less popular sports will be available. You will be able to see several events, such as triathlon, marathon, road cycling, and sailing, free of charge. ■

Olympic Park Station—access to the Olympic site and all major events will be primarily by public transportation.

Olympic checklist

As with all major events, the best advice for prospective spectators is to prepare for the worst and try to keep a large stock of patience on hand. Items you should carry with you include a hat, sunscreen, sunglasses, one to two pints of bottled water, aspirin, a plastic cup, a small cache of filling snack food such as dried fruit or nuts, a small folding stool and/or a small cushion, a light sweater, interesting reading matter, a camera and film, a pocket radio, and a small pair of binoculars.

Don't forget that large crowds attract thieves. Keep your valuables out of sight as much as possible and try to carry only a minimum of money, credit cards, and other valuables. Remember that a purse or handbag is an easy target for a grab and run—and that thieves may try to snatch things right out of your hands.

Finally, allow plenty of time to get to and from venues; delays will be inevitable, but if you plan for them, you shouldn't miss your events.

More information and updates are available from the Sydney Organising Committee for the Olympic Games (SOCOG) (*Tel 13 6363; www.sydney.olympic.org*). ■

A Vietnamese Australian takes a break to enjoy a meal from a street stall in Cabramatta, in Sydney's west, though it feels closer to Ho Chi Minh City.

More places to visit in the Western Suburbs

CABRAMATTA

For a totally different experience, take the train out west to the suburb of Cabramatta. The area around the railway station is given over to Vietnamese shops, restaurants, and businesses, to the extent that it has been nicknamed Vietnamatta. It's as if a piece of the exotic Far East has been transplanted in suburban Sydney. The food here is some of the best Vietnamese cuisine this side of the Ho Chi Minh Trail.
160 A2 Train to Cabramatta Station

CAMPSIE

A little closer to the city than Cabramatta, the same sort of cultural makeover has taken place at Campsie, except here the dominant culture is Korean. Australian and Korean cuisines have a great deal in common—they both have a strong emphasis on barbecuing. The center of the action is on Beamish Street.
161 D2 Train to Campsie Station

DULWICH HILL

If you happen to be passing 425 New Canterbury Road in Dulwich Hill, check out Abla's Pastries. Behind the unassuming-looking shopfront is a wonderful selection of Lebanese specialties. There are gigantic trays of baklava, *makaroun, bourma,* bird's nest, and *kashtah* on display, and an area where you can sit down with the locals to enjoy cake and coffee, Turkish Delight, or ice cream.
161 D3 Train to Dulwich Hill Station or bus 426

MOSMAN

Mosman, although not in the Western Suburbs, is easily reached from the city and is well worth a visit. The area is the northside's answer to the southside's fashionable Double Bay (see p. 146).

The shops along the main thoroughfare, Military Road, are a mix of elegant clothing boutiques and sophisticated cafés and restaurants. Many of the nearby houses are stately federation-style residences surrounded by land that was acquired when values were lower on the north side of the harbor—before the Harbour Bridge was built.
161 E5 Bus 244 or 247 from the city Ferry to Taronga Zoo then bus 238, or ferry to Mosman Wharf and bus 230 or 233 ∎

R inging the city are national parks, pristine waterways, wildlife parks, and historic towns where you can take a picnic for a day, or lose yourself for weeks.

Excursions

A koala enjoys its gum leaf diet.

North

JUST AN HOUR TO THE NORTH OF THE city, a pocket of spectacular wilderness reaches in an almost unbroken chain inland from the coast to the Blue Mountains. It includes a string of beaches, the boating paradises of the Hawkesbury River and Pittwater, and the largely unspoiled succession of national parks that includes Bouddi, Brisbane Water, Kuring-gai Chase, Marramarra, Dharug, and Wollemi. Within the northern suburbs are two smaller national parks, Lane Cove (along one of the upper arms of Sydney Harbour) and Garigal (north from the upper arm of Middle Harbour).

Two pelicans join a fisherman in his search for fish on the coast north of Sydney.

Not surprisingly, the emphasis in many of these areas is on recreation. Pittwater is especially popular for weekend getaways, not least because it is only an hour from the city and can claim some of the best scenery and boating anywhere in the world. Farther west, the Hawkesbury is a beautiful river system with stunning scenery along its lower reaches and historic towns and lush farmlands around the upper reaches.

Throughout this area, you may find that the people tend to be relaxed and largely unstressed (even more than most other Sydneysiders). Perhaps it's hard to get tense about life when you can go for a swim in the sea in the early morning and wet a line after work in the afternoon. Or else it is true that "there is nothing half so much worth doing as simply messing around in boats." ■

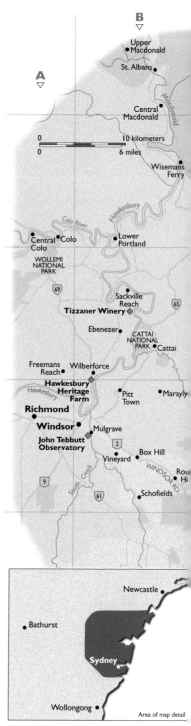

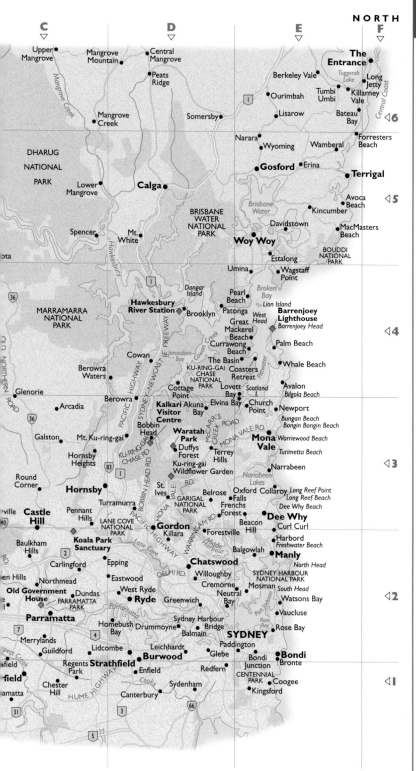

C ▽　　D ▽　　E ▽　　F ▽

Upper Mangrove
Mangrove Mountain
Central Mangrove
Peats Ridge
Berkeley Vale
The Entrance
Tuggerah Lake
Long Jetty
Killarney Vale
Ourimbah
Tumbi Umbi
Somersby
Mangrove Creek
Lisarow
Bateau Bay
Central Coast
◁6

Narara
Wyoming
Wamberal
Forresters Beach

DHARUG
NATIONAL
PARK

Gosford ●Erina
Terrigal

Lower Mangrove
Calga
Avoca Beach
◁5

Spencer
Mt. White
BRISBANE WATER NATIONAL PARK
Brisbane Water
Kincumber
MacMasters Beach

ota

Davidstown
BOUDDI NATIONAL PARK

Woy Woy
Ettalong
Umina
Wagstaff Point

36

Dangar Island
Pearl Beach
Broken Bay
Lion Island

MARRAMARRA NATIONAL PARK
Hawkesbury River Station
Brooklyn
Patonga
West Head
Barrenjoey Lighthouse
Barrenjoey Head

Great Mackerel Beach
Currawong Beach
Palm Beach
◁4

Cowan
The Basin
Whale Beach

Berowra Waters
KU-RING-GAI CHASE NATIONAL PARK
Coasters Retreat

Glenorie
Arcadia
Berowra
Kalkari Visitor Centre
Cottage Point
Akuna Bay
Lovett Bay
Scotland
Avalon
Bilgola Beach

Galston
Mt. Ku-ring-gai
Bobbin Head
Elvina Bay
Church Point
Newport
Bungan Beach
Bongin Bongin Beach

Hornsby Heights
83
Waratah Park
Duffys Forest
Terrey Hills
Mona Vale
Warriewood Beach
◁3

Round Corner
Ku-ring-gai Wildflower Garden
Turimetta Beach

ville
Hornsby
Turramurra
St. Ives
Belrose
Oxford Falls
Collaroy
Narrabeen Lakes
Narrabeen
Long Reef Point
Long Reef Beach

Castle Hill
Pennant Hills
GARIGAL NATIONAL PARK
Frenchs Forest
Dee Why Beach

Baulkham Hills
2
Koala Park Sanctuary
LANE COVE NATIONAL PARK
Beacon Hill
Dee Why
Curl Curl

en Hills
Northmead
Carlingford
Epping
Eastwood
Gordon
Killara
Forestville
Balgowlah
Harbord
Freshwater Beach

Old Government House
Dundas
West Ryde
Chatswood
Willoughby
North Head
Manly

PARRAMATTA PARK
Ryde
Greenwich
Cremorne
Mosman
SYDNEY HARBOUR NATIONAL PARK
South Head
Watsons Bay

Parramatta
Homebush Bay
Drummoyne
Neutral Bay
Port Jackson
Vaucluse

7
Merrylands
4
Lidcombe
Balmain
Sydney Harbour Bridge
SYDNEY
Rose Bay
Rose Bay

Guildford
Leichhardt
Paddington
Glebe
Bondi
Bronte

afield
Regents Park
Strathfield
Burwood
Enfield
Redfern
Bondi Junction
CENTENNIAL PARK
Coogee
◁1

field
Chester Hill
Sydenham
Kingsford

amatta
Canterbury
66

31
3

5

Cottage Point is a boating haven on Cowan Creek in the Ku-ring-gai Chase National Park. Moorings can be hard to find during the summer holidays.

Ku-ring-gai Chase National Park

THE SANDSTONE BUSHLAND OF KU-RING-GAI IS CUT BY deep gorges full of eucalyptuses and ferns tumbling to the water's edge. Many of the gorges are partly inundated by seawater and extend several miles inland. Adjoining Pittwater, the Lower Hawkesbury River, and Cowan Creek, this 44,478-acre (18,000-ha) national park is the second oldest in Australia and has a rich mixture of Aboriginal and European history. It was dedicated in 1894, with further areas added in ensuing years.

Ku-ring-gai Chase National Park
◭ 175 D4
Visitor information
☎ 9457 1049

Bobbin Head
◭ 175 D3
Visitor information
✉ Ku-ring-gai Chase Rd.
☎ 9457 1049

One of the great delights of this magical area is waking up on a boat moored in a small bay with the Australian bush tumbling down steep slopes on all sides. As parrots shriek in the trees and kookaburras give their distinctive laughing cry, remind yourself that you are only an hour from the country's biggest city.

Among the highlights of the park is its Aboriginal rock engravings, many of which are accessible to the public (see p. 151). There are also numerous walking trails and several small towns, marinas, and boat-rental areas, plus plenty of picnic spots in scenic locations.

Accessible by road is **West Head.** Until 1951, this area was in the hands of the Australian Navy, and some of the fortifications from World War II are still visible.

These days, it is a favorite stopping point for visitors because of the spectacular views over Pittwater, Barrenjoey Head, Lion Island, and Broken Bay. From the road running out to West Head, several walking trails lead to secluded beaches and bays on the Pittwater and Cowan Creek sides.

Major visitor facilities can be found at **Akuna Bay** (marina and boat rental) and **Bobbin Head,** which is serviced on Sundays only by Shorelink bus 577 from Turramurra Station (*Tel 9457 8888*). Bobbin Head, located between two drowned river gorges, is a very sheltered spot well inland. It offers kiosks and picnic areas, motorboat, rowboat, and canoe rentals, and ferry cruises.

On the heights above Bobbin Head is the **Kalkari Visitor Centre.** Here you can watch videos about the park or wildlife displays. Kangaroos and emus inhabit the enclosed 20 acres (8 ha) of the **Discovery Trail.** A program of guided walking tours is conducted from Kalkari by volunteers from Chase Alive (*Tel 9457 9853*). Guides to the park's many day walks are also available.

Cottage Point is one of the few waterside villages that can be reached by car as well as boat. You can watch the vessels drifting and motoring by from one of its many restaurants and cafés. Boats can be rented.

Camping (*Tel 9972 7378*) in the park is permitted at The Basin, a sheltered bay on Pittwater accessible by boat or walking trail only. Reservations are required, especially during school vacations. A ferry service, Palm Beach Ferries (*Tel 9918 2747*), is available from Palm Beach.

Several routes enter the park from train stations along the main northern line. From Mount Ku-ring-gai Station, there is access to Bobbin Head; from Berowra a track leads to Waratah Bay; and from Cowan a trail accesses Jerusalem Bay. These trails down to the water are quite steep so be prepared for a climb back to the stations. The park can also be accessed from

Hawkesbury River train station through the town of Brooklyn along a section of the Great North Walk that runs up to Cowan Station (if you prefer an easier walk, set off downhill from Cowan to Brooklyn).

Road access to the park is from Ku-ring-gai Chase Road and Bobbin Head Road, both of which access Bobbin Head. Mona Vale Road and McCarr's Creek Road provide access to Church Point, Akuna Bay, and West Head.

Waratah Park

On the way to Ku-ring-gai, Waratah Park was the home of Skippy, the bush kangaroo and star of the popular 1960s TV series. At the park kangaroos and emus—tame enough to be fed by hand—wander freely in 30 acres (12 ha) of native bush. A koala house, Tasmanian devils, and bird and reptile displays add to the attraction. Picnicking is popular and the bistro restaurant provides do-it-yourself barbecues. Views extend over Ku-ring-gai and Cowan Creek from a lookout in the park. ■

The Baha'i Temple at Ingleside is a prominent landmark, visible from the city and the northern beaches beyond.

Kalkari Visitor Centre
- ✉ Ku-ring-gai Chase Rd.
- ☎ 9454 9853

Waratah Park
- 🅰 175 D3
- ✉ 13 Namba Rd., Duffy's Forest
- ☎ 9450 2377
- 🚌 Buses operate to the park from Chatswood railway station; there is hotel pickup.

Pittwater

IF SYDNEY HARBOUR IS THE CITY'S WORKING PORT, Pittwater is its playground. Lying at the northern extremity of a long series of golden beaches, this huge waterway is protected by the mighty buttress of Barrenjoey Head. It hugs the shore of Ku-ring-gai Chase National Park and extends beyond Lion Island into Broken Bay. When Governor Phillip started exploring the area in March 1788, he called it the "finest piece of water I ever saw." The region comprises such a labyrinth of inlets, coves, and drowned river valleys that it took the first settlers a couple of years to discover the major river that enters it, the Hawkesbury.

NORTHERN BEACHES

Between Sydney Harbour and Pittwater is the region known as the Northern Beaches. Stretching north from Manly, the beaches include Harbord (also called Freshwater), Curl Curl, Dee Why, Long Reef—the 3-mile (4-km) stretch of sand called Collaroy at one end and Narrabeen at the other (nearby **Narrabeen Lakes** is a sheltered waterway popular with dinghy sailors and sailboarders, and boat rentals are also available here)—and tiny Turimetta Beach.

Next come Warriewood, Mona Vale, Bongin Bongin, and Bungan Beaches. At this point, the southern-most reach of Pittwater forms a peninsula, with sheltered waters on one side and ocean on the other. Beaches facing the ocean, on the western side of the penin-sula, include Newport, Bilgola, Avalon, Whale, and, finally, the idyllic **Palm Beach**—the sandy isthmus ending at the imposing **Barrenjoey Head.**

Palm Beach

The peninsula in particular has long been a vacation destination for the well-to-do of Sydney; today, only the very rich can afford to have houses here.

The beach itself is a glorious sweep of sand and dunes that separates the Pacific from Pittwater. It comes to a dramatic stop at the headland topped by **Barrenjoey Lighthouse.** Pedestrian access is via a rough vehicle track up to the lighthouse: the 360-degree views over Palm Beach, the ocean, Broken Bay to the north, West Head, and Pittwater are well worth the long uphill walk. (Note: This is not the place to be in a thunderstorm.)

From atop Barrenjoey you can sometimes see seaplanes taking off or landing on Pittwater. Golfers will notice the pocket golf course on one side of the isthmus.

Sydney Harbour Seaplanes (*Tel 9388 1978*) provides service from Rose Bay in Sydney Harbour—flights that also provide spectacular views of the city, coastline, and Pittwater. Planes pull up at Barrenjoey Beach on the Pittwater side, with Palm Beach just over 100 yards (91 m) away. Taxi services to other sights can easily be arranged, and there are several good-quality restaurants close at hand.

Palm Beach Ferries (*Tel 9918 2747*) is located next to the sea-plane dock and connects with the hamlets of **Great Mackerel Beach, Coasters Retreat,** and **Currawong Beach** (none have road access).

Cottages are available for rent here; get details for Great Mackerel Beach and Coasters Retreat from

Barrenjoey Head with Palm Beach left and Pittwater right—a chain of golden beaches extends from here to Sydney Harbour, 15 miles (24 km) south.

Pittwater
🅰 175 E4

Raine & Horne Palm Beach (*Tel 9974 4311*) and for the Currawong area from Currawong Cottages (*Tel 9974 4141*). There is also a Ku-ring-gai Chase National Park camping area at The Basin (see p. 177).

Barrenjoey Beach is an absolute mecca for sailboarding. The gently shelving beach and prevailing northeasterly wind offers sheltered water and breezes for beginners, while farther out from shore more experienced sailors can get into some serious wind.

Keep an eye out for wind gusts known to locals as Barrenjoey bullets—gusts that roar down off the headland and hit small patches of the water, where they can pick up boards and riders and toss them about like leaves.

Southern Pittwater

While the wind, the scenery, and the lure of the open sea are the attractions at the northern end of Pittwater, most boating activity is based at the southern end. There are several boat-rental operations in the vicinity, plus the Royal Prince Alfred Yacht Club, on Mitala Street in **Newport,** which is the main yachting center for the entire waterway. At most times of the year berths can be arranged here, although in summer, when all of yachting Sydney descends in hordes, vacant dock space becomes extremely scarce (*Tel 9997 1022 for details on affiliations, availability, and assistance finding crew places on boats for twilight or weekend races*).

LION ISLAND

Whether you're on Barrenjoey Head, West Head, or out on the water, you'll be curious to know what the "seated lion" crouched out in the middle of Broken Bay facing the ocean is called. It's Lion Island, which would be Sydney's nominee if they ever hold a world's most beautiful island competition. The island is a wildlife reserve, uninhabited, and has no public access. ∎

Newport Beach, like most of the Northern Beaches, has a holiday atmosphere but is less than 45 minutes from the city center.

Also in Newport is the major pub for the peninsula area, the **Newport Arms Hotel** (*Kalinya St., Tel 9997 4900*). The hotel is a large venue by any standards, with several varying styles of eating areas. The best thing about it is the huge outdoor area overlooking the water. Accommodations are available, although rooms can be noisy until the pub closes.

Across the bay from Newport is **Church Point.** From here ferries (*Tel 9999 3492*) ply to Scotland Island, Lovett Bay, and Elvina Bay (no car access), all of which have several beautiful houses and places to stay (*Ferry Wharf Real Estate, Tel 9999 4961*). There is a youth hostel at Pittwater (*Tel 9999 2196, ferry only from Church Point, reservations, especially on weekends, are essential*) that is highly regarded and extremely popular.

From Church Point, McCarr's Creek Road winds around to Ku-ring-gai Chase National Park, where the inland waterways of Cowan Creek split into numerous steeply sided bush valleys. Although the road provides access to the bush landscape of West Head and the cafés and anchorages of Cottage Point and Akuna Bay, the ideal way to explore this area is by boat.

Vessels of every description, from canoes to cruisers, can be rented from a plethora of companies based from Newport to the Nepean (see p. 181). In Pittwater and around, the major yacht rental companies include Pittwater Yacht Charter (*Tel 9997 5344*) and Ausail Pittwater (*Tel 9999 3477*), while Clipper Cruiser Holidays, Akuna Bay (*Tel 9450 0000*), Skipper a Clipper (*Tel 9979 6188*), and Halvorsen Boats at Bobbin Head (*Tel 9457 9011*) rent out cabin cruisers and motorboats. More companies can be accessed by Internet and the yellow pages directory (*www.telstra.com.au*), and there is a guide to rental boats (*www.charterguide.com.au*).

You do not normally need a special license to rent vessels, although for yachts sailing experience is usually necessary (if it isn't, start worrying about the rental company). Several of the companies mentioned can also provide a sail guide. Alternatively, if your time is limited, it can be just as much fun to rent a dinghy from a marina for an afternoon and try to snag a fish.

An excellent guide to all the harbors, rivers, and ports of Sydney is the *Sydney Waterways Guide* by Alan Lucas (Horwitz Grahame), which lists water depths, charts, hazards, anchorages, items of interest, and picnic spots from Port Hacking to the Central Coast.

Access to Pittwater is by car (one hour), bus, or the aforementioned seaplanes. From the city, bus route L90 runs from Wynyard Station to Palm Beach. Another route involves taking the ferry to Manly (see pp. 98–99), bus 155 or 156 to Mona Vale, then the L90. ■

Hawkesbury River

A CONTINUATION OF THE SPECTACULAR WATERWAY OF Pittwater, the Hawkesbury River is an extensive river system that winds between rugged bushland and rich farmland from well north of Sydney, around to the city's west side, and then back down to the south. It is a scenic river that can be explored for much of its length by car, but the preferable way to see it is from the water. Houseboats can be hired at many points, and in the upper reaches waterskiing gardens are dotted along its banks.

Brooklyn provides food, fuel, restaurants, and more to "boaties" and visitors to the lower Hawkesbury. It is an hour from the city by train.

The first settlers, thinking they had fully explored Pittwater and Broken Bay shortly after their arrival, were surprised to find the river a year later along what "was supposed to be a short creek." The first exploration party, led by Governor Phillip, got 20 miles (32 km) upstream before their supplies ran low and they turned back.

Once it was fully explored, the Hawkesbury River rapidly became an important means of transporting cargo from inland areas down to Broken Bay and a vital link in the spread of settlement north. Some of the earliest towns, buildings, and

structures in Australia are found along its banks.

Starting at the lower reaches, one of the most pleasant towns is **Brooklyn.** It is named after the Brooklyn Bridge Company, which built the rail bridge across the Hawkesbury at the turn of the 19th century. Brooklyn can be reached in exactly an hour by train from Central Station. Note that the station at Brooklyn is called Hawkesbury River.

The town provides full services to cruising people, and a pleasant waterfront area is popular for weekend fishing.

HAWKESBURY/ NEPEAN

When the early settlers first explored the area, they thought the upper and lower reaches of the Hawkesbury were two different waterways. As a result they called the waters upstream from Richmond the Nepean, and those downstream the Hawkesbury. ■

Just offshore, in the center of the river, is **Dangar Island.** A ferry service runs out to the island from Brooklyn, and there is a pleasant café alongside the wharf, also some nice walks and sandy beaches.

Accommodations are available on the island, at Brooklyn, and on the small isolated beaches and coves nearby. Details from Hawkesbury River Tourist Accommodation Centre (*Tel 9985 7090*).

One of the nicest ways to see this part of the Hawkesbury is to ride with the **riverboat postman** (*Tel 9985 7566*). Because there are several communities that can only be accessed by water, a ferry runs the postal service and passengers can go along for the ride while it delivers mail and other supplies. The service operates Monday through Friday at 9:30 a.m. and 1:15 p.m. and on Wednesday and Friday afternoons at 1:30 p.m. The 8:16 a.m. train from Central Station in the city arrives at Hawkesbury River Station in time for the morning ferry. Several cruise companies have their rental offices at Brooklyn.

Access is by road on the Sydney–Newcastle Freeway or by train from the city to Hawkesbury River Station.

Although the ideal way to explore the river is by boat, there is quite a pleasant drive along the northern shores of the river. On the M1 (the Sydney–Newcastle Freeway, one of the great engineering feats of the 1960s with gigantic cuttings and bridges), cross the river and take the exit to Upper Mangrove. Through Mangrove, follow signs to Spencer and Wisemans Ferry and you'll find yourself on a long, winding drive with the river on one side and national parks on the other. There are several camping spots along the way, and some walks, but only limited facilities.

Wisemans Ferry (*Visitor information, 7 Thompson Sq., Windsor, Tel 4577 2310*) is named after Solomon Wiseman, who set up the ferry service in 1827. The Wisemans Ferry Inn was originally his home. Accommodations, camping, and boat rental are available in the township. At Wisemans Ferry the Macdonald River joins the Hawkesbury and two car punts service the north and south banks. If you are coming direct from the city (on the M2 and Old Northern Road), turn left when you come off the main ferry and within a mile (1.5 km) you will see signs to the Great North Road (no car access). The road, now part of **Dharug National Park,** was dug out of the sheer cliff face by convicts between 1826 and 1830. This section, open to walkers only, forms part of the **Great North Walk,** which extends from the city to the Hunter Valley (*details from the Sydney Visitor Centre, see p. 73*). At this point the road features sandstone walls and buttresses, and handmade sandstone drains run beneath the road. The marks of the convict chisels can still be seen on nearly every piece of stone as you ascend the trail, taking in views of the Hawkesbury and the Macdonald Valley. You need only walk for 10 to 15 minutes along the road to find a pleasant spot for a quiet picnic.

Back at your vehicle, continue along the mostly unsurfaced road into the Macdonald Valley and the village of **St. Albans.** This rich farming area was settled soon after it was discovered (only a year after the First Fleet arrived), although amenities such as electricity weren't installed until the late 1960s. Just before the village is a cemetery where seven First Fleeters are buried, although the graves aren't marked.

St. Albans itself is the center of a small community of artists and

smallholders. At the center is the **Settlers Arms Inn** (*Tel (02) 4568 2111*), which dates from 1836 and has intimately rustic accommodations, plus information on several historic sites. The pub was originally built to service Cobb & Co. coaches traveling the Great North Road. These days the area is usually rather sleepy, but the local folk festival brings visitors flocking in at Easter.

MACQUARIE TOWNS

Back at the Hawkesbury River, you can explore numerous villages along its banks; five were established by Lachlan Macquarie in 1810. They are still known as the Macquarie Towns and include **Richmond, Pitt Town, Wilberforce, Castlereagh** (the only town that didn't survive), and **Windsor.**

Richmond and Windsor are the two major centers of the Upper Hawkesbury and can be accessed by rail as well as the M2 tollway from the city.

Many historic buildings can be seen, including **St. Matthew's Church** at Windsor, designed by Francis Greenway and built between 1817 and 1822, and the **Macquarie Arms Inn,** built in 1815 and still

Carless Dangar Island, with the town of Brooklyn at the top of photo. Bird life is particularly abundant.

referred to today. There are tearooms and reception facilities and night tours for groups can be arranged. Independent travelers may be able to join group tours (*Tel (02) 4577 3120/2485*), otherwise Tebbutt's great-grandson, John Halley Tebbutt, may accede to a polite request.

Hawkesbury River cruises are conducted from Windsor Wharf, Wednesdays and Sundays, and there is an occasional cruise that conveys passengers the 75 miles (120 km) to Brooklyn and returns by coach.

Highlights of some of the smaller towns in the area include the oldest church in Australia, the **Presbyterian Church** at Ebenezer, which dates from 1809, and the oldest wooden cottage in the country, **Rose Cottage,** at Wilberforce. Built between 1811 and 1816, this is now within the **Hawkesbury Heritage Farm,** a theme park set near the river. Near Ebenezer, the Tuscan-inspired 1887 **Tizzana Winery** makes a pleasant stop and has a small selection of wines and ports grown in a nearby vineyard.

Also on the river is **Cattai National Park,** which occupies 1,048 acres (424 ha). Here you can see rain forest remnants and historic buildings, and there are picnic areas. Camping is permitted here during school vacations. ∎

The riverboat postman takes passengers on its regular run to the Lower Hawkesbury communities that don't have car access.

Hawkesbury River
🅰 174 B5

Hawkesbury Historic Museum
✉ 7 Thompson Sq.
☎ (02) 4577 2310
💲 $

Hawkesbury Heritage Farm
✉ Rose St., Wilberforce
☎ (02) 4575 1457
🕐 Closed Mon.–Wed.
💲 $$

Cattai National Park visitor information
✉ Cattai Rd., Cattai
☎ (02) 4572 8404

operating. The inn faces Thompson Square, as does the **Hawkesbury Historic Museum** a couple of doors down from the inn. The museum sells a useful publication, entitled "Guide to Windsor and Richmond Historic Buildings." Of particular interest is the beautiful **John Tebbutt Observatory** on Palmer Street in Windsor. The 19th-century astronomer John Tebbutt had a crater on the moon named after him and he is featured on the Australian $100 note. His observations in the mid-19th century, especially of comets, provided valuable data that is still being

Boat rental

Between Brooklyn and Windsor, self-drive dinghies, cruisers, or houseboats can be rented from Brooklyn, Wisemans Ferry, and several of the townships. Companies include: Ripples Houseboat Hire at Brooklyn (*Tel 9985 7333*); Luxury Houseboats, Brooklyn (*Tel 9985 7344*); Holidays Afloat Brooklyn (*Tel 9985 7368*);

Able Hawkesbury River Houseboats, Wisemans Ferry (*Tel (02) 4566 4308*); Glename Yacht Hire (*Tel 9314 5130*); Cruise Craft Houseboats, Berowra Waters (*Tel 9456 2866*); and Windsor River Cruises (*Tel (02) 9831 6630*).

Further details are available on the Internet (*www.telstra.com.au; www.charterguide.com.au*). ∎

The most commonly seen kangaroo in the Sydney region (and its wildlife parks) is the eastern gray (*Macropus giganteus*), which frequents both wooded areas and grasslands.

More places to visit in the north

GARIGAL NATIONAL PARK
About 7 miles (11 km) north of the city center, the 5,367-acre (2,172-ha) Garigal National Park is an impressive pocket of sandstone bushland north from the upper reaches of Middle Harbour. There are facilities at Davidson Picnic Area and a network of walking and horseback-riding trails. Details are available at the entrance.
🅰 175 D3 ✉ Warringah Rd., Forestville ☎ 9451 3479

KOALA PARK SANCTUARY
Northwest of the city, the Koala Park Sanctuary was established in the 1920s on 10 acres (4 ha) of native bushland. Koalas roam free and there are photo opportunities during feeding times (*10:20 a.m., 11:45 a.m., 2 p.m., and 3 p.m.*). The park also has a long-established and successful breeding and study program. Other creatures to be seen—either wandering loose or in enclosures—are dingoes, wallabies, wombats, kangaroos, and cockatoos.

A visit to the park could be combined with a trip to Windsor and the Hawkesbury River (see pp. 181–84), a detour off the M2 tollway.

Tours are conducted from the city twice daily, departing from the Clocktower Centre in Argyle Street, The Rocks, at 9 a.m. and 2 p.m.
🅰 175 C2 ✉ 84 Castle Hill Rd., West Pennant Hills ☎ 9484 3141

LANE COVE NATIONAL PARK
Just 7 miles (11 km) northwest of Sydney city center, 916-acre (371-ha) Lane Cove National Park stretches along the Lane Cove River, which runs into Sydney Harbour. There are picnic areas, two kiosks, and a small visitor center with heritage displays.

Details of trails for bushwalkers are available at the upper and lower entrances. Boating is the preferred way to see the park, however, with rowboats and canoes available for rent. The Lane Cove paddlewheeler conducts short cruises. Swimming above the weir is not encouraged due to submerged rocks and branches. Below the weir, sharks are waiting.

Access is from Lane Cove Road, Delhi Road, and Lady Game Drive. North & Western Bus Lines service 550 from Chatswood station operates to the park (*open 9 a.m. to sunset*).
🅰 175 D2–D3 ☎ 9412 1811 ∎

West & south

JUST WEST OF THE CITY, BETWEEN Sydney Harbour and the Blue Mountains, lies the vast Sydney Basin, an area in which most of the population lives in suburb after suburb of red-tiled, brick houses on "quarter acre blocks." This was the stuff of the Australian dream, the desire to have your own home and block of land, which many people realized in the years after World War II.

Before then, however, there was another dream, and that was to find land that could be used to grow crops to sustain the first settlement. Find it they did, and as a consequence some of the buildings in the western area of Sydney are among the oldest and best preserved in the country.

In this spacious western area wildlife parks, botanic gardens, and recreational amenities preserve, protect, and display some of Australia's rich natural heritage.

The southern region of Sydney may lack the grand scenery or idyllic beaches to be found in the Blue Mountains or the Northern Beaches, but there are several enjoyable excursions to be made.

Botany Bay was almost the cradle of the nation, for example, and several historic sites remain. Just south of the bay, the commercial and recreational center of Cronulla offers beaches, boating, easy walking, and some interesting history.

From Cronulla, a short ferry ride can take you to Royal National Park. The second oldest park in the world, the Royal offers first-class walking, bird- and wildlife watching, and beautiful coastal scenery. ■

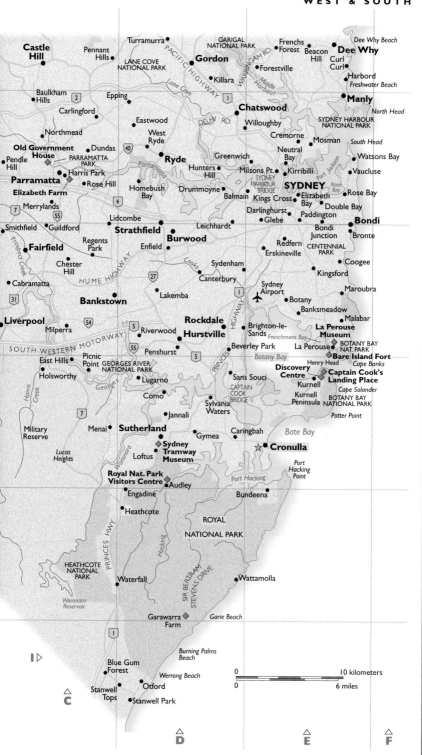

Castle
Hill

Pennant
Hills

Turramurra

GARIGAL
NATIONAL PARK

Frenchs
Forest

Beacon
Hill

Dee Why Beach

Dee Why

Curl
Curl

LANE COVE
NATIONAL PARK

PACIFIC HIGHWAY

Gordon

Killara

Forestville

Harbord
Freshwater Beach

Baulkham
Hills

Epping

Lane Cove

WARRINGAH RD.

Middle
Harbour

Manly

Carlingford

Eastwood

Chatswood

North Head

Northmead

West
Ryde

DELHI RD.

Willoughby

Cremorne

SYDNEY HARBOUR
NATIONAL PARK

Old Government
House

Dundas

Mosman

South Head

Pendle
Hill

PARRAMATTA
PARK

Ryde

Greenwich

Neutral
Bay

Watsons Bay

Parramatta

Harris Park

Parramatta

Hunters
Hill

Milsons Pt.

Kirribilli

Port Jackson

Vaucluse

Elizabeth Farm

Rose Hill

SYDNEY HARBOUR
BRIDGE

SYDNEY

Rose
Bay

Merrylands

Homebush
Bay

Drummoyne

Balmain

Kings Cross

Elizabeth
Bay

Rose Bay

Smithfield

Guildford

Lidcombe

Leichhardt

Darlinghurst

Glebe

Paddington

Double Bay

Bondi

Fairfield

Regents
Park

Enfield

Strathfield

Burwood

Redfern

Bondi
Junction

Bronte

Chester
Hill

HUME HIGHWAY

Sydenham

Cooks

Erskineville

CENTENNIAL
PARK

Coogee

Cabramatta

Canterbury

Sydney
Airport

Botany

Kingsford

Maroubra

Bankstown

Lakemba

Banksmeadow

Milperra

Liverpool

SOUTH WESTERN MOTORWAY

Riverwood

Rockdale

Hurstville

Brighton-le-
Sands

Frenchmans Bay

La Perouse

Malabar

La Perouse
Museum

BOTANY BAY
NAT. PARK

East Hills

Picnic
Point

Penshurst

Beverley Park

Botany Bay

Bare Island Fort

Holsworthy

GEORGES RIVER
NATIONAL PARK

Lugarno

Georges

Como

Sans Souci

CAPTAIN
COOK
BRIDGE

Discovery
Centre

Henry Head

Kurnell

Cape Banks

Captain Cook's
Landing Place

Military
Reserve

Jannali

Menai

Sylvania
Waters

Gymea

Caringbah

Kurnell
Peninsula

Cape Solander

BOTANY BAY
NATIONAL PARK

Lucas
Heights

Loftus

Sutherland

Sydney
Tramway
Museum

Cronulla

Bate Bay

Potter Point

Royal Nat. Park
Visitors Centre

Audley

Port Hacking

Bundeena

Port
Hacking
Point

Engadine

Heathcote

ROYAL

NATIONAL PARK

HEATHCOTE
NATIONAL
PARK

PRINCES HWY.

Hacking

SIR BERTRAM STEVENS DRIVE

Waterfall

Wattamolla

Woronora
Reservoir

Garawarra
Farm

Garie Beach

Burning Palms
Beach

Blue Gum
Forest

Werrong Beach

Stanwell
Tops

Otford

Stanwell Park

0   10 kilometers

0   6 miles

C   D   E   F

A bedroom in Old Government House

Parramatta

PARRAMATTA WAS ESTABLISHED IN NOVEMBER 1788—LESS than a year after the arrival of the First Fleet—as the soils in the area were found to be better suited to farming than those at Sydney Cove. During the early years of the colony, while it was battling for survival, the population of Parramatta was larger than that of Sydney Cove, and a number of buildings from this period have survived.

Parramatta
- 187 C5

Visitor information
- Corner of Church & Market Sts.
- 9630 3703

Parramatta Park
- O'Connell St.
- 9635 8149
- Closed Mon.

Many of the town's historic sites are now almost swamped by development, but they are still worth seeking out.

PARRAMATTA PARK

Parramatta Park, on O'Connell Street, contains several of the buildings that have survived from the early years of the colony in the 18th century. The most significant of these is **Old Government House,** built in 1799 by Governor Hunter and added to by Governor Macquarie in 1815. The building is now in the hands of the National Trust and has been fully restored and decorated with early 19th-

century furniture. There is a gift and coffee shop.

The oldest surviving headstone in Australia, dating from January 1791, is also located on O'Connell Street, in **St. John's Cemetery.** It belongs to Henry Dodd and there are numerous other graves of early settlers, including the "flogging parson," Samuel Marsden.

Parramatta Park was set aside for the public by Lachlan Macquarie. It occupies over 618 acres (250 ha), and its other buildings include the Governor's Dairy, the Tudor gatehouse off O'Connell Street, rotundas, and a bathhouse built by Governor Brisbane in 1822.

Right: Old Government House sits on a hill in Parramatta Park, with views to the Parramatta River.

SAMUEL MARSDEN

Samuel Marsden (1764–1838), a parson, was appointed as a magistrate in Sydney in 1795. He was a stern disciplinarian who gained a reputation for having convicts lashed severely for minor indiscretions. In 1800 he used torture to extract a confession, and did so again after the Vinegar Hill Rebellion in 1804 (see p. 28). ∎

ROSE HILL & HARRIS PARK

On the opposite side of the main shopping and business district are the small suburbs of Rose Hill and Harris Park, where two of the oldest buildings in the country can be found. Rose Hill was the original name given to Parramatta, but Governor Phillip changed the name of the township to the Aboriginal for "places where eels lie down" on June 4, 1791.

In the same year, **Experiment Farm Cottage** (*9 Ruse St., Parramatta, Tel 9635 5655, closed Mon. and Fri.–Sat.*) was built on 30 acres (12 ha) of land granted to convict James Ruse, the first farmer in the colony to declare himself self-sufficient. The surviving cottage homestead—now restored and furnished in period style by the National Trust—was built on the land in 1834 by a surgeon, John Harris.

One of the most significant buildings in the Parramatta district is **Elizabeth Farm** (*70 Alice St., Rose Hill, Tel 9635 9488*), built by John and Elizabeth Macarthur (see p. 28) and the oldest surviving house in the country.

The attractive colonial-style house, part of which dates from 1793, is set in a pleasant garden that was first laid out in 1830. Many of the plants and trees, native and exotic, have significant historical and botanical interest.

As with the Inner City and Eastern Suburbs, a special Explorer bus services the many historic sites around Parramatta. Access is by train from the city or, for a more scenic approach, the Parramatta RiverCat travels through many attractive harborside suburbs, past the Homebush Bay Olympic site (see pp. 166–71) and on to the Charles Street Wharf at Parramatta. Access by car is via the M4 tollway from the city.

The Parramatta Tourist Information Centre on the right-hand side of the second bridge up the river from the ferry wharf has walking and driving guides to the many historic sites in this precinct (some guides are also available at the wharf). "Historic Parramatta" is a small guide sheet detailing 24 buildings along a signposted walking or driving route around the area. ∎

Cape Solander, on the seaward side of Botany Bay National Park. Daniel Solander visited the bay with Captain Cook in 1770, 18 years before the Sydney colony was established.

Botany Bay

ONLY 5 MILES (7 KM) SOUTH OF THE CENTRAL BUSINESS District, Sydney's second major waterway is famous as the intended site of the colony's original settlement. Botany Bay had been visited by Capt. James Cook in 1770, and the historic site where he landed is now part of Botany Bay National Park. Large parts of its shores have been given over to industry, but you will find a few gems tucked away and the western shore is a cycling, walking, and boating haven.

Botany Bay

📖 187 E3

Botany Bay National Park visitor information

✉ Cape Solander Dr.

☎ 9311 3125

Within the **Botany Bay National Park** is **La Perouse Museum** (see p. 158), devoted to the French explorer Comte de la Pérouse, who arrived in Botany Bay shortly after the First Fleet. He and his vessels disappeared not long after his visit and he was mourned as much by the English, whose respect he had earned, as he was by the French. Also in the museum building—a former cable station—is a Botany Bay exhibition, and artifacts crafted by the local Aboriginal community are on sale. Short tours are

conducted in English and French.

Nearby in La Perouse rises the **Bare Island Fort,** built from 1881 to 1885 to upgrade the bay's defense system. You can rent a boat from Frenchmans Bay, below the museum, and there are small beaches at Congwong Bay and Little Congwong.

A tower near the museum was completed in 1822 to watch for smugglers landing in the bay.

Take a stroll or do some bird-watching along the Henry Head walk, where there are a number of places to picnic, fish, and scuba dive. Access is by car along Anzac Parade or bus routes 393 and 394 (L94) from the city.

On the western side of Botany Bay, from the Cooks River down to the Georges River, is an almost continuous stretch of calm water beach-front with walking and biking trails, picnic areas, boat ramps, and netted pools. The bike trails reach around to Cronulla (see pp. 192–93) and (with a few nasty traffic spots) the Olympic venues at Homebush Bay (see pp. 166–71). A bike path to the city along the Alexandra Canal is planned. Meanwhile, cyclists will find plenty of cafés at Brighton-le-Sands, facing Botany Bay.

The main section of the 1,074-acre (435-ha) Botany Bay National Park covers the southern headland of the bay, the site of several significant relics of the Captain Cook landing. Look for the **Discovery Centre** (with Captain Cook and wetlands exhibitions), monuments to Cook and Banks, **Captain Cook's Landing Place,** and the grave of one of Cook's crew, Forby Sutherland, who was buried here after his death in 1770.

As with the north side of the park, there are several picnic areas and quite a few walking trails, plus fishing, swimming, and bird-watching opportunities. ∎

La Perouse Museum is located within an old cable station, built to house operators working on the telegraph line to New Zealand.

La Perouse Museum
- 187 E4
- Cable Station, Anzac Parade, La Perouse
- 9311 3379

Discovery Centre
- 187 E3
- 9668 9111
- Access is by car along Captain Cook Dr. to Kurnell or train to Cronulla Station & bus 67

A walk in Cronulla

The beachside suburb of Cronulla, a precinct of Sydney near the southern section of Botany Bay National Park, adjacent to the northern section of Royal National Park, offers a wealth of recreational opportunity—beaches, inshore waterways, less pressured leisure activity. This route includes headland walking trails, several beaches, and Gunnamatta Bay, with mostly level walking.

Bass and Flinders Point—though only 20 miles (30 km) from Sydney, it took eight years for explorers to reach this area.

From Cronulla Station, cross at the traffic lights and walk down the left-hand side of Munro Park. Follow a lane past the central mall area to **South Cronulla Beach ❶**, where you might be tempted to take your first dive into the Pacific.

If you can resist, turn right and follow the track around Cronulla Point to tiny **Blackwoods Beach ❷**. This is unpatrolled and rather rocky but has a popular surfing spot at the end of a rock shelf half a mile (1 km) offshore. The heights above the beach make a superb vantage point.

Continue on to **Shelly Beach ❸**, another small beach, which has toilets and changing facilities and a large ocean pool with wheelchair access all the way into the water. Onshore is a large picnic area with plenty of shady trees. Farther on still, at **Oak Park,** you'll find another surf break, a small beach, and another pool on Glaisher Point.

At the southern end of the promontory is the **Bass and Flinders Memorial ❹**, a monument to George Bass and Matthew Flinders, who first explored Port Hacking in March 1796 (with a young boy named William Martin) in nothing more than a tiny rowboat, named *Tom Thumb*. Bass Strait, the treacherous stretch of wild water between Victoria and Tasmania, is also named after George Bass, who discovered it in January 1798, thereby reducing the traveling time from London to the colony in New South Wales.

From Bass and Flinders Point enjoy the view across Port Hacking to the township of Bundeena, Jibbon Beach, and Royal National Park's northern edge. All of these are accessible by ferry, which departs from a wharf at the end of this walk.

From the memorial, turn your back on the ocean and start to head inland. Just down the slope you'll notice that the terrain and the vegetation change. Instead of the Norfolk pines of cultivated gardens, eucalyptuses and figs of the Australian bush predominate.

In **Salmon Haul Reserve ❺**, just down the hill, notice the fig tree with its trunk growing sideways due to the strong southerly winds.

🅜 187 E3
► Cronulla Station
↔ 3.5 miles (5.6 km)
⏲ Allow at least 1.5 hours, longer if you can't resist a swim
► Cronulla Station

NOT TO BE MISSED
- Shelly Beach
- Bass and Flinders Memorial
- Gunnamatta Park

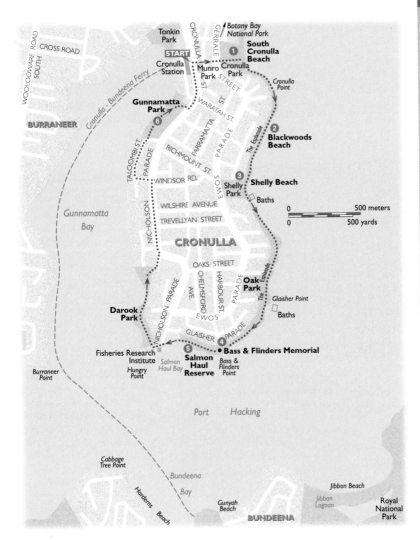

At the end of Salmon Haul Reserve take the stairs on the far side of the large white house and walk through to Nicholson Parade, past the entrance of the Fisheries Research Institute, and continue along the path to **Darook Park.** As you head along the path to the right, notice the holes in the trees that accommodate a variety of parrots, including eastern rosellas and cockatoos.

From here either make your way down to the water where, at low tide, the sand flats in front of the houses and seawall make for fairly easy walking, or continue to the far side of Darook Park and climb up to Nicholson Parade and follow it to Leumeah Street.

Turn left, then right at Taloombi Street through to **Gunnamatta Park 6.** Here there is a mesh enclosed swimming area, a large pavilion, and a vast picnic area. Go through the park to reach the ferry wharf at the head of the bay, just below the railway station, where this walk began.

For more on the ferries to Bundeena and Port Hacking cruises, see page 194. ■

Port Hacking
& Botany Bay cruises

THE GEORGES RIVER AND PORT HACKING, TWO OF
Sydney's lesser known waterways, are both worth exploring for their
scenery. They offer quiet reaches of native bushland and mangrove
wetlands, and Towra Point Reserve, in Botany Bay, is renowned for
waterbirds such as stilts, spoonbills, and pelicans.

TOM THUMB III
17102

*Reservations are advised; note that
cruise times may vary due to tides).*

The M.V. *Tom Thumb III* is
named after the vessel used by
explorers Bass and Flinders (see
p. 192). Cruises take three hours
and explore both the national
park side of the port and river,
with its cliffs and slopes of native
bush and mangroves, and the
opposite bank, where numerous
opulent houses nestle in the bays
or make bold statements on the
hillsides. Light refreshments are
served on board, and albums of
photographs show the development
of the area and its use as a fishing
and oyster port.

Riverboat Cruises (*Tel 9583
1199, 10:30 a.m. Mon.–Sat., 12:30
p.m., 1:30 pm., and 2:30 p.m. on Sun.
from Sans Souci Wharf, on western
side of Captain Cook Bridge, Sans
Souci*) runs tea and coffee cruises
aboard the M.V. *Bass and Flinders*,
M.V. *Martin*, and M.V. *That's Life*.
Choose between exploring the winding Georges River (*Mon., Wed., and
Fri.*), which threads between subur-
bia, golf courses, riverside parks and
mangroves, or Botany Bay (*Tues.,
Thurs., and Sat.*), including some
of the region's most significant bird
sanctuaries. Take bus 302 or 303
from the city.

Towra Point in particular is
one of the most significant coastal
wetlands regions and is vital for
migratory birds from as far away as
China and Siberia. It is also accessible by road via Cronulla. ■

**Ferries connect
Cronulla with
Bundeena, at the
northern end of
Royal National
Park, as well as
provide scenic
cruises around
Port Hacking.**

The ferry wharf and marina below
the Cronulla Station at Tonkin
Street is the base for **Cronulla
National Park Ferry Cruises,**
which operates an hourly service to
and from Bundeena and Royal
National Park (see pp. 195–97).
Cruises around Port Hacking and
up the Hacking River are conducted aboard two quaint wooden
ferries, the M.V. *Curranulla* and
M.V. *Tom Thumb III* (*Tel 9523
2990, Sun.–Mon., Wed., and Fri.
at 10:30 a.m.; and on Sun. afternoons during summer holidays.*

Royal National Park

DiVERSE FLORA AND FAUNA GRACE THE 39,536 ACRES (16,000 ha) of coastal heath, littoral rain forest, and bushland that comprise Royal National Park. Visit rock engravings and hand stencils left by the Dharawal people, or enjoy the beaches and rivers, many of which have enticing swimming pools. A real attraction is the lack of vehicular roads; you can spend an afternoon at an almost deserted beach, or "go native" for days, exploring inland and coastal walks.

Royal National Park

⛺ 187 D2

Located 20 miles (32 km) south of the city, Royal National Park was established in 1879. The park has approximately 12 miles (19 km) of coastline, an inland river, many streams, and a comprehensive network of walking trails. There are camping areas (permits are available from visitor centers), scenic drives, plus several stunning coastal lookouts.

Access to the park is provided by car and train or the ferry from Cronulla to the township of Bundeena (an enclave surrounded by the park on the south side of Port Hacking). Several roads are ideal for cycling, including some—such as fire trails—that are closed to traffic.

Walking trails enter the park from Loftus, Engadine, Heathcote, Waterfall, or Otford railway stations. Roads enter from the Princes Highway on the western side and at Otford in the south. For a particularly scenic drive, enter the park at Audley and follow Sir Bertram Stevens Drive to the southern side of the park

Burning Palms Beach is one of several uncrowded beaches in Royal National Park. Take extreme care if you are swimming on an unpatrolled beach.

Audley visitor
information center
✉ Audley Rd., Audley
☎ 9542 0648

where, at Otford Lookout and Stanwell Tops, hang gliders launch off the hilltop and soar out over the Pacific Ocean, which beats against the rocks far below. The view from here extends south well down the coast to the city of Wollongong, and all the way up to the northernmost headland of the park.

BY CAR

Visitors arriving by car usually start at **Audley,** at the crossing of the Hacking River. Here you'll find a visitor center, displays on the park, a shop, and information on walks within the park. Nearby are wide expanses of picnic areas, safe swimming areas, and rowboat and canoe rental. There is road access to a number of beaches within the park, several of which are patrolled, including **Garie, Era,** and **Burning Palms.** With only a few basic facilities, they make quite a contrast to the city beaches with their busy shopping and food strips. Smaller picnic areas with road access are tucked away all over the park.

Car camping is only permitted at **Bonnie Vale,** facing Port Hacking. Nude bathing is permitted at **Werrong Beach,** on the southern edge of the park, a mile (1.5 km) from Otford Lookout.

ON FOOT

Walking trails within the park are designed to suit every level of fitness and desire for adventure. One of the shortest trails, the **Garawarra Farm to Burning Palms Beach walk,** is less than a mile. Some walks follow streams or escarpments through the inland areas of the park.

The premier walk in the park is a two-day coast route that starts from the ferry at Bundeena and follows the headlands and beaches south to Otford Railway Station. The views of beaches, rugged headlands, heath, and rain forest are superb. Along the way you'll find camping sites that comply with the park requirement that sites must be at least half a mile (1 km) from roads and picnic grounds. If you are very energetic, it is possible to cover this route in a day, but it is far better to take two days to give yourself time to swim and enjoy the sights. Some sections of the track are also quite steep. Note, too, that permits from a visitor center are required. They can be obtained in advance, along with maps and advice on your intended trip. For information, contact NPWS South Metropolitan District (*P.O. Box 44, Sutherland, NSW 1499, Tel (02) 9542 0648*). For noncampers, the park is open during daylight hours. ■

Opposite: The
figure-eight pool
south of Burning
Palms Beach was
formed by wave
action and stones
grinding away the
soft sandstone of
the rock shelf.

Sydney Tramway Museum

Near the Loftus entrance to Royal National Park is the Sydney Tramway Museum (*Map 187 D3, corner of Rawson Ave. and Princes Hwy., Loftus, Tel 9542 3646, closed Mon.–Tues., and Thurs.–Sat., except public holidays*), featuring relics from the days when Sydney had a comprehensive tramway system. These include the R-class *Commodore* and the oldest electric tram in the Southern Hemisphere, a C-class dating from 1894. The expression "he was off like a Bondi tram" refers to the way the trams flew down the hill to the beach.

The museum also features examples of vehicles from several other Australian cities, as well as from overseas. Short rides are conducted, including trips into Royal National Park. ■

Wildlife of the Sydney region

Whether you have penetrated into the wilds of one of the national parks, or are wandering through Hyde Park in the middle of the city, the rich diversity of wildlife in the Sydney area is never far away. You'll be surprised how many of the creatures on these pages you'll be able to check off even during the briefest of stays. Visitors seeking a longer list than is presented here could consider the guide *Burnum Burnum's Wild Things*, a pocket guide that has many more of the birds and animals of the Sydney region. A large part of this volume also covers the wide variety of native plants. For bird-watchers, there are several excellent field guides available from bookstores in the city.

Australian pelican (*Pelecanus conspicillatus*)
Ungainly on the ground, with short legs, large body, and long bill on a long neck, these birds are superb flyers. Sexes are similar. Growing to 64 inches (1.6 m), they are found all over Australia in shallow marine and inland waters. They can rise to great heights on thermals and glide huge distances to reach food. They tend to forage rather than plunge dive. There is often a flotilla of them loitering around the docks at the Sydney Fish Market.

Little penguin (*Eudyptula minor*)
The only species of penguin found on Australian mainland waters, the little penguin can be found as far north as sub-tropical Queensland. They are slate blue in color, with a white chest. Sexes are similar, though the male has a heavier bill. They grow to 16 inches (40 cm). There is a colony near Manly and they can be seen around Manly Cove and the heads. They may also be seen on Gordon's Bay, near Coogee in the Eastern Suburbs.

Black swan (*Cygnus atratus*)
Graceful bird, common on inland waters, can often be found on the lakes at Centennial Park, and the Royal Botanic Gardens' ponds. The Black swan grows to 50 inches (1.3 m) and has a black, sometimes brownish, plumage, and a red bill with a white tip. Males have slightly thicker necks than females and hold them straighter when they swim. They make a honk or bugle sound and hiss when they are protecting their territory. It is best to keep clear of them when they have young.

Eastern rosella (*Platycercus eximius*)
One of many beautiful parrots found around
Sydney. Common. At 11–12 inches (28–30.5
cm), they are slightly larger than a budgerigar
and quite a lot more colorful. Sexes are alike.
They are frequently seen in open country
and the parks and gardens of the city. They
are great flyers and quite quick, so you may
hear their shrill screech and only catch a
flash of color as they pass. Also commonly
seen around Sydney is the crimson rosella,
which has a red head and body with blue
cheeks and wings.

Rainbow lorikeet
(*Trichoglossus heamatodus*)
Striking parrot commonly found in Sydney,
growing to 10–12 inches (25.5–30.5 cm). It is
the only lorikeet with a blue head. Sexes are
alike. The lorikeet is a noisy bird that can usually be seen in flocks and heard chattering when
feeding. These birds tend to be arboreal and
feed on flowering trees and shrubs. Like cockatoos and parrots, they have a hooked beak, but
they are also equipped with an adapted brush-
like tongue which helps them feed on nectar.

Kookaburra (*Dacelo novaguineae*)
Famous for its laugh, the kookaburra is commonly seen around bushland areas. It grows to
18 inches (45.5 cm) and both sexes are similar.
The most distinguishing feature of this rather
handsome bird is its laughing call, which
sounds like it has just heard the best joke ever
told. Kookaburras are predatory birds, hunting small reptiles and mammals, and can often
be seen in a conspicuous position on the edges
of forest clearings watching the ground for a
prospective meal.

Silvereye (*Zosterops lateralis*)
This small but very attractive bird is
common on coastal heaths and in the coastal
forest understory from South Australia to
Queensland. It grows to four inches (10 cm);
males and females are similar. Interestingly,
there are mainland Australian silvereyes and
Tasmanian silvereyes, and while the mainland
birds are nonmigratory, the Tasmanians are
sometimes seen on the mainland, although
they do not breed while visiting. The silvereye's diet consists of insects, fruit, and nectar.

Sulphur-crested cockatoo
(*Cacatua galerita*)
Big and raucous, with a deafening scraping screech, the sulphur-crested cockatoo is common, particularly in riverside areas and timbered countryside, such as Centennial Park. Growing to 20 inches (51 cm), it has a distinctive yellow crest that it lifts in an impressive display that at a stretch resembles the sails of Sydney Opera House. Sexes are similar. A sulphur-crested cockatoo holds the record for the oldest known bird: It was 80 years old when it died at London Zoo in 1982.

White-bellied sea eagle
(*Haliaeetus leucogaster*)
Glorious predatory bird found patrolling seas, lakes, and rivers. White-breasted with gray to dark gray wings and back; males grow to 30 inches (76 cm), females to 34 inches (86 cm). They can be seen on the Hawkesbury waterways, often perched on dead tree branches. The sea eagle is one of 24 raptors that inhabit Australia and is so superbly adapted to hunting that it only spends a few minutes each day seeking its food.

Koala (*Phascolarctos cinereus*)
Generally nocturnal, these arboreal marsupials tend to sleep very high in the trees, which means they are far easier to find in wildlife parks than in the wild. Sometimes referred to as "koala bears," they are not bears and naturalists will be quick to correct you if you call them so. Eating a diet of eucalyptus leaves, these creatures are just under two to three feet (61–91 cm) fully grown, but have an intestinal pouch (appendix) up to 23 feet (7 m) long to help their digestion.

Short-beaked echidna
(*Tachyglossus aculeatus*)
An egg-laying mammal that lives on termites, the echidna is shy and difficult to find, but there is a good exhibit at Taronga Zoo. With the long-beaked echidna (a native of New Guinea, to the north of Australia) and the one species of platypus, the short-beaked echidna is one of only three living monotremes (egg-laying mammals) on the planet. Echidnas live on ants and termites caught by means of a long, sticky tongue.

Swamp wallaby (*Wallabia bicolor*)

The swamp wallaby prefers forest areas where it browses on foliage. It is elusive, but can be spotted on walks away from built-up areas. There are swamp wallabies in the Discovery enclosure at the Kalkari Visitor Centre in Ku-ring-gai Chase National Park, but even there they are shy. Wallabies, kangaroos, and rat-kangaroos belong to the marsupial family *Macropodidae* (meaning large-footed) and are characterized by large, powerful hind legs that are used for hopping. An adult swamp wallaby is five and a half feet tall (1.7 m) when fully grown.

Gray-headed flying fox
(*Pteropus poliocephalus*)

A huge bat. Look closer and you'll see that they have quite foxlike faces. Most Sydneysiders love them and think they're cute. These guys are harmless and live on fruit and nectar. To see them, just look up at night or listen for their raucous chatter in the Moreton Bay fig trees and flowering eucalyptuses in all the city parks. There is a colony just behind the kiosk/café in the Royal Botanic Gardens right next to the Central Business District.

Eastern gray kangaroo
(*Macropus giganteus*)

This is the most common species of kangaroo in the Sydney region. They are often seen in the national parks and are a standard item in all wildlife parks where you can feed them, pat them, and have your photo taken with them. Kangaroos are marsupials, which means that the young are born highly underdeveloped and are then suckled in the mother's pouch until they are able to survive. Of 19 marsupial families, 16 are found in Australia.

Ringtail possum (*Pseudocheirus peregrinus*)

This is the most common of several possums found around Sydney. They take their name from American opossums, which they resemble, but when he named them in 1770, Capt. James Cook omitted the "o." Possums are nocturnal creatures and enjoy insects, blossoms and pollen, and fruit left out by Sydneysiders who encourage them around their houses. There are several of them in Hyde Park, which you can sometimes see hopping about the grass.

Platypus (*Ornithorhynchus anatinus*)
The platypus is a strange-looking creature: It has a duck's bill, a rabbit's body, webbed feet, and a short but thick, beaverlike tail, and as a monotreme, it also lays eggs. The first specimen sent to England was denounced as a hoax. They are difficult to find in the wild, where they are highly susceptible to any disturbance to their environment, but Taronga Zoo has some good examples The platypus's bill finds invertebrate prey by sensing electrical fields. Note: The small spurs on the ankles of adult males are poisonous.

Blue-tongue lizard (*Tiliqua scincoides*)
You only get to see this lizard's tongue, which is a remarkably vivid blue, if it pokes it out to ward off predators. For the blue-tongue lizard, running away certainly isn't an option; like quite a few members of the skink family (190 Australian species can be found from the tropics to deserts to subalpine zones), blue-tongues have heavy bodies and short legs, and virtually drag themselves along the ground. They are quite common in suburban gardens around bushland areas.

Lace monitor (*Varanus varius*)
A species of goanna (a corruption of iguana), lace monitors can grow to over six feet tall (2 m). They climb trees and feed on birds and eggs, mammals and insects. They are often seen scavenging around picnic areas in the bush. Though not dangerous and usually quite timid, a lizard this big isn't something you'd want to annoy. If they do bite, the wound tends to become infected and can often require dozens of stitches. The largest goanna is the perentie (*Varanus giganteus*), found in central Australia.

Red-bellied black snake
(*Pseudechis porphyriacus*)
This snake is venomous, but not particularly aggressive, and can usually be found near water. It grows to five feet (1.5 m) in length. Australia has the world's most venomous land snakes and is unique in being the only continent where venomous snakes outnumber nonvenomous snakes. For comparison, there are 18 Australian snakes more dangerous than rattlesnakes. Most fatalities in Australia occur when a person attempts to kill the snake. So live and let live.

Bird-watching & bush walking

In the Sydney region, there are more than 350 species of birds. There are study centers in several national parks and wetland areas and bird-watching clubs include NSW Field Ornithologists Club (*NSWFOC, Tel 9660 8062*) and Royal Australasian Ornithologists Union, commonly known as Birds Australia (*Tel 9290 1810; www.vicnet.net.au/-birdsaus*). Both clubs have details of numerous bird sanctuaries in and around Sydney.

Bush walkers can link with several clubs that organize walks almost every weekend through outdoors and camping stores. Tour companies offering a range of walking experiences include Aussie Bush Discoveries (*Tel 9622 1557*), Aus Walk (*Tel 6457 2220*), and Oz Trek Adventure Tours (*Tel 9360 3444*). ■

Humpback whale

(*Megaptera novaeangliae*)
Hundreds of whales migrate up the coast annually in June and July, then head south from September to November, sometimes very close to shore. Other species can also be seen, such as right, blue, and sperm whales. Radio stations often broadcast details of their presence, so tune in if you are keen to observe them. Whaling stations once dotted the Australian coast, but since 1980 whaling in Australia has been banned and their numbers are recovering.

Blue-ring octopus

(*Hapalochleana maculosa*)
Frequents ocean and harbor rockpools, but is extremely difficult to find. The blue-ring octopus is small (its body is only up to three inches/6 cm long), but it is venomous and its bite has been fatal. (Bites have only been inflicted when the creature was being handled.) Normally a plain brown camouflaged color, they display the blue rings and spots when disturbed. Victims usually recover if artificial respiration is given for approximately 12 hours.

Bottle-nosed dolphin

(*Tursiops truncatus*)
Dolphins are increasingly common around Sydney as efforts to clean up waterways produce results. They are starting to venture into the harbor and may be glimpsed around the heads. Bottle-nosed dolphins are one of 13 species found in Australian waters. They usually travel in small groups in coastal waters. The most famous colony of bottle-noses is a group in Western Australia, at Monkey Mia, which have been handfed since 1964.

More places to visit in the west & south

AUSTRALIAN WILDLIFE PARK

The Australian Wildlife Park lies within the 500-acre (202-ha) amusement park called **Australia's Wonderland.** It can be visited separately and has exhibits that range across birds, mammals, and reptiles, as well as dry land and wetland habitats. The animals are not just on show, however; many form part of the park's educational program or research and breeding programs that are ensuring the species' survival.

As well as seeing the usual kangaroos, wallabies, and emus, you can walk through aviaries and koala enclosures. Here several nocturnal houses and habitat displays present animals such as wombats and goannas in their underground burrows. Another enclosure contains little penguins (often referred to as fairy penguins), pythons, and venomous snakes.

One of the ever popular crocodile exhibits is a large saurian that originates from the tropical north of Australia and goes by the name of Maniac. You can also see flying foxes close at hand, or visit the petting zoo or kangaroo feeding station.

A recent addition is the Outback Woolshed, a reconstruction based on turn-of-the-century sheds where sheepshearing demonstrations are held along with whip-cracking and stock-handling displays. Elsewhere in the park, educational talks and presentations about reptiles, koalas, and crocodiles take place several times a day. There are two restaurants, and a gift and souvenir shop.

The park is located just off the M4 freeway between Parramatta and the foot of the Blue Mountains. A shuttle bus service runs direct to the park from Rooty Hill railway station and buses operate from the city with hotel pickup (*details from your hotel's reception or the park*). 🅰 186 B5 ✉ Wallgrove Rd., Eastern Creek ☎ 9830 9187

FEATHERDALE WILDLIFE PARK

Featherdale contains the largest private collection of native fauna in Australia, with particular emphasis on bird life. It has more than 200 species of native birds, including a wide variety of stunningly plumaged parrots. The park also boasts one of the largest koala colonies in New South Wales.

You can walk among the kangaroos and see penguins, crocodiles, wombats, possums, Tasmanian devils, and more. Educational talks and tours cover koalas, kangaroos, wombats, crocodiles, and reptiles. And you'll find everything you need for an Aussie-style barbecue in the restaurant area.

Featherdale is located between Blacktown and Doonside railway stations and could be combined with a trip to the Blue Mountains (see pp. 217–23) or Parramatta (see pp. 188–89). Tours that include the park operate from the city, picking up from city hotels.

Access from the M4 motorway Reservoir Road exit. Bus 725 from Blacktown station stops at the park. 🅰 186 B5 ✉ 217 Kildare Rd., Doonside ☎ 9622 1644

MOUNT ANNAN BOTANIC GARDEN

Opened in 1988, the Mount Annan Botanic Garden is a branch of the Royal Botanic Gardens (see pp. 52–53). Its main role is to accommodate the bulk of the Royal Botanic Gardens' collection of native plants. Originally occupied by a group of dairy farms settled by Scottish immigrants, the site is named after the Scottish town of Annan.

The 1,000-acre (405-ha) garden features walking trails, ornamental lakes, and, of course, one of the world's finest collections of Australian native plants—bottlebrushes, wattles (more than 300 species), banksias, and eucalyptuses. There are wetland areas, beds of annuals, and the Terrace Garden, which features 2,500 species of plants. The ultimate aim of the garden is to display most of the 25,000 species of plants known to exist throughout Australia.

Facilities include picnic areas, free gas barbecues, a café, a visitor information center, and an education center.

Access is from Narellan Road, via the southwestern freeway (route 31). Bus 896 leaves from Campbelltown Station. 🅰 186 B2 ✉ Mount Annan Dr., Mount Annan ☎ (02) 4648 2477 ∎

Spend a couple of days enjoying the mountain scenery, cruising pristine water-ways, or sampling some of the world's finest wines. All lie within a couple of hours of the city. And beyond? An entire continent is waiting for you.

Farther afield

Wine grapes, Hunter Valley

Farther afield

WHEN YOU NEED A RESPITE FROM THE DELIGHTS OF SYDNEY, THE OPTIONS are boundless. Within one to three hours' drive of the city there is a world of waterways, beaches, and mountain scenery to be discovered. Visit some of the best wineries in the world, or swim, surf, sail, hike, or ride in an idyllic setting.

The Central Coast offers numerous beaches and seaside villages where the most you'll have to worry about is deciding what strength sunscreen to use or how to sink a difficult putt. Then there are the wineries of the Hunter Valley, just a little over two hours away and one of the premier districts in a country whose winemaking has definitely come of age. Nondrinkers can enjoy the lovely scenery of rolling hills covered in vines, lunch in superb garden settings, join a cycle tour, or go ballooning.

To the west of the city, the rugged Blue Mountains present spectacular scenery, mountain villages, and cooler-climate flora and fauna. One of the great attractions for Sydneysiders is to spend a weekend in winter snuggled up in front of a roaring fire, enjoying a real taste of the season. To the south-west, the Southern Highlands are less rugged but no less attractive, and the tulip festival is a highlight every year.

The coast south of Sydney and Wollongong is possibly even quieter than that to the north, and there are some delightful unspoiled bays and beaches to discover. And, of course, there are the wonderful cheeses from the thriving dairy industry.

The capital of Australia, the ornamental city of Canberra, is nearly four hours to the southwest, and features one of the country's finest art galleries, a spectacular annual flower festival, and ready access to the snowfields of the Snowy Mountains. As the seat of national government, it also features major institutions housed in stunning architecture. ∎

Gulgong
Bylong
Denman
East Gresford
Dungog

Mudgee
Jerry Plains
Hunter
Singleton
Hunter Valley
Branxton

Lue
Bulga
15

Hargraves
Rylstone
Lake Windamere
Howes Valley
Blaxlands Restaurant & Wine Centre
Maitland
1

Kandos
Hungerford Hill
Kurri Kurri
Raymond Terrace

Cessnock
Kurri

Ilford
Bogee
WOLLEMI
YENGO
Newcastle

Hill End
Sofala
NATIONAL
NATIONAL
Lake Macquarie
Belmont

86
Capertee
Glen Davis
PARK
PARK
Morisset
Swansea

Portland
Macdonald
DHARUG N. P.
Wyong
Budgewai

Bathurst
Wallerawang
Australian Reptile Park & Wildlife Sanctuary
Forest of Tranquility
Tuggerah Lake
The Entrance

32
GREAT WESTERN HIGHWAY
Mount Wilson
Wisemans Ferry
Old Sydney Town
Gosford
Terrigal

Lithgow
Bell
BRISBANE WATER
Avoca
Brisbane Water

Grovetts
Perrys Lookdown
N. P.
Pearl Beach
Broken Bay
BOUDDI NATIONAL PARK

yney
Hydro-Majestic Hotel
Mt. Victoria
Leap
Evans Lookout
Windsor
Cowan
Palm Beach
Pittwater

Rockley
Oberon
Blackheath
Medlow Bath
Richmond
Springwood
Mona Vale

Explorers Marked Tree
Leura
Glenbrook
Hornsby

Black Springs
Jenolan Caves
Katoomba
Blue Mts
Echo Point
Penrith
Manly

Trunkey Creek
Three Sisters
Jamison Valley
Wentworth Falls
Parramatta
Port Jackson

KANANGRA BOYD NATIONAL PARK
Lake Burragorang
Liverpool
SYDNEY

Tuena
Abercrombie
BLUE MOUNTAINS NATIONAL PARK
Camden
Botany Bay

Campbelltown
Sutherland

Picton
Audley
ROYAL NATIONAL PARK

Laggan
Tahmoor
31
Stanwell Park

Taralga
ILLAWARRA HWY.
Bargo
Bulli

Crookwell
Berrima
Unanderra
Wollongong

Grabben Gullen
TARLO RIVER NATIONAL PARK
Moss Vale
Southern Highlands
Mittagong
Dapto
Port Kembla

Bowral
Fitzroy Falls
Shellharbour

Marulan
31
Exeter
Bundanoon
Jamberoo
Minnamurra Rainforest

Goulburn
Kangeroo Valley
Kiama

Bungonia
Berry
Gerringong
Gerroa

nning
Bomaderry
Seven Mile Beach

Collector
23
MORTON
1
Nowra

Lake Bathurst
NATIONAL

Lake George
Tarago
Huskisson
Jervis Bay

ton
PARK
Jervis Bay

Bungendore
Charleyong
PRINCES HIGHWAY
Milton

eanbeyan
Shoalhaven
BUDAWANG NATIONAL PARK
Ulladulla

oogong eservoir
Braidwood
Clyde

ERRY IONAL SERVE
Captains Flat
Termeil
1

Nelligen
0   60 kilometers
0   40 miles

DEUA NATIONAL PARK
Batemans Bay

tains
Moruya

C   D   E   F

Hunter Valley

TWO HOURS NORTH OF SYDNEY IS A BROAD AND FERTILE valley—perhaps the closest thing Australia has to the land of milk and honey. It extends more than 100 miles (160 km) inland; near the coast a wide alluvial plain gives way to rolling hills, to farms and vineyards. Its edges are defined by the steeply wooded slopes of the Great Dividing Range. Coal mining is also a major industry in the region, as the entire area sits on a gigantic seam of coal.

Hunter Valley
🗺 207 E6
Wine Country information center
✉ Aberdare Rd., Cessnock
☎ (02) 4990 4477

In the latter half of this century, the Hunter Valley's main attraction for tourists has been as one of the premier wine-growing districts of the world. Grapes have been grown in the area since 1824, when James Busby, among the fathers of Australian viticulture, took up a grant of 2,000 acres (809 ha) on the Hunter River between Branxton and Singleton. These days wineries are found in the Lower and Upper Hunter Valley, primarily growing semillon and shiraz, although the locally popular Chardonnay is increasingly prevalent.

The gateway to the region is the town of **Cessnock** (*Visitor*

Left: Each year, new vineyards spring up in the Hunter Valley, acknowledged as one of the best wine-growing areas in the country.

Below: A sampling of some of the valley's better known labels

information, Aberdare Rd., Tel (02) 4990 4477), where the vineyards reach right to the edge of town. Here the Wine Country information center has details about all the wineries, accommodations, and activities in the area. A full calendar of events throughout the year includes concerts in the vineyards, food festivals, and the **Hunter Valley Vintage Festival** held in February.

Because of its proximity to Sydney, numerous day and weekend tours are conducted to the Hunter Valley from the city (*Sydney Visitor Centre, Tel 9255 1788*).

The hospitality at the wineries is what you would expect from Australians—friendly and very helpful. Tastings at most venues are free, and there is no pressure to buy (at least not that you would notice). The main restriction is that most wineries prefer groups to reserve visits in advance, so they don't get overwhelmed by six tour buses at once. Most wineries can organize shipment to any location on the planet, and some can even set up a regular delivery service of their latest vintages, which means you can "revisit" the Hunter year after year.

Apart from the wineries, the valley offers pleasant scenery and is dotted with restaurants, intimate cottage accommodations, and motels. You can also follow pursuits such as ballooning, horseback riding, and cycling. ■

A drive to the Hunter Valley wineries

The following Lower Hunter wineries, just a short drive from Cessnock, include some of the major players in the region and are located in some of the most scenic areas. Around McDonalds Road, between the Broke Road and Marrowbone Road, you'll find more than a dozen wineries large and small. Don't hesitate to make detours. With another 40 or so wineries in the Hunter Valley, it is likely you'll run out of time before you run out of places to visit.

Leave Cessnock and drive north on the Allandale Road to reach the Broke Road and the **Hunter Valley Wine Society** ❶ (*Tel (02) 4998 7397*). This is a good starting point, as you can taste wines here from many of the wineries throughout the region.

Petersons Champagne House (*Tel (02) 4998 7881*), just behind the Wine Society, is a beautiful building with a good selection of sparkling wines and very informative talks for booked groups.

Farther along the Broke Road, turn off to **Pepper Tree Wines** ❷ (*Halls Rd., Tel (02) 4998 7539*). The winery and restaurant are set on 25 acres (10 ha) of beautiful gardens where the **Convent Guesthouse** stands. This former nunnery was transported to the site from the New South Wales country town of Coonamble.

Return to the Broke Road to reach **Blaxlands Restaurant & Wine Centre** (*Tel (02) 4998 7550*). Here a wine list of 80 local wines, including its own Chardonnay, semillon, and shiraz, complements some of the valley's specialties such as fresh Maitland asparagus, grain-fed eye fillets with a shiraz juice, or lobster wasabi.

At McDonalds Road, turn right then left onto unsurfaced Gillards Road, which leads to **Scarborough Wines** ❸ (*Tel (02) 4998 7563*). Ian Scarborough certainly knows how to make Chardonnay, and the winery enjoys one of the prettiest locations in the area.

Return once again to the Broke Road. Turn off to reach **Tyrrell's Vineyards** ❹ (*Tel (02) 4998 7000, closed Sun.*). Murray Tyrrell is one of the major forces in Australian wines, with a family tradition going back to 1858.

Return along the Broke Road to the intersection with McDonalds Road and

McGuigan Cellars (*Tel (02) 4998 7402*) and the **Hunter Valley Cheese Company** (*Tel (02) 4998 7744*), which share the same premises. The cheese company is one of the largest cheese producers in the valley, and its great selection of strongly-flavored cheeses is a superb complement to the local wines.

Next door to McGuigan, on McDonalds Road, is **Brokenwood Wines** ❺ (*Tel (02) 4998 7559*). Brokenwood has a reputation for producing wines of great quality from grapes grown in the valley and other districts. The prices are a notch higher than most of the other wineries, but it's hard to argue with quality like this.

Across McDonalds Road is the **Small Winemakers Centre** (*Tel (02) 4998 7668*), which represents some of the valley's boutique wineries either set in remote locations or without their own cellar doors.

Turn left onto McDonalds Road from the Small Winemakers (heading away from the Broke Road) to **Tamburlaine Wines** ❻ (*Tel (02) 4998 7570*). The staff here is passionate about wine and spend time passing on their interest to visitors. Much of the business here is

---

🗺 207 E6

▶ Cessnock

🔁 20 miles (30 km)

🕐 Allow 4–6 hours

▶ Cessnock

NOT TO BE MISSED
- Hunter Valley Cheese Company
- View from picnic area between Tamburlaine Wines and Lindemans Winery

POKOLBIN

Scarborough Wines ③

GILLARDS ROAD

BROKE ROAD

Tyrell's Vineyards ④

McGuigan Cellars

Brokenwood Wines ⑤

BROKE ROAD

Small Winemakers Centre

CYPRESS LAKES COUNTRY PARK

MCDONALDS ROAD

Tamburlaine Wines ⑥

Blaxlands Restaurant & Wine Centre

Petersons Champagne House

Pepper Tree Wines ②

Convent Guesthouse

BRANKTON ROAD

Black Creek

Hunter Valley Wine Society ①

LOVEDALE ROAD

DEBEYERS ROAD

Lindemans Winery ⑦

Hungerford Hill Wines

POKOLBIN MOUNTAINS ROAD

Drayton's Family Wines

OAKEY CREEK ROAD

McWilliams Mount Pleasant Estate ⑧

MARROWBONE ROAD

ALLANDALE ROAD

The Convent guesthouse was once a nunnery.

GOLF CLUB

MOUNT VIEW ROAD

START

CESSNOCK

ABERDARE STREET

0 — 3 kilometers
0 — 2 miles

---

mail order (to anywhere in the world), and group tastings are particularly well run.

A short drive beyond Tamburlaine takes you to the best picnic spot in the Hunter, atop a small hill with a scattering of gazebos and a parking area. You may even have live music for your picnic if there is an outdoor function at **Lindemans Winery** ⑦ (*Tel (02) 4998 7684*) just below. Lindemans is one of the stalwarts of the region, established in 1843.

Next door, in a quaint former church, is **Hungerford Hill Wines** (*Tel (02) 4998 7666*), one of the innovative players in Australian winemaking with a range of wines made from grapes from a number of New South Wales regions such as Cowra, Mudgee,

and Tumbarumba. Turn left, then right at the end of McDonalds Road to reach Oakey Creek Road and **Drayton's Family Wines** (*Tel (02) 4998 7513*). Established in 1853, the fifth generation has recently shown its skill by sweeping Hunter Valley wine shows.

Just off nearby Marrowbone Road is a comparative newcomer, **McWilliams Mount Pleasant Estate** ⑧ (*Tel (02) 4998 7505*), established in 1921 in an idyllic setting. The company has an enviable reputation as a large winemaker with skills in equal measure, producing consistently good wines. To return to Cessnock, continue along Marrowbone Road, turn right at Oakey Creek Road, then take the first left, onto Mount View Road. ∎

Australian wine

Once considered a laughingstock by the international winemaking community (the Monty Python comedy team did a memorable sketch deriding it), Australia's long but isolated tradition of great winemaking has blossomed in the last two decades. And the world has reaped the benefits.

The history of Australian wine reaches all the way back to Governor Phillip and the First Fleet. Shortly after his arrival in 1788, Phillip became the country's first vigneron when he had vine cuttings and grape seeds that had

Grapes were first grown in the governor's garden at Sydney Cove, seen here in 1791 in a painting by William Bradley.

been brought with the fleet from England planted in the garden of Government House.

The site of Phillip's vineyard is thought to be where the Hotel Inter-Continental, in the Treasury Building on Macquarie Street, stands (see p. 66). The hotel retains a close connection with its viticultural past: An exhibition in the hotel's One One Seven restaurant traces the planting and harvesting of the first grapes, and the restaurant is the setting for regular lunches with local wine luminaries.

Start of the industry

In fact, the vines first planted in Sydney, attacked by fungal disease in the humid climate, did poorly, whereas the vineyards in Parramatta and farther west flourished and gradually began to produce wines that were noticed in Europe. A fortified red from a

vineyard at Eastwood, in northwest Sydney, won a silver medal in London in 1823, for example. The vineyard was owned by Gregory Blaxland, one of the explorers who had pioneered the route over the Blue Mountains. William Macarthur also established a commercial vineyard on the banks of the Nepean.

James Busby's vineyard on his 2,000-acre (809-ha) land grant was the first in the Hunter Valley, and Busby also established an agricultural institute that taught viticulture and winemaking in Liverpool, in Sydney's southwest. During the wine industry's early development, immigrants brought with them winemaking skills and new grape varieties.

Today's market

In recent years, there has been an increase in the number of vineyards in Australia as the quality of the local product has gained acceptance here and overseas, especially in Britain, the United States, and Canada. The growth of the industry has meant that the latest methods and technologies have been installed in the new wineries, and Australian wines are now in demand in several foreign countries.

In New South Wales, the main winegrowing region is the Hunter Valley (see pp. 208–211). Other regions include Mudgee, Cowra, and the Southern Highlands areas around Canberra and Tumbarumba.

In Victoria, Rutherglen is highly regarded for its fortified wines, the Yarra Valley attracts the likes of Domaine Chandon with its Chardonnay, and the Mornington Peninsula is great Sauvignon Blanc country, as are the Pyrenees and western Victoria.

Neighboring South Australia is also blessed with some great wine-growing areas. There are parts of Coonawarra (Cabernet Sauvignon), the Clare Valley (Cabernet and shiraz), and the mighty Barossa Valley (Cabernet and shiraz, including Penfold's Grange and Henschke's Hill of Grace) that are comparable with Bordeaux in France.

Over in the west, vineyards prosper in the Margaret River region, with Rieslings, Chardonnays, and reds that are on a par with wines from the eastern state winemakers. ∎

Above: Harvesting grapes in the Hunter Valley takes place around March each year.

Right: A basket press at the Wyndham Estate winery in the Hunter Valley

Below: Picking grapes in the world-renowned Barossa Valley, South Australia

Newcastle

THE HUNTER VALLEY ISN'T ALL WINERIES, HOWEVER. AT the mouth of the Hunter is Newcastle, the second largest city in New South Wales after Sydney. Traditionally a coal and steel town, it is only a short drive from the vineyards and has undergone something of a renaissance as a tourist center since heavy industry has contracted.

Newcastle

🅰 207 F5

Newcastle Tourism

✉ 92 Scott St.

☎ (02) 4929 9299

Bar Beach is one of several surfing beaches close to the center of the city of Newcastle.

A chain of sparkling beaches stretches north and south of the city (see pp. 215–16), and Newcastle's central precinct, with a number of historic buildings, has been extensively refurbished. The waterfront area now features restaurants and pedestrian walkways, and there is a **Maritime and Military Museum** (*Fort Dr., Tel (02) 4929 2588*) at Fort Stratchley.

Escaped convicts were the first to reach the area, in 1791, where they found coal protruding from the riverbanks. The Hunter was named Coal River in 1796 and a penal station established in 1801. The settlement was named Newcastle in 1804, and interesting historic buildings in the area include **Newcastle East Public School** (1908), **East Newcastle Gaol** (1817–18), the hospital (1817), **Christ Church Anglican Cathedral** (1883), and the **Courthouse** (1822).

Newcastle Tourism has information on everything that this pleasant, breezy city and the surrounding district has to offer. Access is by rail, road, or tours from Sydney (*details from Sydney Visitor Centre, Tel 9255 1788*). ■

Central Coast

FROM THE NORTH SIDE OF BROKEN BAY, THE CENTRAL COAST extends to Newcastle and the Hunter Valley in a succession of beachside towns and resorts. Here you can sunbathe and surf on clean, sandy beaches, try to catch a fish, or navigate the many sheltered waterways.

Across the north shore of the Hawkesbury and Broken Bay, several national parks offer superb scenery, quiet tracks and beaches, and Aboriginal carvings. These include **Brisbane Water National Park** and **Bouddi National Park.**

Between these two parks is the exclusive **Pearl Beach.** There are views across to Lion Island (see p. 179) and the entrance to Brisbane Water and the town of **Gosford** (*Visitor information, Mann St., Gosford, Tel (02) 4385 4430*), where boats can be rented.

Just east of Gosford, the beachside towns of **Avoca** (*Visitor information, 18–20 The Boulevard, Woy Woy, Tel (02) 4385 4430*) and **Terrigal** (*Visitor information, Rotary Park, Terrigal Dr., Tel (02) 4385 4430*) offer two different paces of life, Avoca being quieter than the larger Terrigal. The Avoca beachside movie theater has screenings at reasonable prices. Behind the beach, a small lake with boat and windsurfer rentals is popular with families.

Terrigal's resort caters to all needs, with swimming pools, a sheltered lagoon, spas, water sports

Bouddi National Park offers spectacular views of these unusual sandstone cliffs.

Brisbane Water National Park
 207 E5

Bouddi National Park
207 E4

National Parks & Wildlife Service
Central Coast District Office, Suites 36–38, 207 Albany St. N., Gosford
(02) 4324 4911

Places to visit

If you want a break from swimming and fishing, visit **Old Sydney Town** (*Pacific Hwy., Somersby, Tel (02) 4340 1104, closed Mon.–Tues., except during school vacations*), reached from the Gosford exit of the freeway. This is a reconstruction of Sydney in the era 1788 to 1810, and the 50-acre (20-ha) site features a windmill (the original stood on Observatory Hill, see pp. 78–79), a church, and workmen's cottages. Costume reenactments take place throughout the day, and there is a native animal park with kangaroos and koalas.

These creatures can also be seen at the **Australian Reptile Park and Wildlife Sanctuary** (*Pacific Hwy., Somersby, Tel (02) 4340 1022*). The specialty here is reptiles, especially snakes. You can handle some of the nonvenomous varieties and watch venomous snakes being milked of their poison. This is part of the park's research programs to improve antidotes.

Near Gosford is the **Forest of Tranquility** (*Ourimbah Creek Rd., Ourimbah, Tel (02) 4362 1855, closed Mon.–Tues., except during school vacations*), a natural rain forest laced with walkways. There are more than 120 species of birds, plus wallabies and other native animals.

For accommodations and other visitor information contact Central Coast Tourism (*Tel (02) 4385 4430 or 1800 806 258*). ∎

Lake Macquarie, four times the size of Sydney Harbour, is a popular boating location.

facilities, boat rental, health clubs, cafés, and boutiques.

For superb coastal views, walk to **The Skillion** headland. Farther north is **The Entrance** (*Visitor information, The Waterfront Parade, Tel (02) 4385 4430*), the mouth of Tuggerah Lake, another safe boating area with surf and sand. Pelicans are fed daily at 3:30 p.m. in the Memorial Park.

Lake Macquarie, Australia's largest saltwater lake, is the major lake of the region. Large areas are navigable, although sand flats exist in some areas. It is ideal for houseboats, which can be rented from Lake Macquarie Holiday Cruisers (*Tel (02) 4973 5770*), Luxury Afloat (*Tel (02) 4958 3044*), or Newcastle Holiday Houseboats (*Tel (02) 4952 2343*). Plenty of affordable waterside accommodations are available, and there are some relaxed resorts. On the eastern side of the lake, the beaches are never far away. ∎

Blue Mountains

THE BLUE MOUNTAINS ONCE FORMED AN IMPENETRABLE barrier between Sydney and the interior of New South Wales. When seen from the heights of the city, the mountains are unmistakably blue due to the fine mist of eucalyptus oil exuded by the eucalyptus forests. These days the region is a haven for visitors, offering incredible scenery, clear mountain air, and attractive English-style gardens.

The mountains form part of **Blue Mountains National Park,** one of Australia's principal and most accessible national parks. Covering 610,000 acres (247,021 ha), the park is characterized by extensive areas of 1,000-foot-high (305-m) sheer cliffs with lookouts that offer sweeping panoramas and views into shadowy precipitous gorges with dramatic waterfalls.

The varied mountain environments range from windswept outcrops of rock and poor sandy soil to sheltered, well-watered valleys with rich volcanic soil, and the range of microclimates supports an incredibly diverse range of plant species.

Numerous well-marked walking trails of varying lengths fan out from the mountain towns. Use extreme caution near the edge of cliffs, however, as the local sandstone is notorious for breaking away without warning.

AROUND KATOOMBA
One of the premier attractions of the park is the upper mountains area around the town of Katoomba. Here the highlights include **Echo Point,** a stunning viewpoint overlooking the **Three Sisters** and **Jamison Valley.**

The Three Sisters are three enormous sandstone pillars that tower

The most famous feature of the Blue Mountains is the Three Sisters, which stand sentinel looking south over the rugged beauty of Jamison Valley.

Blue Mountains
◭ 207 D4
Visitor information
✉ Great Western Hwy., Glenbrook
☎ (02) 4739 6266

Katoomba
◭ 207 D4
Echo Point Visitor Centre
✉ Echo Point Rd., Katoomba
☎ (02) 4739 6266

above the precipices that drop 1,000 feet (305 m) into the valley below. This is one of the must-see destinations for tours of every description; at night the Sisters are floodlit.

The **Prince Henry Cliff Walk** connects Echo Point and the Three Sisters along a spectacular trail (allow at least two hours).

You can descend to the valley from Katoomba by way of the **Giant Stairway,** a steep 860-step staircase cut into the rock. From there you can return to the cliff top at Echo Point by the **Scenic Railway** (*Tel (02) 4782 2699*), formerly used to transport coal miners from the valley below. The railway has one unique feature—it runs up the cliff on rails that are nearly vertical, making it the steepest tourist railway in the world. If that doesn't get your pulse racing, the **Scenic Skyway** (*Tel (02) 4782 2699*) traverses a spur of the Jamison Valley at a height of 676 feet (206 m).

Getting to the Blue Mountains

Access to the Blue Mountains is by car from the city (a journey of about two hours) along the M4 motorway. A frequent rail service stops at all the mountain towns mentioned, except Mount Wilson, Jenolan Caves, and localities on the Bell's Line of Road. Several bus tours and ecotours depart Sydney daily for the main Blue Mountains sites. Transfers can be arranged from most city hotels, and information on accommodations and tours is available from the Sydney Visitor Centre *(Tel 9255 1788),* the Echo Point Visitor Centre, and the Blue Mountains information center. ∎

Cliff Drive, a 5-mile (8-km) road with viewpoints, connects Katoomba with the small mountain town of **Leura.** Its main street, with neat wooden buildings, antique shops, and a relaxed pace, has hardly changed since the 1950s. On the first Saturday in October, many of the houses open for the **Leura Gardens Festival.** The colder climate makes for some attractive English-style gardens. For details of this and other mountain events, call the Blue Mountains information center.

Another attraction in Katoomba is **The Edge** (*225–237 Great Western Hwy., Tel (02) 4782 8928*), a Maxivision theater featuring a 38-minute film about the Blue Mountains and the ecology of the area. The film captures much of the scenic beauty of the region on a screen 60 feet (18 m) high and 80 feet (24 m) wide and features several items not on the usual visitor itinerary, including great footage of the Wollemi pine's secret valley (see p. 53).

The lookout on the northern side of Govett's Leap Road takes in the ramparts of the Grose Valley.

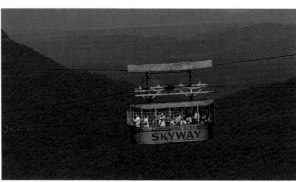

The Scenic Skyway's round-trip journey across a chasm of the Jamison Valley takes about six minutes, which can seem like a lifetime.

The slope on the Scenic Railway's journey into the Jamison Valley is 52 degrees, the steepest gradient in the world.

East of Katoomba, just a short distance from the town of **Wentworth Falls,** are the waterfalls of the same name that plunge into the Jamison Valley. One of the most enjoyable ways of reaching the falls is along the **Darwin Walk,** named after

CHRISTMAS IN JULY

Numerous resorts and hotels in the Blue Mountains participate in one of the mountains' recent innovations, Yulefest. As Christmas falls in the middle of Sydney's summer, it is now popular to have a Christmas festival in the mountains during the Australian winter, complete with dinner and all the trimmings. ∎

English naturalist Charles Darwin (1809–1882), who visited the area during an excursion ashore from H.M.S. *Beagle* in 1836. The route starts from a small park just down the hill from the railway station and is about an hour of easy walking each way, following the stream down to the falls along fern- and tea-tree-filled gullies.

A mile (0.5 km) past Katoomba on the Great Western Highway, heading toward Blackheath, is the **Explorers Marked Tree.** The tree, now just a stump protected by a small shelter, had a blaze cut into it by explorers Gregory Blaxland, William Wentworth, and William Lawson in 1813 as they passed by on the first successful crossing of the mountains.

A little farther on is the **Hydro–Majestic Hotel** (*Medlow Bath, Tel (02) 4788 1002*), which has long been a mountain institution. Because the eucalyptus-laden air was believed to have therapeutic powers, hoteliers hoped guests would come to take the waters as well. It is one of the most popular places for a romantic weekend and features an impressive ballroom. If you are just passing through, the coffee lounge and restaurant are wonderful places to contemplate the superb view of the Megalong Valley.

Blackheath, farther west, is another peaceful mountain village. It has access to breathtaking scenery at Govetts Leap, Evans Lookout, Pulpit Rock, Perry's Lookdown, and Anvil Rock. The **Blackheath Heritage Centre** (*Govetts Leap Rd., Tel 4787 8877*) provides a wealth of information on the flora, fauna, and indigenous culture of the mountains, and the **Fairfax Heritage Track** leads to Govett's Leap lookout. The center is the main source of information on the national park, with interactive displays, an art exhibition, walking track guides, maps, and books on the mountains, the region's flora and fauna, and the local Aborigines. Refreshments are available.

The most westerly of the mountain villages is **Mount Victoria,** listed as an urban conservation area and classified by the National Trust. It features typical mountain houses—wooden chalets with shady verandas that both catch the sun and block the wind. Shortly after passing through the village, the highway starts its descent to the western plains. At Mount Victoria the highway is joined by **Bell's Line of Road,** an alternative route back to the city through the mountains via the towns of Richmond and Windsor (see p. 183).

PLACES ON THE BELL'S LINE OF ROAD

The first place you will come to along the Bell's Line of Road is **Mount Wilson** (*turn off 5 miles/ 8 km E of Bell*). The mountains have long been a popular destination for Sydneysiders seeking great scenery and a milder climate, and during the last century Mount Wilson became an enclave of the well-to-do, who created mini-estates among the bushland setting and a rare patch of fertile land.

Mount Wilson's **Cathedral of Ferns**, just under a mile (1 km) from the village center, is a natural rain-forest area that displays yet another facet of the diverse flora and fauna of the mountains. You explore it via a 20-minute walk.

One of the best gardens in the Mount Wilson area is **Yengo** (*Tel (02) 4756 2002, closed Mon.–Fri. and June–Aug. and Jan.–March*) on Queens Avenue, designed between 1877 and 1880 by Charles Moore, the first director of the Royal Botanic Gardens. It is a walled garden featuring azaleas and rhododendrons, with Catalan wrought-iron grills and an oak door dating from the 16th century.

Here you will also find a fenced reserve for a group of parma wallabies, a safe haven for them since the 1950s. Ask the staff here for information about opening times of other gardens in the area such as **Nooroo,** which was featured on Australian stamps and is more than a century old.

The Bacchante Gardens at Blackheath blend azaleas and rhododendrons in an Australian setting of eucalyptus.

The major garden on the Bell's Line of Road is **Mount Tomah Botanic Garden** (*Tel (02) 4567 2154*), the cool-climate garden annex of the Royal Botanic Gardens (see pp. 52–53). The gardens are beautifully landscaped with ponds and waterfalls and have the bonus of sumptuous views to the north over the Grose Valley. There are a visitor center with a shop, a good restaurant, and a popular picnic area with barbecue grills. Access is from Bell's Line of Road, involving a pleasant drive through apple and soft-fruit orchards, then through native bush and rocky escarpments from Richmond up to Mount Victoria.

Along the Bell's Line of Road between Bell and Lithgow is the **Zig Zag Railway** (*Tel (02) 6353 1795*). Built in the 1860s to transport coal from the rich deposits of Lithgow, the railway has a system of tunnels, viaducts, and cuttings to negotiate the Blue Mountains. The 10-mile (16-km) ride is quite memorable. On weekends the train is hauled by steam locomotive, during the week by vintage diesel rail motor. Call to check the daily timetable, which often varies to accommodate groups.

The Bell's Line of Road also offers a scenic route back to the city that takes longer than the highway but has some great views of the Grose Valley. Along the way is the town of **Bilpin**, center of a major apple-growing area with many roadside stalls.

JENOLAN CAVES

About 34 miles (55 km) southwest of Mount Victoria, one hour by car, are the **Jenolan Caves** (*turn off the Great Western Hwy. just past the historic village of Hartley*). Discovered in 1838 by the bushranger James McKeown, an escaped convict, the caves are located at the end of a scenic if slightly nerve-racking road that runs through a stunning gorge, a grand cavern, and a tunnel.

Nine caves are open to the public, with limestone chandeliers and columns, and underground lakes and river systems. Ladders and well-constructed paths provide ready access to guided tours and group sizes are limited so that the caves can be enjoyed in comfort and safety. Access is by guided tour only (*group tours should be pre-booked*). Tours average 1.5 hours and operate daily. Specialist tours for the energetic—involving lamps, crawling, and climbing—are also available but need to be reserved at least a month in advance. Contact the guides office.

About 5,970 acres (2,416 ha) of nature reserve surround the caves, with several walking tracks that, given the steeply sloping terrain, can be quite strenuous.

Accommodations are plentiful here, but the best option is Jenolan Caves House (*Tel (02) 6359 3322 or 1800 068 050*), which has cabins and a lodge in addition to the main building.

In the lower mountains, the **Glenbrook** area is dotted with picnic areas, swimming holes, walking tracks, and lookouts. The Blue Mountains information center is based here. Car camping is available at **Euroka Clearing** (*Tel (02) 4588 5247, Mon.–Fri.*). ■

Below: The Angel's Wing and Gabriel's Wing in the Temple of Baal, Jenolan Caves

South Coast

STRETCHING SOUTH FROM SYDNEY TO THE BORDER WITH the state of Victoria, the New South Wales South Coast has a milder climate than that of the North Coast, and a distinctly different character. One of the major industries here is dairying, and numerous cheese companies can be found along the southbound Princes Highway.

Wollongong

🅰 207 E3

Visitor information

✉ 101 Crown St.

☎ (02) 4228 0300

Kiama

🅰 207 E3

Visitor information

✉ Blowhole Point, Terralong St.

☎ (02) 4232 3322

Shoalhaven Tourist Centre

✉ 254 Princes Hwy., Bomaderry (2 miles/ 3 km N of Nowra)

☎ (02) 4421 0778

OVERNIGHT

A good two-day trip is to take in the South Coast sights down to Jervis Bay on day one, then either stay overnight in Huskisson or continue up to the resorts of the Southern Highlands (see pp. 226–27), just 50 miles (80 km) away. From there you can take in the sights en route back to Sydney. In the summer months, book ahead. ■

Opposite: Sea-weeds such as Neptune's necklace cling to the rocks in the sheltered, crystal clear waters of Jervis Bay.

WOLLONGONG & AROUND

Within close range of Sydney, the city of Wollongong, like Newcastle (see p. 214), is heavily industrialized, but it also has a pleasant harbor area with a fish co-op and cafés. As an alternative to the freeway, drive through **Royal National Park** (see pp. 195–97) via Audley, then along a spectacular, snaking, coastal cliff road. Eventually the cliffs give way to the **Illawarra** region, a scenic coastal plain that starts just south of Royal National Park and continues south beyond Wollongong.

Just south of Wollongong (via Jamberoo on the Princes Highway, past the turnoff to the Illawarra Highway—a direct route to the Southern Highlands) is the **Minnamurra Rainforest** (*Map 207 D3, Tel (02) 4236 0469*), a small pocket of subtropical rain forest with an award-winning environmental center. From an elevated boardwalk, you can study the ferns and orchids that compete for light in the rain-forest canopy and watch the bird-life feeding.

KIAMA TO JERVIS BAY

Farther down the coast is **Kiama,** famous for its blowhole that sends up large geysers of water from an ocean cavern. These days the hole has eroded and the water doesn't spurt particularly high unless the tides and waves are right, but it can be quite exhilarating when the conditions are good.

From Kiama, the route winds south through rugged headlands

and dairy country, via the prettily located headland town of **Gerroa,** to **Seven Mile Beach.** Here there are camping grounds and expanses of empty sand, ideal for beachcombing and being alone with nature.

Inland lies the picture-postcard town of **Berry** and the turnoff to **Kangaroo Valley** (see p. 227).

Continue down the Princes Highway to **Nowra** (*information from Shoalhaven Tourist Centre*). Just across the bridge over the Shoalhaven River is Nowra's oyster co-op, and the area's cheese shops are definitely worth stopping by for a sample. Vacation resorts can be found at the southern end of Seven Mile Beach and at **Jervis Bay** (*Map 207 D2*), 15 miles (24 km) south of town.

Jervis Bay is one of the most beautiful pieces of protected waterway on the South Coast and a deservedly popular destination. Guarded by the striking precipice of Point Perpendicular, the crystal clear waters of the bay are ideal for boating, fishing, scuba diving, and snorkeling. The sands of the beaches are reputed to be among the cleanest and whitest anywhere in the world, and there are waterside villages and camping areas.

The main center of the bay is the town of **Huskisson,** a former boat-building and fishing town. These days there are Dolphin Watch Cruises (*Tel (02) 4441 6311*), which also take in penguins, and the **Lady Denman Heritage Complex** (*Tel (02) 4441 5675*), with a museum, walks, and fish feedings. ■

Southern Highlands

Exhibits in the Bradman Museum relive the life and times of the cricketer known simply as The Don.

LOCATED TO THE SOUTHWEST OF SYDNEY, TWO HOURS BY road, the highlands differ from the Blue Mountains in having a gentler terrain of rolling hills, more suited to farming. The area reminded Lachlan Macquarie of England when he visited it in 1820.

Since then the area has been gentrified by wealthy businessmen from the city who fancy themselves as lords of the manor and weekend farmers. There are several English-style gardens with flowering annuals, rhododendrons, and azaleas.

The principal towns are Mittagong, Bowral, Moss Vale, and Berrima, while villages such as Bundanoon and Exeter are worth exploring for their fruit stalls and antique shops.

A network of country roads laces through the area, making a pleasant alternative to the main highways and providing cyclists with options for short rides from town to town. As in the Blue Mountains, many of the hotels in the area host Yulefest dinners (see p. 220) from June to August.

BOWRAL

One of the main attractions of Bowral is the annual **Tulip Time Festival** (*Tel (02) 4871 2888*), staged over two weekends and a week in late September and early October. During this time numerous parks and gardens around the town become a riot of floral color, music, foods, and country wares. Flower festivals and garden open days also take place in the town in summer and fall.

The **Bradman Museum** honors Australian cricket's greatest batsman and Bowral's most famous son, Sir Donald Bradman (1908–). There are photos, films, memorabilia, tearooms, and a view over the Bradman Oval, where commemorative and gala matches are sometimes played. Follow the Bradman Walk from the museum past Bradman's nearby former home and other haunts.

BERRIMA

Several of the buildings in the historic town of Berrima date from the 1830s. One not to miss is the Georgian-style **Courthouse** (*Tel (02) 4877 1505*), designed by colonial architect Mortimer Lewis (1836–38). **Berrima House** is where Ben Hall (1837–1865), a farmer who became a notorious bushranger in the region after persecution by the law, is reputed to have stayed. Visit the low security **Berrima Gaol**, and **Harpers Mansion** (*Tel (02) 4861 2402,*

closed Tues.–Fri.), a National Trust building, and the **Surveyor-General Inn** (*Tel (02) 4877 1226*), first opened in 1835. A leaflet with a self-guided walking tour is available from the Courthouse and many of the stores.

AROUND THE HIGHLANDS

Getting to the Southern Highlands can be an adventure in itself. If driving direct from the city via Liverpool, a diversion to Camden takes you past the **Mount Annan Botanic Garden** (see p. 204). From there the road climbs to Picton, where there is a boutique brewery, **Scharer's Little Brewery,** in the George IV Hotel. Dances take place on Friday and Saturday nights at the **Wool-Away Woolshed** (*Tel (02) 4677 1379*).

A tour of the South Coast (see pp. 224–25) could be combined with a drive through the scenic **Kangaroo Valley,** visiting the 250-foot (76-m) **Fitzroy Falls** near Moss Vale, then continuing to the Southern Highlands and back to Sydney. The falls, a short walk from the parking lot, can be disappointing after a long dry spell, but are well worth a visit after heavy rain.

The **Cockatoo Run** steam train trip travels the scenic 37 miles (59 km) from Port Kembla on the coast to Robertson and Moss Vale in the highlands—three hours each way. The train departs at 9:30 a.m. Saturday through Tuesday (*Tel 9699 2737 or 1800 643 801*).

You could also combine the sights of the Southern Highlands with a tour to the nation's capital, **Canberra** (see pp. 228–30). ■

Fitzroy Falls drop from the Southern Highlands to the coastal lowlands. There are walks on either side and a camping area nearby.

Canberra

AS A CITY WHOSE MAIN INDUSTRY IS GOVERNMENT, Canberra is extremely tidy and well manicured. Neat gardens, streets, and buildings present an attractive facade, but you may find that after spending time in Sydney, Canberra lacks the lively hustle and bustle of a major city. Still, there are several must-sees here—art galleries, museums, and scenic lookouts in particular.

Canberra
🗺 206 B2
Visitor information
✉ 330 Northbourne Ave., Dickson
☎ (02) 6205 0044
www.canberratourism.com.au

National Gallery of Australia
✉ Parkes Place, Parkes
☎ (02) 6240 6502

Australia's capital city is situated 175 miles (280 km) southwest of Sydney, between the Southern Highlands and the Snowy Mountains.

In 1909, after much bickering between Sydney and Melbourne as to which of the two cities should be the capital, it was decided to create an entirely new city, on what was at the time a prosperous sheep farm. It was named Canberra, the local Aboriginal word for "meeting place." Perhaps a word meaning "compromise" might have been a better choice. Nevertheless, the city designed by Chicago landscape architect Walter Burley Griffin

(1876–1937) in 1913 has become one of the most picturesque in the country, with a population of just over 300,000. The city plan includes an extensive system of bike paths.

Aside from the major public buildings associated with government, national institutions include the National Library, the National Gallery of Australia, and the Australian War Memorial.

The **National Gallery of Australia,** located in what is referred to as the Parliamentary Triangle, is the newest of the nation's major galleries (it opened in its current building in 1982). It already has 100,000 works in its

collection, encompassing traditional forms, textiles, costumes, and much more. Aboriginal and Australian art is well represented, and there are fine examples of Impressionist and contemporary European and American art.

Major touring exhibitions—works from the Russian Hermitage or Turner paintings, for example—bring together significant works from all over world.

Outside the gallery, the Sculpture Garden presents works by Auguste Rodin, Henry Moore, and others among eucalyptuses and ponds. The gallery has coffee shops and an excellent restaurant.

Right next door to the gallery in King Edward Terrace is the **High Court of Australia** (*Tel (02) 6270 6811*), the premier court of Australia. Inside, large murals depict the founding of Australia and its constitution. The court is open for inspection most days and court sittings can be attended by the public.

Also on King Edward Terrace is **Questacon** (*Tel (02) 6270 2800*), the National Science and Technology Centre. Questacon is oriented toward children and features many interactive demonstrations of scientific principles. Don't miss Brain and Senses (sight, hearing, and touch), the Force Gallery, complete with an earthquake machine, or the musical instruments. Constantly changing shows and demonstrations take place, too.

Next door to Questacon is the **National Library of Australia** (*Tel (02) 6262 1111*). Housed in an imposing building, the library has one of the largest collections of books and manuscripts in the country. It frequently mounts exhibitions illuminating both local and national events and people.

The Commonwealth of Australia's **Parliament House** (*Tel (02) 6277 5399*) sits back from Lake Burley Griffin on Capital Hill. The hill was excavated to hold the bulk of the house that lies partly

Balloons drift over Lake Burley Griffin during the Canberra Balloon Festival.

The National Gallery of Australia has several paintings from Sidney Nolan's Ned Kelly series. Kelly is Australia's most famous bushranger (highway robber), and part of local folklore.

Australian War Memorial

✉ Anzac Parade, Campbell

☎ (02) 6243 4211

submerged in the landscape and is partly roofed with grass. The understated design is then contradicted by a four-legged, 260-foot (79-m) flagpole that straddles the entire structure.

The building looks down on the "temporary" Parliament House that was used from 1927 until the current house opened as part of the national Bicentennial celebrations in 1988.

Parliament House contains both houses of the federal government, the House of Representatives and the Senate; the Great Hall; and the offices of the politicians and their staffs. It is open to the public every day, and you can watch the affairs of state from the public galleries whenever the houses are sitting.

The building at the end of the grand boulevard of Anzac Avenue is the **Australian War Memorial.** This is one of the most visited attractions in the country, a testimony to the loss of life throughout Australia due to war. There are numerous exhibits that use film, sound, and interactive displays to depict the many conflicts Australia has participated in, usually as an ally of England or its post-World War II security partner, the United States. One of the Midget submarines that attacked Sydney Harbour in 1942 (see p. 102) can also be seen here. However, the main function of the memorial is as a monument to the fallen, and its courtyard and shrine of remembrance bear quiet witness to their sacrifice.

Black Mountain, topped by a large communications tower (*Tel 1800 806 718*) with a viewing platform and the revolving Black Mountain Tower Restaurant (*Tel (02) 6248 6162*), is the major scenic viewpoint of the city. The view over the city to the distant mountain ranges provides a magnificent panorama that extends for more than 50 miles (80 km).

Lake Burley Griffin, ringed by bike paths and parks, provides a focus for the recreational activities of Canberrans. The major parks in the city include **Black Mountain Reserve,** with barbecue facilities, picnic areas, and swimming areas (note that the lake's water is not considered safe to drink and isn't terribly inviting to swim in); and **Weston Park,** which has similar facilities, plus a kiosk and model-train rides.

Opposite the Parliamentary Triangle, **Commonwealth Park** is the closest park to the Central Business District. A restaurant and café overlook the water and the Captain Cook memorial water jet. The park is also the venue for Canberra's annual spring flower festival, Floriade (*Tel (02) 6205 0044*). This spectacular event, held from mid-September to mid-October, consists of massed plantings throughout the park, with marquee restaurants and food outlets, music and entertainment. ■

Travelwise

Sydney's monorail

TRAVELWISE INFORMATION

PLANNING YOUR TRIP

WHEN TO GO

CLIMATE
Sydney has a warm, temperate climate virtually year-round. The city is usually free of extremes of heat or cold. Close to the coast, frosts and heat waves are rare and some restaurants have outdoor dining at night even in winter. Farther inland frosts may occur and temperatures can climb above 100°F (37°C). In the Blue Mountains the winters are colder, with temperatures falling to around 45°F (7°C) and occasional snow. The summers tend to be milder, but century temperatures are not unheard of.

The average temperatures for Sydney are:

Spring	September to November	63°F (17°C)
Summer	December to February	72°F (22°C)
Fall	March to May	64°F (18°C)
Winter	June to August	55°F (13°C)

Rainfall is moderate (approximately 30 inches/73 cm a year) with the most rain falling in winter months and the least falling in spring.

MAIN EVENTS
See also Holidays (p. 236)

January
Sydney Festival, Tel 8248 6500: International, month-long festival held in midsummer (January), including theater, dance, music, and visual arts. There are numerous free events, including major outdoor performances in The Domain (opera, classical, jazz).

Sydney International Tennis Tournament, Tel 9331 4144:

Major international tennis stars feature in this event, traditionally held at White City in mid-January. The tournament is a lead up to the Australian Open grand slam event, held in Melbourne. Beginning in 2000, the tournament will be held at Sydney Olympic Park, Homebush Bay.

Chinese New Year: Fireworks, dragon dances, and processions.

February
Sydney Gay & Lesbian Mardi Gras, Tel 9557 4332, www.mardigras.com.au.: The parade, usually at the end of February, is the culmination of the month-long Mardi Gras festival (see pp. 140–41).

March
Archibald, Wynne, and Sulman Prizes: Announced mid-March, the Archibald (portraiture), Wynne (landscape), and Sulman (subject painting or mural) Prizes attract plenty of local attention. The winners and top contenders are displayed at the Art Gallery of New South Wales (see pp. 56–59) until mid-April, and there is an opportunity to register your personal tastes for a People's Choice award.

April
Sydney Royal Easter Show, Tel 9704 1000: Held during the first two weeks of April, at Homebush Bay, the Easter Show is a display of New South Wales agricultural excellence, plus sideshows and a diverse range of exhibits and performances.

June
Sydney Film Festival, Tel 9660 3844: Held in early June, this two-week film fest features local and international films shown in Australia for the first time. It is also a great opportunity to get into the spectacular State Theatre and admire the interior.

Sydney Food and Wine Festival, Tel 9931 1111: All the best chefs

and winemakers demonstrate their skills before the public in a series of dinners, seminars, and workshops.

Manly Food and Wine Festival, Tel 9977 1088: Usually held on the first weekend of June, this gastronomic festival turns the Manly Corso into one long food stall, with music and entertainment to boot.

Yulefest Blue Mountains, Tel (02) 4739 6266: From June to August, numerous guesthouses and restaurants serve Christmas dinners with all the trimmings so that Australians and others can have the Southern Hemisphere equivalent of a cold Christmas.

September
Carnivale, Tel 9251 7974: A festival of artistic and cultural events is held at locations around the city with the emphasis on cultural understanding.

Festival of the Winds, Bondi Beach, Tel 9130 3325: In mid-September, all manner of kites take to the skies over the beach, with kite shops and workshops held among food stalls and wandering entertainers.

September–October
Floriade, Canberra, Tel (02) 6205 0044: From mid-September to mid-October, a stunning floral display of tulips and annuals can be seen in the national capital's Commonwealth Gardens.

Bowral Tulip Time Festival, Tel (02) 4871 2888: One of the oldest garden festivals sees many gardens open throughout the Bowral area of the Southern Highlands, displaying masses of tulips.

October
Manly International Jazz Festival, Tel 9977 1088: Held the first week of October, with over 70 indoor and outdoor concerts.

Opera in the Vineyards, Hunter Valley, Tel (02) 4990 4477: In mid-October great performers attend this popular event, which is considerably more than an excuse to visit the vineyards. But if you need one...

Jazz in the Vines, Hunter Valley, Tel (02) 4938 1345: Held late October, for those who don't go in for opera (see above).

October–November

Blue Mountains Spring Gardens, Tel (02) 4739 6266: Throughout October and November, tremendous floral displays can be seen and many of the best gardens are open on most weekends. Mount Wilson is a little out of the way, but well worth a visit at this time.

December

Carols by Candlelight, Tel 9265 0444: Held outdoors in The Domain, usually two weeks prior to Christmas, this annual event is extremely popular with families.

Sydney to Hobart Yacht Race, Tel 9363 9731: For over 50 years, the spectacular start to Australia's leading ocean race on Boxing Day (December 26) has drawn huge crowds of spectators onto the water and the headlands around the city. The Sydney to Hobart Yacht Race is one of the world's bluewater sailing classics, and the start of the race sees Sydney at its most colorful, with giant maxi yachts and pocket racers being followed by a gigantic spectator fleet. Check with ferry operators (Tel 13 1500) for transportation.

WHAT TO TAKE

Sydney's temperate climate and natural setting mean that you should be prepared for weather that is mild to warm. Among the must-brings are comfortable walking shoes, a hat to keep off the sun (a baseball cap may not be adequate if you have sensitive skin), and a swimsuit. It is possible to get sunburned even in the middle of winter, so sunscreen with a protection factor

of 15+ is recommended. Insect repellent is also needed, especially in the evening. Hats, sunscreen, and bug repellent are available from all drugstores (known in Australia as chemists).

In late spring, summer, and early fall, lightweight clothing is all you'll need during the day and a light pullover for the rare cool evening. In the winter months in the city, you may need a jacket, although the temperature rarely gets below 46°F (8°C). However, if you are visiting the Blue Mountains be prepared for temperatures that can go below freezing.

For evening wear, neat, casual attire is acceptable in most venues. For men, a jacket and tie may be required for theater and top-class restaurants, for women semi-formal clothing is appropriate. In cosmopolitan venues, black is practically a uniform.

Just before you head for the airport, check you have your passport, visa or ETA, driver's license, airline ticket, traveler's checks, and insurance papers.

INSURANCE

Before your visit you should arrange sufficient medical and travel insurance. Ensure the policy is adequate to cover costs for ambulance or helicopter rescue, emergency surgery, or transportation home.

If you are hiring a car, compulsory third party insurance is included in the rental. Additional insurance should be considered, especially to reduce your costs in the event of windshield damage if you are planning to travel on country roads.

Should you need to make a claim for property theft, report the matter to the police, obtain a copy of the report, and refer the matter to the insurer via the emergency phone number they provide with your policy.

ENTRY FORMALITIES

VISAS

Many travelers not holding an Australian or New Zealand passport may now obtain authority to enter Australia through the Electronic Travel Authority (ETA) system, which replaces the need for an Australian visa. The free tourist ETA is valid for multiple entries into Australia (each entry to a maximum of three months) over a period of one year. A business ETA can be purchased for around $A80 ($50), allowing multiple entries into Australia for the life of your passport. Restrictions apply. ETAs should be obtained by phone from your travel agent or airline at least ten days prior to your trip.

Visitors not eligible for an ETA and those wishing to stay for longer than three months, or to work, must obtain a visa to enter. Further advice and application forms may be obtained from your travel agent, or from the Australian embassy, high commission, or consular office.

CUSTOMS

Customs controls at all Australian ports of entry are tight, and you should expect to have your personal luggage searched. Visitors over the age of 18 are also restricted to a duty-free limit of one liter of liquor and 250 cigarettes plus other goods such as perfume and jewelry to the value of $A400 ($260). Travelers under 18 may bring gifts to the value of $A200 ($130) without paying duty.

CURRENCY RESTRICTIONS

There is no limit to the amount of Australian or foreign currency you can bring in for personal use, though sums in excess of $A10,000 ($6,400), or its equivalent, should be declared on the appropriate inbound customs forms. You must gain prior permission to export hard currency exceeding the value of $A5,000 ($3,200).

QUARANTINE

Australia is free from many pests and diseases that could cause irreparable damage to the country's agriculture or environment. To prevent their entry, the importation of fresh or packaged food, fruit, eggs and egg products, vegetables, seeds, cultures, animals, plants, and plant products is strictly controlled. Declare any of these products upon entry.

DRUGS & NARCOTICS

Searches for a range of prohibited substances are frequently made by customs control, often with sniffer dogs. Penalties for drug importation are severe. You should clearly label medicines for personal use and obtain a statement from your doctor if you are importing a large number of pharmaceuticals, or if they are of a restricted type.

HOW TO GET TO SYDNEY

AIRLINES

Sydney is the main destination for inbound flights to Australia, with connections to and from most countries in Asia, Europe, and North and South America. Australia's major carrier is Qantas, with connections to all continents. From the United States, the major carriers also include United Airlines and Air New Zealand. The flight time from Los Angeles is 14 hours. From the United Kingdom, British Airways, Singapore Airlines, and Cathay Pacific also operate regular flights.

Useful numbers in Sydney:
Air New Zealand, Tel 13 2476
British Airways, Tel 9258 3300
Cathay Pacific, Tel 13 1747
Qantas, Tel 13 1211
Singapore Airlines, Tel 13 1011
United Airlines, Tel 13 1777

AIRPORTS

Almost all arrivals to Sydney are via the international Kingsford

Smith Airport, the only major airport. It is located 7 miles (11 km) from the city and is serviced by bus, rail, and taxi. The airport has two main terminal complexes at two separate locations: the international terminal and the domestic terminal. Shuttle buses and rail services connect the two.

The Airport Express bus runs to the city (route 300) from the international terminal, stopping at the domestic terminal, Central Station, Town Hall, and Circular Quay. Route 350 operates from the international terminal to the domestic terminal, Central Station, Kings Cross, and Elizabeth Bay. A round-trip fare costs about $A8 ($5). Many city hotels operate their own shuttle buses direct to their doors. Fees may apply in some instances. Other hotels feature limousine pickups.

The taxi trip to the city takes 30 minutes or less and costs about $A15 ($10). In rush hour, from and to the airport delays should be anticipated.

The rail service operates to Central Station and the Eastern Suburbs. Change at Central Station for services to other destinations.

GETTING AROUND

TRAVELING IN & AROUND SYDNEY

BY CAR

Visitors can drive in New South Wales on a valid driver's license from their country of origin for the same class of vehicle. The license and the driver's passport must be carried when driving. If the license is not in English, a translation must also be carried. In other states, the visitor's license may have to be presented to the motor registration authority on arrival. An international driver's permit is not sufficient on its own; it must be accompanied by a valid driver's license.

Renting a car

Vehicle rental is cheap compared to many other countries with daily rates starting from as low as $A25 ($15) for a good-quality, small vehicle.

The major international companies are represented, and all have desks at the airport. There are also several budget-rental companies in the city and Kings Cross area.

Reservations
Avis, Tel 9353 9000
Budget, Tel 13 2727
Hertz, Tel 13 3039
Thrifty, Tel 9380 5399

Campers, motorhomes, and four-wheel drives are available from Brits Rentals, Tel 1800 331 454; Budget, Tel 1800 643 985; and Hertz, Tel 9647 2766.

Driving information

In Australia, traffic drives on the left-hand side of the road. Details of regulations and road signs are available from Roads & Traffic Authority offices (Tel 13 2213) located throughout the city. The National Roads and Motorists Association (Tel 13 2132) is known as the NRMA and can also provide information from its office at 151 Clarence Street, Sydney, and regional offices throughout N.S.W.

Breakdown assistance The NRMA has reciprocal arrangements with most international motoring associations and provides a 24-hour emergency breakdown service (Tel 13 1111). It is also a good source for touring maps.

Drink-driving It is an offense to drive while under the influence of alcohol or other prohibited substances. A blood alcohol level above 0.05 percent is sufficient to lose your license for three months and face a fine of $A1,000 ($640) or more. Random breath testing (drivers can be pulled over without the police being required to have a reason or reasonable suspicion) is widespread, seven days a week, and at all hours of the day and night. If you have an accident while under the influence of alcohol, it is likely to invalidate your car's insurance. As a guide, if you have more than two full-strength beers, or two glasses of wine, or a nip of spirits, don't drive. And if you have been drinking the night before, don't drive the following morning if you suspect you may still have too much alcohol in your system.

Gas Gasoline (petrol) comes in leaded (regular and super) and unleaded (regular and premium) grades and is sold by the liter (approximately one-fifth of a gallon) and costs between 70 and 80 Australian cents a liter ($A3.50–$4.00 a gallon). Diesel is also available.

Maps Road atlases for the Sydney area are available from bookshops and most service stations and are well worthwhile if you are planning to do a lot of local driving.

Seatbelts The wearing of seatbelts is compulsory, in both the front and back seats. Children must also be suitably restrained.

Speed limits Usually 35 mph (56 kph) in urban areas (25 mph/40 kph in the vicinity of schools during school hours), 60 mph (96 kph) in the country, and 68 mph (109 kph) on certain freeways.

BY PUBLIC TRANSPORTATION
Sydney's public transportation system extends well into nearly all the areas described in this travel guide.

Timetable information
Details for government-run buses, trains, and ferries are available from 6 a.m to 10 p.m. daily, Tel 13 1500. Brochures and timetables are available from information counters at Circular Quay.
Bus Private and government

buses cover the entire city area; tour buses operate to sites in the north, south, and west. Regular Sydney buses are blue and white and operate between the city and the suburbs. Route numbers prefixed with "X" are express services that run between the outer suburbs and the city. Those beginning with "L" are limited-stop services operating longer routes.

Special bus services include the Sydney Explorer bus and the Bondi & Bay Explorer bus. The Sydney Explorer bus operates on a 20-mile (32-km) circuit to 24 different stops and attractions around the city, Darling Harbour, and Kings Cross, approximately every 20 minutes from 8:40 a.m. to 7 p.m. daily. Commentary is provided along the way, and tickets allow you to board and disembark as often as you like.

The Bondi & Bay bus route extends for 28 miles (45 km) with 19 stops and takes in Watsons Bay, Bondi, and other Eastern Suburbs beaches down to Coogee and Centennial Park. Buses run at 30-minute intervals. A SydneyPass is valid for three, five, or seven days and covers buses, trains, ferrys, Explorer buses, Airport Express, ferry cruises, and the RiverCat to Parramatta.

Ferry Traveling by ferry is the most convenient, inexpensive, and pleasurable way to take in the harbor sights. Ferry services operate to the uppermost reaches of nearly every waterway and all depart from the Circular Quay Ferry Terminal.

Rail CityRail trains serve much of the Central Business District as well as the outer suburbs. Services run from 4:30 a.m. to midnight. Interurban trains run to the South Coast, Newcastle, and the Blue Mountains.

The Monorail acts primarily as a sight-seeing trip for visitors. Trains complete the 2-mile

(3-km) circuit in just over ten minutes and run every five minutes. For a map of the rail network, see the inside back cover.

Ticket information The most expensive ticket option is usually a single ride ticket. Numerous other tickets are available at discount rates. For buses, the TravelTen ticket allows 10 trips in peak hours or off peak. Day tickets are also available that provide unlimited trips. FerryTen tickets provide 10 harbor trips at a discounted rate. On the rail system off-peak tickets, purchased after 9 a.m. and on weekends, are substantially less expensive than peak hour tickets. Day tickets are available that provide unlimited trips within the inner city area. Day and weekly tickets that provide unlimited trips on ferry, train, and bus are also available. The SydneyPass is valid for three, five, or seven days, and covers buses, trains, ferrys, Explorer buses, Airport Express, ferry cruises, and the RiverCat to Paramatta. All of the above tickets are available from outlets at Circular Quay. Most of the above tickets are available from train stations but tickets such as TravelTen for buses are available from designated outlets around the city, such as newsstands.

Taxis Meter-operated taxi cabs travel across the Sydney metropolitan area and in the various regions described in this guide. Taxi stands can be found at airports, most train stations, and major ferry stops such as Circular Quay and Manly. Taxis can also be hailed from the street, or you can call the following major companies for reservations or immediate pickup:

Taxis Combined Services,
  Tel 9332 8888
Legion Cabs, Tel 13 1451
Premier Radio Cabs, Tel 13 1017
RSL Cabs, Tel 13 1581

Taxis that cater to those with disabilities are also available,

Tel 1800 043187. Private rental car companies operate in the city and there are water taxis operating on the harbor: Taxis Afloat, Tel 9955 3222. Taxi drivers do not expect to be tipped but will accept gratuities offered.

PRACTICAL ADVICE

COMMUNICATIONS

POST OFFICES
Sydney's General Post Office (G.P.O.) is on Pitt Street, near Martin Place. It is open from 8:15 a.m. to 5:30 p.m. weekdays, 8:30 a.m. to noon Saturday. There are several other post offices at key locations around the city. Apart from selling stamps and stationery, post offices operate as branches for some banks and as points at which bills can be paid. Services at some offices include facsimile and e-mail. Sydney G.P.O.'s poste restante address is c/o G.P.O. Sydney, NSW 2000, Australia. For postal inquiries, Tel 13 1317.

TELEPHONES
Public phones take either coins, credit cards, or phonecards ($A5, $A10, $A20, and $A50 denominations) that are available from newsstands, post offices, and service stations. Local calls cost 40 cents for unlimited conversation. Calls outside the local area are timed and require further coins to continue the conversation. Rates are cheaper after 7 p.m. and on weekends. Sydney has analogue, digital, and Iridium mobile phone coverage. Check with your supplier to ensure your mobile phone's compatibility.

Using the telephone
Most Australian telephone numbers comprise eight digits and there are only nine area codes covering the entire country. There is plenty of room for confusion when dialing area codes. To call Sydney from overseas: Dial 61 for the country and 2 for Sydney and other areas with the 02 area code, followed by the number. When calling Sydney from other parts of Australia, dial 02. If you are in the 02 area, you do not need to dial the code.

To make an international call from Sydney, dial 0011, then the country code (1 for the U.S. and Canada, 44 for the U.K.), then the area code (without the leading zero), followed by the number.

Calls to six-digit telephone numbers beginning with 13 are charged at the local rate, no matter where you are calling from. Numbers prefixed with 1800 are toll-free.

Useful telephone numbers
Directory assistance: local and national 1223
Interpreter service: 13 1450
Operator: 1234
Time: 1194
Weather: 1196

CONVERSIONS

Australia uses the metric system of weights and measures. Speed and distances are in kilometers:
1 mile = 1.6 km

Weights are in kilograms and tonnes:
1 kg = 2.2 lbs
1 tonne = 0.98 tons

Volumes are in liters:
1 liter = 1.75 pints

Temperatures are in centigrade:
0°C = 32°F

ELECTRICITY

Australian electricity operates at 240 volts, and a three-pin adapter is needed for most non-Australian appliances. U.S. appliances require a voltage transformer. Many hotels provide 110-volt shaver sockets. Note that an electric shock from an Australian power supply is likely to be fatal.

HOLIDAYS

On public holidays, banks, post offices, and government and private offices generally close, as do most shops. Public transportation operates on a Sunday schedule, but many restaurants, bars, and tourist attractions remain open. Nearly everything shuts down for Good Friday and Christmas Day. The following are public holidays in Sydney and New South Wales:
January 1 (New Year's Day)
Fourth Monday in January (Australia Day)
Late March/Early April (Good Friday, Easter Saturday, Easter Monday)
April 25 (Anzac Day, varies slightly from year to year)
Second Monday in June (Queen Elizabeth II's birthday)
First Monday in August (Bank Holiday, banks only; not a statewide closure)
First Monday in October (Labor Day)
December 25 (Christmas Day)
December 26 (Boxing Day)

LIQUOR LAWS

It is against the law for anyone under the age of 18 to buy alcohol or consume alcohol in public. Service hours for public bars are generally Monday to Saturday 10 a.m. to 10 p.m.; Sunday hours vary. Restaurants, clubs, and hotel lounges have more flexible hours. Alcohol is sold at hotels, liquor stores, and other licensed premises. Many restaurants are licensed to sell alcohol. Some venues are only able to sell alcohol with a meal. Others are B.Y.O. (Bring Your Own). Most restaurants, licensed or otherwise, will allow you to B.Y.O.; they may apply a small corkage fee for opening the bottle and serving it.

MEDIA

NEWSPAPERS
Sydney is served by three major metropolitan dailies (Monday to Saturday). There are two quality

broadsheet newspapers, the *Sydney Morning Herald* and the *Australian*. The former has a strong local focus, the latter is oriented toward national interests. Both are heavily weighted to local news, but both have daily international news sections and some international sports results (English soccer, American football, baseball, and basketball, for example). The third metropolitan newspaper is the tabloid *Daily Telegraph,* the more sensationalist of the three, although it is fairly restrained compared to some of the newspapers published in Britain or the United States. There are two Sunday papers: the *Sunday Telegraph* and the *Sun Herald*.

TELEVISION
Sydney has five free-to-view television stations. There are three commercial networks (seven, nine, and ten), the government-owned but substantially independent Australian Broadcasting Corporation (ABC, channel 2), and the similarly established multicultural broadcaster, SBS. There are two cable networks, Foxtel and Optus Vision, which feature sports channels, movie channels, and news channels such as CNN.

RADIO
There are numerous radio stations on the AM and FM bands with specializations such as news and talkback (2GB and 2BL), popular music (2WS, 2DAY-FM and MMM), the youth station (JJJ), and classical (ABC-FM and 2MBS).

MONEY MATTERS

Australian currency is decimal with the dollar as the basic unit of currency. There are 100 cents to the dollar. Notes, which are plastic and have a clear window and a hologram (quite a good souvenir in themselves), come in $100, $50, $20, $10, and $5 denominations. Coins come in 5c, 10c, 20c, 50c, $1, and $2. Transactions involving 6, 7, 8, or 9 cents are rounded up or down to

the nearest multiple of 5 cents. The price is rounded down for 6 and 7 cents and rounded up for 8 and 9 cents. So if something costs $1.67, you'll be charged $1.65; if it costs $1.68, you'll pay $1.70. There are currency exchanges at the international airport (5:30 a.m. to 11 p.m.), Pitt Street Mall, Circular Quay, and numerous locations around the city (usually 9 a.m.–5 p.m.). The major banks and hotels also provide exchange facilities in all major currencies. Traveler's checks include American Express, Thomas Cook, Visa, Barclays, Bank of America, and Mastercard.

Automatic Teller Machines (ATMs) may also be used if your card has international access. Contact your bank at home for details of availability and the service charges that may apply.

OPENING TIMES

Thursday nights are late-night shopping nights. Most stores close on Saturday afternoons and Sundays; however, many major department stores and some specialty stores are open daily. Banks are generally open from 9:30 a.m. to 4 p.m, although some operate later on Fridays and many in the city are open on Thursday nights and all or part of the weekends, especially in the busier shopping centers.

RELIGION

Christianity is the most widespread faith; however, there are also Jewish and Muslim congregations. Your hotel should be able to provide details of the nearest places of worship. Features of some of the following churches are described in this guide.
Anglican: St. Andrews Cathedral, Town Hall; St. James, Queens Square, Macquarie Street
Baptist: Central Baptist Church, 619 George Street
Jewish: Great Synagogue, 189 Elizabeth Street
Muslim: Islamic Council of N.S.W., Tel 9742 5752

Roman Catholic: St. Mary's Cathedral, College Street
Presbyterian: Scots Church, 44 Margaret Street

TIME DIFFERENCES

The time differential from Greenwich mean time (GMT) is +11 hours in summer, +10 hours during the rest of the year. From Los Angeles the difference is +19 (summer) and +18 hours (winter). Daylight saving in N.S.W. operates from the last Sunday in October until the last Sunday in March. Other states observe different arrangements, and some don't have daylight saving at all.

TIPPING

Tipping is not a widespread custom in Australia, and hotels and restaurants do not add service charges to accounts. Porters at airports, taxi drivers, and hairdressers do not expect tips. However, if you think they have provided good service a gratuity is an acceptable form of thanks. The same applies in restaurants where tips up to 10 percent are more common. In all cases, tipping is entirely at your discretion.

TRAVELERS WITH DISABILITIES

Australia is very aware of the need for facilities for the disabled and is a signatory to international treaties ensuring equality of access. Most airlines, hotels, and transportation offices can arrange the best possible assistance when given advance notice and details of your needs. Restaurants and cinemas are often well equipped to assist with your requirements, and most modern buildings provide wheelchair access.

VISITOR INFORMATION

Information on the city's many attractions, current events, and activities can be obtained from a range of sources, including the

Sydney Visitor Centre,
106 George Street, The Rocks,
Tel 9255 1788.

Daily newspapers also have
the latest in what's on in and
around the city. The main
Sydney broadsheet newspaper,
the *Sydney Morning Herald,* has
a daily entertainment section
detailing performances and
cinema screenings. The newspaper's Friday supplement gives
comprehensive details of just
about everything that is
happening over the weekend
and ensuing week. Other
sources include the *Australian*
and the *Daily Telegraph.*

Tourist information centers are
to be found in even the smallest
towns across Australia. They
provide information and advice
free of charge and are indicated
by the international "i" sign.

TOURIST OFFICES

The Australian Tourist
Commission (A.T.C.) operates
tourist information offices in
most countries.

United States
2121 Avenue of the Stars
Suite 1200
Los Angeles, CA 90067
Tel 310/552-1988
Fax 310/552-1215

Chicago Helpline, Tel 708/296-
4900, Fax 708/635-3718

United Kingdom
Gemini House
10–18 Putney Hill
London SW15 6AA
Tel 0181-780 2227
Fax 0181-780 1496

INTERNET INFORMATION

The Australian Tourist
Commission and the Office of
National Tourism give travel and
reservations advice at the
following addresses:

www.aussie.net.au
www.tourism.nsw.gov.au
www.australian.com

EMERGENCIES

EMBASSIES IN SYDNEY

Most embassies are located in
the national capital, Canberra,
but many countries also have
consular offices in Sydney:
U.S. Consulate, 39 Castlereagh
Street, Tel 9373 9200
U.K. Consulate, Level 16, Gateway
Building, 1 Macquarie Place,
Tel 9247 7521
Canadian Consulate, Level 5,
111 Harrington Street,
Tel 9364 3000

EMERGENCY PHONE NUMBERS

Ambulance, fire, or police, Tel 000
Emergency Prescription Service,
Tel 9235 0333
Dental Emergency Information
Service, Tel 9369 7050
Lifeline, Tel 13 1114
Prince of Wales Hospital
Emergency, High Street,
Randwick, Tel 9382 3960
St. Vincents Hospital Emergency,
Victoria Street, Darlinghurst,
Tel 9361 2520
Sydney Hospital Emergency,
Macquarie Street, Sydney,
Tel 9382 7111
**Lost or stolen traveler's
checks or credit cards:**
American Express: Cards, Tel
9271 8666; Cheques, Tel 9271
8689
Bank of America, Tel 9931 4200
Mastercard, Tel 1800 120113
Thomas Cook Mastercard,
Tel 1800 127 495
Visa, Tel 1800 805341

WHAT TO DO IN A CAR ACCIDENT

In the event of a car accident
police must be called if the
damage exceeds $A500; for
insurance purposes you should
call them in any circumstance. If
people are injured the police
must be called immediately and,
if necessary, call an ambulance.
In all cases an accident must
be reported to the police within
24 hours. You should exchange

details with the other driver if
another vehicle is involved—
name, address, telephone number,
registration number of the
vehicle. Note that the driver's
details are contained on his/her
license which also has his/her
photo on it. You should also seek
the details of any independent
witnesses. Inform your insurance
company as quickly as possible.

HEALTH

Visitors are permitted to bring
reasonable quantities of pre-
scribed (non-narcotic) medica-
tion into the country. Drugs
should be clearly labeled and
identifiable. If large quantities are
being carried, a doctor's certificate is advisable for presentation
to customs and/or an Australian
doctor if required. Australian
pharmacies (called chemists) can
fill most prescriptions, but they
must be written by an
Australian-registered doctor.

Vaccinations are not required if
you are traveling direct to
Australia, unless you have come
from or visited a yellow fever-
infected country or zone within
six days prior to arrival. You do
not need a health certificate to
enter Australia.

Most overseas travelers are not
covered by the government
Medicare service, Tel 13 2011.
Emergency medical treatment is
available under the local Medicare
system for visitors from the U.K.,
Malta (for six months from date
of arrival), Italy (six months),
Sweden, the Netherlands, and
Finland. There is no coverage for
U.S. visitors: Take out a health
insurance policy prior to your
visit to cover the period of your
stay (see p. 233).

Health risks are no greater than
any other advanced western
country. Despite scares with
Sydney's water supply in 1998, it
is generally considered safe to
drink. If in doubt, plenty of bottled water is available throughout the city.

HOTELS & RESTAURANTS

Compared to other major cities of the world, prices for accommodations in Sydney are quite reasonable. It is possible to spend a small fortune and be treated like royalty—several Sydney hotels have pampered princesses and presidents—but very comfortable lodgings can be found that have equally comfortable tariffs. However, even budget travelers should consider saving up for a big night at one of the hotels that has a sweeping harbor view. You haven't lived until you've seen the sun go down or rise over one of the world's great waterways.

Most hotels are to be found in the central city area, The Rocks, Kings Cross, and Darlinghurst. If you're keen on the beach, a few hotels from Bondi to Coogee have been included. There are many motels in suburban areas but these are not usually frequented by overseas travelers.

Farther afield, areas such as the Hunter Valley and the Blue Mountains tend toward boutique-style accommodations, which are very popular with Sydney people, especially on weekends. Savvy travelers visit these areas during the week, when tariffs are lower, or book well in advance if they are planning a weekend break.

RESTAURANTS

When it comes to restaurants, Sydney has a quite dazzling range of cuisines and settings to choose from. As with accommodations, prices compare favorably with other cities. Here, though, you'll find many eateries that can provide an outstanding meal for a handful of coins. An emphasis on fresh produce and palate-cleansing flavors reflects the warm year-round climate and the preference for lighter meals. Just as refreshing, it is usually fairly easy to get a table at Sydney restaurants. Only a handful are booked out months ahead.
L = Lunch
D = Dinner
B.Y.O. = Bring your own (wine)

Hotel and restaurants are arranged alphabetically within a price range in each district.

PRICES

HOTELS
An indication of the cost of a double room without breakfast is given by **$** signs.

$$$$$	Over $280
$$$$	$200–$280
$$$	$120–$200
$$	$80–$120
$	Under $80

RESTAURANTS
An indication of the cost of a three-course dinner without drinks is given by **$** signs.

$$$$$	Over $80
$$$$	$50–$80
$$$	$35–$50
$$	$20–$35
$	Under $20

CIRCULAR QUAY & EAST

HOTELS

SHERATON ON THE PARK
$$$$
161 ELIZABETH ST.
TEL 9286 6000
FAX 9286 6686
One of the city's finest hotels, facing Hyde Park and close to all city attractions. Rooms are stylish and contemporary; of the 49 suites, 23 have balconies that overlook the park. A brasserie offers à la carte dining and a famed buffet. Gekko, the hotel's signature restaurant, offers the best Australian produce—scallops, prawns, quail, rack of veal, roasted barramundi, yellowfin tuna, tenderloin of beef. The entrance to Gekko is through a "wine library" showcasing many choice Australian wines: 26 Chardonnays for instance, and 17 vintages of Penfolds Grange Hermitage.
🛏 557 🅿 200 🔁 🕉 🈯
🚆 🍷 💳 All major cards

HOTEL INTER-CONTINENTAL
$$$
117 MACQUARIE ST.
TEL 9230 0200
FAX 9240 1240
Located minutes from the CBD, Opera House, Sydney Harbour, and the Botanic Gardens. A modern tower is linked to the preserved 1850s Treasury Building (see p. 66) via the Cortile—a dramatic glass-domed sandstone courtyard that serves as the hotel's central meeting place. Rooms and suites are classically elegant, and many have harbor views. Restaurant One One Seven serves a selection of hot and cold meze dishes followed by local seafood, beef, venison, spatchcock, duck—each matched with a specially selected Australian wine by the glass or bottle. The humidor in Pierpont's bar keeps 30,000 cheroots in tip-top condition.
🛏 498 🅿 131 🔁 🕉 🈯
🚆 🍷 💳 All major cards

HYDE PARK PLAZA
$$$
38 COLLEGE ST.
TEL 9331 6933
FAX 9331 6022
Apartment-style suites are available in this well-appointed hotel on the eastern side of Hyde Park, close to the city, the Australian Museum, Oxford Street, and transportation.
🛏 182 🅿 50 🕉 🈯
🚆 🍷 💳 All major cards

MARRIOTT
$$$
36 COLLEGE ST.
TEL 9361 8400
FAX 9361 8599
Luxury hotel on the eastern

HOTELS & RESTAURANTS

side of Hyde Park. Elegant contemporary decor. Rooms have microwaves, wet bars, computer data ports, voice-mail, fax lines, work desks. In the restaurant overlooking the park, the short dinner menu might include coriander marinated prawns in wonton pasty, followed by kangaroo loin and emu wrap, finishing with white chocolate passion-fruit gâteau.

ⓘ 241 🅿 150 🔁 ⊘ ⑤
⬛ 📺 🚫 All major cards

🏨 THE REGENT SYDNEY
$$$
199 GEORGE ST.
TEL 9238 0000
FAX 9251 2851
Great location right on Circular Quay, next door to The Rocks. This large hotel was undergoing major refurbishment as this guide went to print. Luxurious rooms are spacious, and bathrooms have Italian marble.

ⓘ 594 🅿 110 🔁 ⊘ ⑤
⬛ 📺 🚫 All major cards

🏨 RENAISSANCE SYDNEY
$$$
30 PITT ST.
TEL 9372 2233
FAX 9251 1122
Luxury hotel just behind Circular Quay. The decor, in keeping with the name, is all rich colors, reds, golds, blues; tapestries, gilt, mirrors. Rooms have separate bath and shower, large writing desks, data plugs. A 150-year-old pub on the site has been retained.

ⓘ 579 🅿 40 🔁 ⊘ ⑤
⬛ 📺 🚫 All major cards

🏨 RITZ-CARLTON
🍴 SYDNEY
$$$
93 MACQUARIE ST.
TEL 9252 4600
FAX 9252 4286
A short stroll from the Opera House and the Royal Botanic Gardens, one of the city's most elegant hotels, furnished with chandeliers, silk-paneled

walls, antiques, and fine art. Spacious rooms and suites, some with French doors opening onto balconies. Fine restaurant offers dishes such as seared scampi tails dusted in Thai spices or roasted duck breast with fig and red cabbage compote.

ⓘ 106 🅿 50 🔁 ⊘ ⑤
⬛ 📺 🚫 All major cards

🏨 WENTWORTH SYDNEY
$$
61–101 PHILLIP ST.
TEL 9230 0700
FAX 9227 9133
A highly regarded hotel in the city—and one of the more affordable—with a high level of elegance and service.

ⓘ 424 🅿 175 🔁 ⊘ ⑤
📺 🚫 All major cards

RESTAURANTS

> **SOMETHING SPECIAL**

🍴 FORTY ONE
One of Sydney's best restaurants. On level 41 of the Chifley Tower in the CBD. Decor is plush but understated, the view is over the botanical gardens, the harbor, and out to sea. Chef Dietmar Sawyere's food is a judicious blend of classical European and Asian styles and flavors: a warm salad of Chinese roast duck with sea scallops and Vietnamese dressing; crown roast of wild hare with braised Belgian endive. A huge wine list (close to 900 wines), mainly of premium Australian and French wines, with a few New World ones.

$$$$
LEVEL 41
CHIFLEY TOWER
CHIFLEY SQ.
TEL 9221 2500
🚭 134 🚋 Train: Martin Place, Wynyard 🕐 Closed Sun. & Sat L. ⑤ ⑤
🚫 All major cards

🍴 BANC
$$$
53 MARTIN PLACE
TEL 9233 5300
CBD dining on the premises of a former bank. Modern Australian cuisine with elegance and obvious French influences.
🚭 85 🚋 Train: Martin Place
🕐 Closed Sun. & Sat. L ⑤
⑤ 🚫 All major cards

🍴 BENNELONG
$$$
SYDNEY OPERA HOUSE
BENNELONG POINT
TEL 9250 7548
This premier restaurant under the Opera House's small sails is split-level. One area is fine dining, a wide selection of the local produce cooked simply with a Mediterranean influence: seafood, game, beef, vegetarian dishes (reservations essential). The upper level is a cocktail lounge for a drink or a light meal at the Crustacea Bar (oysters, yabbies, lobster, crabs, smoked salmon, and one or two alternatives for the anti-fish folk). Live jazz on most nights, spectacular harbor views (reservations not required).
🚭 140 🅿 3,000 🚋 Train: Circular Quay 🕐 Closed L & Sun. ⑤ ⑤ 🚫 All major cards

🍴 BOTANIC GARDENS
$$$
ROYAL BOTANIC GARDENS
MRS. MACQUARIES RD.
TEL 9241 2419
A splendid setting amid the gardens with indoor and out-door areas serving Modern Australian cuisine with a Mediterranean influence.
🚭 142 🚋 Train: Martin Place, Circular Quay
🕐 Closed D ⑤ 🚫 All major cards

🍴 KABLE'S
$$$
THE REGENT SYDNEY
199 GEORGE ST.
TEL 9255 0226

Signature restaurant at the Regent Sydney. In the past it has had a reputation for varied and innovative modern Australian cuisine. Along with the rest of the hotel it is undergoing a reincarnation, but details are sketchy.

⊞ 120 🅿 200 🚆 Train: Circular Quay 🕐 Closed Sun.–Mon. & Sat. L 🅢 🅢 🅢 All major cards

🍴 PAVILION ON THE PARK
$$$
1 ART GALLERY RD.
THE DOMAIN
TEL 9232 1322
A striking setting in The Domain. Dine indoors in a light and airy space or outdoors, under the vines. By night the Pavilion is adrift in the dark, with the art gallery, looming Moreton Bay fig trees, and the city skyline spotlit. Food is classically based but adventurous. Flavors are robust and ingredients season-driven. In winter, there might be a crispy pig's head salad, or Imam Bayaldi, which translates as "the priest fainted." Warm weather dishes might include a tartare of tuna, swordfish, and crustacea, or roasted swordfish wrapped in prosciutto with truffle and sorrel purée. There's also a quick café (open 9 a.m.–5 p.m.). They offer 180 wines (40 by the glass from Europe and the U.S., but concentrate on Australian ones).

⊞ 100 🚆 Train: Martin Place 🕐 Closed Sun. D–Wed. & Sat. L 🅢 🅢 🅢 All major cards

🍴 IMPERIAL HARBOURSIDE
$$
15 CIRCULAR QUAY W.
TEL 9247 7073
You just can't beat the harborside setting with the great view of the Opera House and Harbour Bridge. The Asian-influenced cuisine is among the best in town.

⊞ 650 🚆 Train: Circular Quay 🅢 🅢 🅢 All major cards

🍴 SYDNEY COVE OYSTER BAR
$$
1 CIRCULAR QUAY E.
SYDNEY COVE
TEL 9247 2937
Delightful harborside stopping point on the concourse between Circular Quay ferries and the Opera House. Alfresco, informal dining and local seafood.

⊞ 140 🚆 Train: Circular Quay 🅢 🅢 All major cards

THE ROCKS

HOTELS

🏨 OBSERVATORY
$$$$$
89–113 KENT ST.
TEL 9256 2222
FAX 9256 2233
Set in the heart of The Rocks, this hotel re-creates the atmosphere of a grand Australian home, to luxury standard, with views of the entrance to Darling Harbour.

🛏 100 🅿 20 🅢 🅢 🅢 🛎 🅢 All major cards

🏨 PARK HYATT SYDNEY
The ultimate. Absolute luxury in an absolutely prime position on the harbor. Catering to a large corporate clientele, there is infrared internet access through TV sets in rooms. The upscale restaurant is in the final stages of a major revamp as this guide goes to press.

$$$$$
7 HICKSON RD.
TEL 9241 1234
FAX 9256 1555
🛏 158 🅿 55 🅢 🅢 🅢 🛎 🅢 🛎 🅢 All major cards

🏨 ANA HOTEL SYDNEY
Great harbor views from every room at this luxury hotel. On level 36 is the Unkai restaurant (see p. 242). There is a sushi corner and a brasserie for all-day dining. Two restored 1890s buildings in the complex contain The Rocks Teppanyaki and the traditional Australian Harts pub. The hotel also has a well-equipped business center.

$$$$
176 CUMBERLAND ST.
TEL 9250 6000
FAX 9250 6250
🛏 570 🅿 120 🅢 🅢 🅢 🛎 🛎 🛎 🅢 All major cards

🏨 QUAY WEST SYDNEY
🍴 $$$$
98 GLOUCESTER ST.
TEL 9240 6000
FAX 9240 6060
Luxury apartment/hotel complex with prime-position views of the main harbor and Opera House. Units have kitchenettes with sink, stove, and microwave; also washers and dryers. Decor is smart cream and navy, marble, granite, and wood. Harrington's restaurant does a fixed-price lunch and dinner offering dishes such as spring rolls filled with crab meat and Asian vegetables; chicken tandoori; roasted lamb rump; or char-grilled beef sirloin.

🛏 132 🅿 40 🅢 🅢 🅢 🛎 🅢 All major cards

🏨 HARBOUR ROCKS HOTEL
$$$
34–52 HARRINGTON ST.
TEL 9251 8944
FAX 9251 8900
Renovated 150-year-old building in the heart of The Rocks. Comfortable and affordable with shopping at hand.

🛏 54 🅿 🅢 🅢 All major cards

🏨 OLD SYDNEY PARKROYAL
$$$
55 GEORGE ST.
TEL 9252 0524
FAX 9251 2093
This charming hotel in the middle of The Rocks has views from the rooftop pool and spa that will take your breath away.
🛏 174 🅿 50 ▫ 🚭 🚫 ▨ 🚫 All major cards

RESTAURANTS

🍴 QUAY
$$$$$
UPPER LEVEL, OVERSEAS PASSENGER TERMINAL
CIRCULAR QUAY W.
TEL 9251 5600
Stupendous views of the Opera House and modern Australian cuisine combine to make this an excellent dining experience. The cooking is delicate and inspired: Try foie gras caviar or basil-infused tuna with mustard seed and soy vinaigrette.
🪑 85 🅿 16 🚈 Train: Circular Quay ⏰ Closed L Sat.–Sun. 🚭 🚫 🚫 All major cards

🍴 MCA CAFÉ
$$$$
MUSEUM OF CONTEMPORARY ART
140 GEORGE ST.
TEL 9241 4253
Contemporary art and contemporary Australian cuisine sit side by side in this eatery. Indoor and outdoor dining in a heritage building with a view across Sydney Cove. Mediterranean inspired, mainly fish, lunch menu, also afternoon teas and breakfasts on the weekend. Run by Neil Perry's Rockpool group (see below).
🪑 150 🚈 Train: Circular Quay ⏰ Closed D 🚫 🚫 All major cards

🍴 ROCKPOOL
$$$$
107 GEORGE ST.
TEL 9252 1888
Superlative chef Neil Perry is presently carving out for himself a restaurant and catering empire, of which his multi-award winning, 10-year-old Rockpool restaurant is the jewel in the crown. Food has a strong emphasis on seafood, and frequent use of Asian flavors such as galangal, lemongrass, chili, coriander, and lime. Try slow-cooked abalone with a fine noodle and fungi salad; herb and spice crusted medium-rare seared tuna on an aubergine salad; and the famed date tart. Perry cultivates a close relationship with Australian winemakers, and offers an extensive menu of premium Australian and imported wines.
🪑 100 🚈 Train: Circular Quay ⏰ Closed Sat. L & Sun. 🚫 🚫 All major cards

🍴 BEL MONDO
$$$
LEVEL 3, ARGYLE STORES
12–24 ARGYLE ST.
TEL 9241 3700
On the third floor of Sydney's original Metcalf Bond Store in the historic Rocks precinct. A dramatic space with cathedral ceilings, a kitchen on a stage, and views of the Harbour Bridge and the Opera House. Chef Manfredo cooks fine Australian produce in the northern Italian style. Try gnocchi with truffles, burnt butter, and parmesan; roast Murray cod with spinach, pine nuts, and sultanas; or chocolate and nougat tartuffo.
🪑 160 🚈 Train: Circular Quay ⏰ Closed Sat. L & Sun. 🚫 🚫 All major cards

🍴 UNKAI
$$$
ANA HOTEL
36TH FLOOR
176 CUMBERLAND ST.
TEL 9250 6123
Some local food critics consider this the best Japanese restaurant in town. Given the competition, that's quite a statement. Nevertheless, the standard of the food, the service, and the view put it squarely in the first rank.
🪑 75 🚈 Train: Circular Quay ⏰ Closed Sat. L 🚫 🚫 🚫 All major cards

🍴 WHARF RESTAURANT
$$$
PIER 4, HICKSON RD.
WALSH BAY
TEL 9250 1761
A personal favorite of the author. A tribute to the days of sail, this converted pier, with its soaring tree trunks supporting the roof, straddles the water, its walls of glass and balconies overlook the inner harbor. Lots of arty activity here; the Sydney Theatre Company foyer is the restaurant's bar area. The Wharf has a small kitchen and a short menu of brasserie-style food with a Mediterranean influence, and always three or four seafood items. The small but select wine list concentrates on New South Wales wines.
🪑 100 🚈 Train: Circular Quay ⏰ Closed Sun. 🚫 All major cards

SYDNEY HARBOUR

HOTELS

🏨 RADISSON KESTREL
🍴 **$$$**
8–13 SOUTH STEYNE
MANLY
TEL 9977 8866
FAX 9977 8209
Intimate boutique hotel at the southern end of Manly Beach. Every room has a balcony and an ocean view. The restaurant opens onto a pergola-covered terrace. Small, innovative menu: Try steamed crab wonton with zucchini noodles and Thai coconut broth; beef tenderloin poached in red wine stock; or chocolate crepe tower with layers of mixed berry mascarpone. Soups, risotto, pizzas for lunch.
🛏 82 🅿 50 ▫ 🚭 ▨ 🍴 🚫 All major cards

CENTRA NORTH SYDNEY
$$
17 BLUE ST.
TEL 9955 0499
FAX 9922 3689
Affordable hotel on the north side of the harbor, with views over the water and city. Transportation to the city takes a matter of minutes.
[i] 210 [P] 60 🔲 🚭 🟦 🟦
🅰 All major cards

SOMETHING SPECIAL

MANLY PACIFIC PARKROYAL
Popular hotel overlooking Manly Beach and the Pacific Ocean. Half the rooms face east over the beach, the other half have westerly views over Manly. All rooms have balconies. Lobby bar and two restaurants. The whole hotel was being extensively altered and updated as this guide was going to press.
$$
55 NORTH STEYNE
MANLY
TEL 9977 7666
FAX 9977 7822
[i] 170 [P] 80 🔲 🚭
🚭 🟦 🟥 🅰 All major cards

RYDGES NORTH SYDNEY
$$
54 MCLAREN ST.
TEL 9922 1311
FAX 9922 4939
Great views from this refurbished hotel set in the heart of the North Sydney business district.
[i] 167 [P] 45 🔲 🚭 🟦
🅰 All major cards

MANLY BEACH RESORT
$
6 CARLTON ST.
MANLY
TEL 9977 4188
FAX 9977 0524
Resort-style accommodations close to the beach, restaurants,

shopping, and entertainment of Manly.
[i] 40 [P] 30 🚭 🟦 🟦
🅰 All major cards

SOMETHING SPECIAL

🍴 BATHERS PAVILION
Delightful site at water's edge. Spanish Mission-style Heritage building recently completely renewed by restaurateur Victoria Alexander. Perfect for a sunny stroll, in winter warmed by open fires. Chef is the renowned Serge Dansereau, who has trained many of the best chefs in Sydney since the 1970s. Known for his close rapport with small producers, he combines a mature and modern approach to food with traditional techniques such as slow cooking in wood fired ovens and grilling on vine leaves. Fixed-price menu for three courses.
$$$
THE ESPLANADE
BALMORAL
TEL 9968 1133
🍴 250 in all venues
🚢 Water taxi, or ferry to Mosman Wharf then bus 233 🚭 🅰 All major cards

RESTAURANTS

🍴 JOHN CADMAN CRUISING RESTAURANT
$$$$
CAPTAIN COOK CRUISES
NO. 6 JETTY
CIRCULAR QUAY
TEL 9206 6666
Beef 'n' reef or surf 'n' turf; steak, seafood, and pasta dishes cater to all tastes if dining afloat is your desire. For other waterborne dining options, check out the tour operators located around Circular Quay and the city side of Darling Harbour.
🍴 650+ 🚆 Train: Circular Quay 🕐 Closed L 🚭 🟦
🅰 All major cards

HOTELS

🍴 SYDNEY HILTON
$$$
259 PITT ST.
TEL 9266 2000
FAX 9265 6065
One of the older international hotels, in the center of the city with cinemas and shopping close by. Two restaurants: The San Francisco Grill has a gentlemen's clubby feel with booth seating, warm Outback colors, and a piano player. The food is classically inclined but adventurous, from steak tartare to crocodile to buffalo. Their coffee brûlée with cointreau and brandy drizzled down an orange rind and set alight is an occasion in itself. The large Market Place serves everything from a bowl of noodles to a buffet with seafood on ice. The 106-year-old Marble Bar is a glorious relic of an earlier hotel
[i] 585 [P] 1,000 🔲 🚭
🚭 🟦 🟥 🅰 All major cards

CENTRAL PARK
$$
185 CASTLEREAGH ST.
TEL 9283 5000
FAX 9283 2710
Small boutique hotel with studio and loft apartments close to tourist attractions, transportation, the Central Business District, and shopping.
[i] 35 [P] 5 🚭 🟦 🟦
🅰 All major cards

FURAMA HOTEL CENTRAL
$$
28 ALBION ST.
SURRY HILLS
TEL 9281 0333
FAX 9281 0222
One of two Furama Hotels in the southern end of town, this one is in a quiet area slightly away from the action but close to Central Station, Chinatown, and Surry Hills.

An all-day brasserie serves Thai and Indian dishes as well as Western food.

🛈 270 🅿 200 🔲 ◎ ▣ ⊠ 🔳 ◎ All major cards

🏨 ROYAL GARDEN
🍴 INTERNATIONAL
$$

431–439 PITT ST.
TEL 9281 6999
FAX 9281 6988
Modern hotel at the southern end of town. Rooftop pool with view of city. Rooms are adequate in size and well-appointed. The Kampung Malaysian restaurant offers authentic Malaysian cuisine; house specialties include spicy satays, also beef rendang, chili crab, curry laksas, and rice dishes. Continental, Thai, and Chinese dishes also.

🛈 215 🅿 10 🔲 ◎ 🔳 ⊠ ◎ All major cards

🏨 AARON'S HOTEL
$

37 ULTIMO RD.
HAYMARKET
TEL 9281 5555
FAX 9281 2666
Budget accommodations close to Chinatown, Darling Harbour, and entertainment complexes. Recently renovated. On two levels only.

🛈 86 🅿 Unlimited 🔲 ◎ ⊠ ◎ All major cards

🏨 CITISTAY WESTEND
$

412 PITT ST.
TEL 9211 4822
FAX 9281 9570
Affordable small heritage hotel within walking distance of restaurants, entertainment, and Darling Harbour.

🛈 90 🔲 ◎ 🔳 ⊠ ◎ All major cards

RESTAURANTS

🍴 CBD RESTAURANT
$$$

75 YORK ST.
TEL 9299 8911
On the first floor of the heritage-listed Hotel CBD.

The other three floors have bars, a Raffles-style club lounge, and a billiards room. The restaurant has polished floors, high ceilings, lots of glass, wooden chairs, and white tablecloths, and features the work of contemporary Australian painters on the walls. The current chef describes the seasonal menu as "simple, honest, passionate flavors with a classic French provincial influence": from roast-suckling pork rump with parsnips, English spinach, and parsley jus to confit of Atlantic salmon with saffron potatoes, fennel, and bouillabaisse-style sauce.

🪑 85 🚆 Train: Wynyard 🕐 Closed Sat. & Sun. ◎ 🔳 ⊠ All major cards

🍴 SUNTORY
$$$

529 KENT ST.
TEL 9267 2900
Traditional Japanese cuisine; part of an international chain. It has the dramatic colors and lines of a samurai's house in a garden setting. A Teppanyaki room—the chef cooks with a flourish in front of guests—a *shabu shabu* and sukiyaki area—traditional pot cooking style on hot plates in table centers—and a tatami room (shoes off, sitting on tatami mats) with service by kimono-clad waitresses.

🪑 110 🅿 25 🚆 Train: Town Hall 🕐 Closed Sat. L & Sun. 🔳 ⊠ All major cards

🍴 GOLDEN CENTURY
$$

393–399 SUSSEX ST.
TEL 9212 3901
One of the innumerable good-quality Chinese restaurants in this area. All encompassing *yum cha* during the day and an impressive range of dishes, specializing in seafood, at night.

🪑 600 🅿 🚆 Train: Town Hall, Central, & Sydney Light Rail to Haymarket ◎ ▣ ⊠ All major cards

🍴 BODHI
$

187 HAY ST.
TEL 9212 5071
Chinese vegetarian upstairs in a former gambling den. It's a little down at heel, but the *yum cha* (10 a.m.–3 p.m.) is mouthwateringly good and perfect for the budget traveler or adventurous diner. Dinners make it worth persevering with the service, which has a Buddhist leaning and could do with some enlightenment.

🪑 150 🚆 Train: Central & Sydney Light Rail to Haymarket ◎ ⊠ All major cards

🍴 CAPITAN TORRES
$

73 LIVERPOOL ST.
TEL 9264 5574
One of the Spanish Quarter's several restaurants with tapas (bar snacks), paella, seafood, and pork dishes.

🪑 300 🚆 Train: Town Hall ◎ ⊠ All major cards

🍴 DIETHNES
$

336 PITT ST.
TEL 9267 8956
Often called "the Greeks," this is wonderfully noisy,

chaotic, and fun. Traditional Greek fare, cabbage rolls, moussaka, stuffed vine leaves, salads with feta cheese, and olives. Big servings, great value.
🛗 200 🚇 Train: Museum 🕐 Closed Sun. ⊘ ❄
🆑 All major cards

🍴 SOUP PLUS
$
383 GEORGE ST.
TEL 9299 7728
Not just a restaurant, also a popular jazz venue. The specialty is soup, but the fare covers most Italian standards.
🛗 120 🚇 Train: Wynyard or Town Hall 🕐 Closed Sun. ❄ 🆑 No credit cards

🍴 SUPERBOWL
$
41 DIXON ST.
CHINATOWN
TEL 9281 2462
The cheaper of the two Superbowl food courts (the other is at 39 Goulburn St.). The specialty here is congee (rice porridge) in all its savory forms—king prawn, fish head, frog, beef, and more. Both venues are open from break-fast to late-night supper.
🛗 70 🚇 Train: Town Hall & Monorail or Sydney Light Rail to Haymarket ❄
🆑 AE, MC, V

DARLING HARBOUR

HOTELS

🏨 STAR CITY
$$$$
80 PYRMONT ST.
PYRMONT
TEL 9777 9000
FAX 9657 8680
Staying in this sort of luxury isn't a gamble, even though you're in Sydney's only legal casino. Serious harbor views, restaurants, and entertain-ment are contained in the one vast facility (see p. 132).
🛏 470 (139 apts.) 🅿 2,500
⇄ ⊘ ❄ 🏊 🛡 🆑 All major cards

🍴 THE GRACE
$$$
77 YORK ST.
TEL 9272 6888
FAX 9299 8189
On the Darling Harbour side of the city, this beautifully restored commercial gothic hotel was originally modeled on the Chicago Tribune building. Features such as stairwells, elevators, pressed metal flooring, marble flooring, and decorative ironwork have been retained. Rooms come with voice mail, computer data ports, and interactive TV. The Brasserie with its high ceilings, atrium, and tall windows serves a simple, fairly hearty Pacific Rim cuisine: crispy-skinned snapper fillet with baby bok choy; roasted veal cutlets with beer-glazed onions and potato mash; banana, macadamia nut, and chocolate-chip pudding with caramelized banana compote.
🛏 382 🅿 60 ⇄ ⊘ ❄
🏊 🛡 🆑 All major cards

🏨 ASTOR GOLDSBOROUGH APARTMENT HOTEL
$$$
243 PYRMONT ST.
PYRMONT
TEL 9292 5000
FAX 9292 5699
Housed in wool stores built in 1883, the apartments offer luxury hotel facilities with plenty of space in the rooms. Overlooks Darling Harbour.
🛏 500 🅿 1,000 ⇄ 🏊 🛡
⊘ ❄ 🆑 All major cards

🏨 HOTEL NIKKO DARLING HARBOUR SYDNEY
$$$
161 SUSSEX ST.
DARLING HARBOUR
TEL 9299 1231
FAX 9299 3340
Very large luxury hotel on the Darling Harbour side of the city. Built in 1991, the hotel was designed to echo the feel of a 1920s ocean liner. The foyer has marble floors and wood

paneling; furnishings in rooms and suites echo the art deco, nautical feel. Site includes two heritage-listed buildings dating from the 1850s, the Corn Exchange (now a shopping arcade) and the Dundee Arms pub. The informal Corn Exchange restaurant specializes in seafood and also has a full Japanese menu.
🛏 645 🅿 30 ⇄ ⊘ ❄
🛡 🆑 All major cards

🏨 NOVOTEL ON SYDNEY HARBOUR
$$$
100 MURRAY ST.
PYRMONT
TEL 9934 0000
FAX 9934 0099
Superior accommodations with all facilities, including a tennis court, right in the middle of the Darling Harbour entertainment precinct.
🛏 527 🅿 60 ⇄ ⊘ ❄
🏊 🛡 🆑 All major cards

🏨 ALL SEASONS PREMIER MENZIES
$$
14 CARRINGTON ST.
TEL 9299 1000
FAX 9290 3819
Centrally located in the city, facing Wynyard Park with transportation literally at the door. The lobby is in rich maroons with crystal chandeliers and black granite floors. Rooms have fax, data ports, and internet access through TVs. There is a seafood buffet restaurant, a bar showing sports on satellite TV, and a brasserie and wine bar.
🛏 446 🅿 ⇄ ⊘ ❄
🏊 🛡 🆑 All major cards

🏨 CARLTON CREST HOTEL SYDNEY
$$
169–179 THOMAS ST.
TEL 9281 6888
FAX 9281 6688
Large rooms and some Darling Harbour views from this well-appointed hotel in the Chinatown entertain-ment district.

HOTELS & RESTAURANTS

📱 252 🅿 600 ⬛ ⬛ ⬛
⬛ ⬛ All major cards

🏨 COUNTRY COMFORT SYDNEY CENTRAL
$$
CORNER OF GEORGE & QUAY STS.
TEL 9212 2544
FAX 9281 3794
Affordable hotel with good facilities close to Central Station, Chinatown, and Darling Harbour.
📱 114 🅿 40 ⬛ 50%
⬛ ⬛ All major cards

🏨 FURAMA HOTEL DARLING HARBOUR
$$
68 HARBOUR ST.
TEL 9281 0400
FAX 9281 1212
The second Furama, this one across from the Entertainment Centre. There's a brasserie in an 1850s wool store with a heritage-listed ironbark roof, and a bar and stone grill where food is cooked at the table on a granite hot plate.
📱 266 🅿 Valet ⬛ ⬛
⬛ ⬛ All major cards

🏨 HOTEL IBIS DARLING HARBOUR
$$
70 MURRAY ST.
PYRMONT
TEL 9563 0888
FAX 9563 0899
Affordable hotel accommodations with great city views and Darling Harbour entertainment at the door. Modern, with basic facilities and compact rooms, but linked with the next door, more upscale Novotel; Ibis guests may use Novotel's facilities.
📱 256 🅿 40 ⬛ ⬛ ⬛
⬛ All major cards

🏨 PARKROYAL AT DARLING HARBOUR
$$
150 DAY ST.
TEL 9261 1188
FAX 9261 8766
Fully appointed hotel on the Darling Harbour side of the

city with views over the water.
📱 295 🅿 50 ⬛ ⬛ ⬛
⬛ ⬛ All major cards

🏨 SYDNEY VISTA
$$
7–9 YORK ST.
TEL 9274 1222
FAX 9274 1230
Well-located hotel with train and bus at the door. Decor has natural colors, wood, limestone floors, lots of glass. Rooms are quite large; some family rooms, suites, apartments, and balcony rooms. Brasserie-style restaurant menu that includes barramundi with lemon myrtle butter, Singapore noodles, and a fish stew.
🛏 268 🅿 40 ⬛ ⬛ ⬛
⬛ ⬛ All major cards

SOMETHING SPECIAL

🍴 TETESUYA'S
The danger with recommending this restaurant is that someone will try to lure Tetsuya Wakuda away from Sydney. Don't do it, he's ours. You'll need to reserve well ahead if you want to discover the genius of his French/Japanese fixed-price eating experience—a six-course degustation delight.
$$$$
729 DARLING ST.
ROZELLE
TEL 9555 1017
🛏 55 🚌 Bus: 433, 452
🕐 Closed Sat. D–Mon.
⬛ ⬛ All major cards

RESTAURANTS

🍴 WOCKPOOL RESTAURANT & NOODLE BAR
$$$$
SOUTHERN PROMENADE
DARLING HARBOUR
TEL 9211 9888
Another arm of the onslaught by inimitable Neil Perry (see Rockpool, p. 242) on the Sydney food scene, in a

stunning setting on the ground floor of the IMAX theater, with indoor and outdoor dining overlooking Darling Harbour. Food inspired by Thai, Chinese, and Indonesian cuisines. Try wok-fried crab omelette, Szechuan duck confit with mandarin pancakes and hoisin sauce, or steamed fish with ginger and shallots.
🛏 200 🅿 Valet 🚈 Monorail to Convention ⬛ ⬛
⬛ All major cards

🍴 JORDONS
$$$
197 HARBOURSIDE
TEL 9281 3711
Upscale fish restaurant. Indoor and outdoor dining awash with the fruits of the ocean and a view across Darling Harbour to the city skyline.
🛏 600 🚈 Monorail or Sydney Light Rail to Harbourside ⬛ ⬛ ⬛ All major cards

🍴 DOYLES AT THE FISH MARKET
$$
SYDNEY FISH MARKET
BLACKWATTLE BAY
PYRMONT
TEL 9552 4339
No prizes for guessing the cuisine here, and the fish is served with typical Doyles skill. Indoor and outdoor dining; often very busy.
🛏 120 🅿 500 🚈 Sydney Light Rail to Fish Market
🕐 Closed Sun.–Thurs. ⬛
⬛ ⬛ D, MC, V

EASTERN SUBURBS

HOTELS

🏨 MEDUSA
$$$
267 DARLINGHURST RD.
DARLINGHURST
TEL 9331 1000
FAX 9380 6901
Contemporary hotel with plenty of urban chic and a courtyard with an elegant reflecting pool. Quiet location,

---

HOTELS & RESTAURANTS

and close to all transportation.

🚻 18 🚭 ❄️ 💳 All major cards

🏨 RITZ-CARLTON
🍴 DOUBLE BAY
$$$
33 CROSS ST.
DOUBLE BAY
TEL 9362 4455
FAX 9362 4744

In the heart of classy Double Bay, with an air of slightly faded Victorian grandeur; antiques, patterned carpets, and fine art. Guest rooms have mahogany beds, marble bathrooms, and armchairs. Most have balconies. Restaurant is contemporary continental; say seared foie gras with grilled mango and ginger citrus beurre blanc, then pan-fried jumbo prawns scented with vanilla and served with a pineapple risotto. Premium Australian wines and French champagnes.

🚻 140 🅿️ 120 🚭 ❄️ 🏊 💳 All major cards

SOMETHING SPECIAL

🏨 🍴 SEBEL OF SYDNEY

Built in the early '60s, when it hosted entertainers and movie stars, the Sebel still attracts the film and entertainment crowd. Timber-paneling gives it a clubby feel. Guest rooms have harbor and streetscape views, a quarter with balconies. Discreet but attentive service. An elegant restaurant: Try lamb cutlet with roast capsicum frittata; pan-fried barramundi fillet; or white chocolate crème brûlée with hazelnut shortbread. Wide selection of mainly Australian wines.

$$$
23 ELIZABETH BAY RD.
ELIZABETH BAY
TEL 9358 3244
FAX 9357 1926

🚻 165 🅿️ 200 🚭 ❄️ 🏊 💳 All major cards

🏨 BOULEVARD HOTEL
🍴 SYDNEY
$$
90 WILLIAM ST.
TEL 9383 7222
FAX 9356 3786

Between the city and Kings Cross, with sweeping views of The Domain, the Opera House, and the harbor. Modern decor with a retro feel. Relaxed fine dining in the 25th-floor restaurant. A seven-course menu showcases some of the flavors of Aboriginal Australia: Try char-grilled fillet of barramundi with lemon myrtle fettucini, limes, and rosella beurre blanc.

🚻 272 🅿️ 25 🚭 ❄️ 🏊 💳 All major cards

🏨 CHATEAU SYDNEY 42
$$
14 MACLEAY ST.
POTTS POINT
TEL 9358 2500
FAX 9358 1959

Spacious rooms and an intimate boutique style. City or harbor views. Close to Kings Cross restaurants and entertainment.

🚻 94 🅿️ 33 🚭 ❄️ 🏊 💳 All major cards

🏨 COOGEE BAY
BOUTIQUE HOTEL
$$
9 VICAR ST.
COOGEE
TEL 9665 0000
FAX 9664 2103

Art deco-style accommodations away from the bustle of the city, with the usually sheltered waters of Coogee Beach nearby. Some suites have kitchen facilities.

🚻 83 🅿️ 100 🚭 ❄️ 🏊 💳 All major cards

🏨 GAZEBO
$$
2 ELIZABETH BAY RD.
ELIZABETH BAY
TEL 9358 1999
FAX 9356 2951

The distinctive bon-bon shaped tower of the late '60s Gazebo hotel remains a

---

Sydney landmark. The 17-story building offers quality affordable accommodations with great harbor views. All rooms have balconies. The tower culminates in a glass dome with heated swimming pool, a restaurant offering fresh local seafood, steaks, and pasta dishes in an elegant atmosphere, and a bar with retro '70s chic—all with an outlook on the harbor.

🚻 395 🅿️ 100 🚭 ❄️ 🏊 💳 All major cards

SOMETHING SPECIAL

🏨 HOLIDAY INN
COOGEE BEACH

Seven floors of well-appointed accommodations close to Coogee Beach. Over half the rooms have balconies and panoramic ocean views, as do the pool terrace and the Brasserie, which opens onto an outdoor dining area shaded by sails. The Brasserie has a large menu; seafood buffets are popular. Wine list emphasizes New South Wales wineries.

$$
242 ARDEN ST.
COOGEE
TEL 9315 7600
FAX 9315 9100

🚻 207 🅿️ 200 🚭 ❄️ 🏊 🏋️ 💳 All major cards

🏨 HOTEL CAPITAL
$$
111–139 DARLINGHURST RD.
KINGS CROSS
TEL 9358 2755
FAX 9358 2888

Well-appointed rooms, many with harbor views and most with bathtubs, a plus for the non-shower minded. There is a traditional Korean bathhouse, with Ginseng spas, baths, and saunas. The hotel's Amrang restaurant specializes in Korean and Japanese food.

🚻 226 🅿️ 60 🚭 ❄️ 🏊 🏋️ 💳 All major cards

🏨 KIRKETON
$$
229 DARLINGHURST RD.
DARLINGHURST
TEL 9332 2011
FAX 9332 2499
Ultra-contemporary hotel by Sydney's leading designer, Ian Halliday. Casual atmosphere and reasonable prices. Award-winning Sydney celebrity chef Luke Mangan has his restaurant, Salt (see p. 250), downstairs.
ⓘ 40 🅿 10 🔁 🔲 🛎
🏊 All major cards

🏨 LANDMARK PARKROYAL SYDNEY
$$
81 MACLEAY ST.
POTTS POINT
TEL 9368 3000
FAX 9357 7600
Located in the heart of the Kings Cross/Potts Point area, this hotel has full facilities and superb views of the city.
ⓘ 470 🅿 300+ 🔁 🔲
🔲 🏊 🛎 All major cards

🏨 MEDINA ON CROWN
$$
359 CROWN ST.
SURRY HILLS
TEL 9360 6666
FAX 9361 5965
Located in the pleasant village atmosphere of Surry Hills, these apartments are spacious and facilities of a high standard. Plenty of good restaurants close at hand.
ⓘ 85 🅿 60 🔁 🔲 🔲
🏊 🛎 All major cards

🏨 SAVOY DOUBLE BAY
$$
41–45 KNOX ST.
DOUBLE BAY
TEL 9326 1411
FAX 9327 8464
Family-oriented boutique hotel in the heart of the shopping and restaurant belt of ritzy harborside Double Bay. Built in the 1960s and still evolving. Breakfasts only.
ⓘ 39 🔁 🔲 🔲 🏊 All major cards

🏨 THE REX
$$
50–58 MACLEAY ST.
POTTS POINT
TEL 9383 7788
FAX 9383 7777
In the restaurant strip around the corner from brassy Kings Cross. Affordable, quality hotel, recently built, technologically up-to-date. A few rooms have outdoor terraces. Decor is natural wood and warm colors. A relaxed restaurant serves simple but tasty risottos, pasta dishes, club sandwiches, grills.
ⓘ 255 🅿 100 🔁 🔲 🔲
🏊 🛎 All major cards

🏨 🍽 SWISS GRAND HOTEL BONDI BEACH
$$
CORNER OF CAMPBELL PARADE & BEACH RD.
BONDI BEACH
TEL 9365 5666
FAX 9365 5330
New architecture facing Bondi Beach. All suites, most with balconies overlooking the water. Grand lobby with a high atrium. The well-lit restaurant provides both a buffet and a menu with an international feel, from seared kangaroo fillets to wok-style noodle dishes with seafood.
ⓘ 203 🅿 200 🔁 🔲 🔲
🏊 🏊 🛎 All major cards

🏨 DE VERE
$
44–46 MACLEAY ST.
POTTS POINT
TEL 9358 1211
FAX 9358 4685
Good quality, affordable accommodations in the middle of the lively Kings Cross entertainment and restaurant scene.
ⓘ 100 🔁 🔲 🏊 All major cards

🏨 MANHATTAN PARK INN INTERNATIONAL
$
6–8 GREENKNOWE AVE.
ELIZABETH BAY

PRICES

HOTELS
An indication of the cost of a double room without breakfast is given by **$** signs.
$$$$$	Over $280
$$$$	$200–$280
$$$	$120–$200
$$	$80–$120
$	Under $80

RESTAURANTS
An indication of the cost of a three-course dinner without drinks is given by **$** signs.
$$$$$	Over $80
$$$$	$50–$80
$$$	$35–$50
$$	$20–$35
$	Under $20

TEL 9358 1288
FAX 9357 3696
Art deco-style and traditional service in an affordable package. Some harbor views.
ⓘ 142 🅿 100 🔁 🔲 🔲
🏊 All major cards

🏨 OXFORD KOALA
$
CORNER OF OXFORD & PELICAN STS.
DARLINGHURST
TEL 9269 0645
FAX 9267 6107
Affordable rooms and apartments on Oxford Street, with nightlife, restaurants, and shopping at the door.
ⓘ 330 🅿 80 🔁 🔲 🔲
🏊 All major cards

🏨 RAVESI'S ON BONDI BEACH
$
CORNER OF CAMPBELL PARADE & HALL ST.
BONDI BEACH
TEL 9365 4422
FAX 9365 1481
Small boutique hotel right on the esplanade of Australia's most famous beach. It was developed by gutting an old hotel. Arched doors open out onto balconies overlooking the water. Large first-floor

restaurant has a relaxed atmosphere. Terrace dining, log fire in winter. Unpretentious hearty fare: oysters, salads, soup of the day, mussels, pasta, fish and chips, steak, and lamb shanks.

🚹 16 🔄 🔲 🔲 All major cards

🏨 SYDNEY STAR ACCOMMODATION
$
275 DARLINGHURST RD. DARLINGHURST
TEL 9331 1000
FAX 9380 6901
Casual atmosphere in affordable accommodations in the midst of the stylish Darlinghurst area. No private bathrooms.

🚹 10 🔲 All major cards

🏨 TOP OF THE TOWN
$
227 VICTORIA ST. KINGS CROSS
TEL 9361 0911
FAX 9361 4972
Just to one side of the hustle and bustle of the center of Kings Cross, this hotel offers high-standard rooms, some with harbor and city views.

🚹 101 🅿 50 🔄 🔲 🔲 All major cards

RESTAURANTS

🍴 CICADA
$$$
29 CHALLIS AVE. POTTS POINT
TEL 9358 1255
Chef/owner Peter Doyle is a prominent member of Sydney's small but talented food mafia. Polished floors, white walls, and sculptural lighting on the ground floor of a Victorian terrace house a couple of blocks away from the Kings Cross buzz. Food is inspired by the Mediterranean. A meal here might be rockfish, saffron, and harissa soup; pot-au-feu of squab in porcini bouillon with cabbage rolls; and cavolo nero or passionfruit soufflé. Huge and

ever evolving wine list, mainly Australian with some French and Italian, designed to complement Doyle's food and to preempt new wine trends.

🍴 90 🅿 Valet 🚆 Train: Kings Cross 🕐 Closed Sun. & Sat. L–Tues. 🔲 🔲 🔲 All major cards

🍴 DARLEY STREET THAI

The best Thai food in Sydney. But the head chef is Australian, and the restaurant isn't on Darley Street. David Thompson is totally committed. He uses local produce in the authentic Thai manner. Favorite dishes: Saeng Wa, grilled scallops with kaffir lime sauce; Gaeng Sap Nok: curry of chopped bird (quail, guinea fowl). The short wine list is selected to enhance the food. Design is minimalist (Burley Katon Halliday), but with warm colors, Charles Eames chairs, and a glass wall opening onto the street.
$$$
28–30 BAYSWATER RD. KINGS CROSS
TEL 9358 6530
🍴 80 🚆 Train: Kings Cross 🕐 Closed L 🔲 🔲 All major cards

🍴 BISTRO MONCUR
$$$
WOOLLAHRA HOTEL
116 QUEEN ST. WOOLLAHRA
TEL 9363 2782
The only fault with Damien Pignolet's French bistro is that you can't make reservations, but if you have to wait for a table it will be worth it. Dishes include French onion soufflé and Barossa chicken bollito misto with chicken sausage, celery hearts, and carrots.
🍴 106 🚌 Bus: 327, 389 🕐 Closed Mon. 🔲 🔲 All major cards

🍴 NIELSEN PARK KIOSK

Stylish Italian cuisine in a lovely harborside setting, doing mainly lunch, a Sunday breakfast, and dinner on three nights. Try a medley of starters: house-smoked tuna salad, marinated octopus, eggplant and ricotta pasta. Follow with tenderloin of veal with mustard, then almond and chocolate cake with vanilla gelato. In summer, take swimming things for a pre-meal plunge. B.Y.O.
$$$
GREYCLIFFE AVE. VAUCLUSE
TEL 9337 1574
🍴 100 (25 outdoors) 🅿 100 🚌 Bus: 325 from Edgecliff railway station 🚤 Water taxi 🕐 Closed Mon. & D Tues.–Thurs. 🔲 🔲 All major cards

🍴 MG GARAGE RESTAURANT
$$$
490 CROWN ST. SURRY HILLS
TEL 9383 9383
Not a drive-in restaurant, more a drive-out restaurant that combines Modern Australian cuisine with, of all things, a sports car dealership. It sounds bizarre, but it's chic and very popular.
🍴 110 🅿 Valet 🚆 Train: Central 🕐 Closed Sat. L & Sun. 🔲 🔲 🔲 All major cards

🍴 PARAMOUNT
$$$
73 MACLEAY ST. POTTS POINT
TEL 9358 1652
A longish, narrow space, somewhat hard edged despite pearly light. Famed chef Christine Manfield has a no-nonsense, assured, and highly individual approach. Try grilled tails of Moreton Bay bug (a

local crustacean) with tamarind, chili, cape gooseberries, and trout roe; or tea-smoked Szechuan duck, spiced duck sausage, smoked eggplant, and rocket. Wine list has boutique Australian wines with hard-to-find gems. Try the tasting menu with matching wines.

🔢 65 🚆 Train: Kings Cross 🕐 Closed L 🚭 💳 💳 All major cards

🍴 SALT

$$$
KIRKETON
229 DARLINGHURST RD.
DARLINGHURST
TEL 332 2566

Another of the author's personal favorites. First solo venture for hot young star, Luke Mangan, on the ground floor of the Kirketon Hotel. Clean lines; silvers, grays, and lilacs; black and white polished terrazzo floors; bustling but not deafeningly noisy. Mangan, who is classically trained, approaches his art with individual flair and a light hand. You might order raw tuna belly with soy, ginger, and shallot dressing and a Japanese egg custard, followed by salt-encrusted squab pigeon with Italian spiced potato, shallot, and sherry stock. Extensive, award-winning wine list 50-50 Australian wines and imports from New and Old Worlds.

🔢 75 🅿 Valet 🚆 Train: Kings Cross 🚭 💳 💳 All major cards

🍴 BAYSWATER BRASSERIE

$$
32 BAYSWATER RD.
KINGS CROSS
TEL 9357 2177

Nothing fazes the staff in this lively brasserie-style eatery that is a favorite of the hip Eastern Suburbs crowd. Indoor and outdoor dining.

🔢 150 🚆 Train: Kings Cross 🕐 Closed Sun. 🚭 💳 All major cards

🍴 CENTENNIAL PARK CAFÉ

$$
CORNER OF GRAND DR. & PARKES DR.
CENTENNIAL PARK
TEL 9360 3355

Café is hardly the word, with a range of cuisines on the menu and a respectable wine list. Dishes might include fresh figs with prosciutto and goat's cheese ricotta; linguine with steamed mussels and baby clams in garlic butter; and blueberry ice cream. Indoor and outdoor dining where you can watch joggers, horseback riders, and cyclists sweep by.

🔢 150 🚌 Bus: 378, 380 🕐 Closed D 🚭 All major cards

🍴 DOYLES ON THE BEACH

$$
11 MARINE PARADE
WATSONS BAY
TEL 9337 2007

The Doyle family has been feeding Sydneysiders great fish for decades. They have restaurants all over the harbor, but it all started here. They also have take-out, pub fare, and the restaurant itself. Open air.

🔢 450 🅿 70 🚌 Bus: 324, 325 ⛴ Ferry: from Circular Quay for lunch, water taxi 🚭 💳 DC, MC, V

🍴 FISHFACE

$$
132 DARLINGHURST RD.
DARLINGHURST
TEL 9332 4803

Upscale fish and seafood restaurant that creates a seaside fish shop atmosphere, but the quality of the produce would have them lining up out to sea. Menu depends on market availablility, but might include panfried cuttlefish or tempura prawns with sweet soy pepper.

🔢 40 🚆 Train: Kings Cross 🕐 Closed L Mon.–Wed. summer, Mon.–Sat. winter 🚭 💳 💳 No credit cards

---

PRICES

HOTELS
An indication of the cost of a double room without breakfast is given by **$** signs.

$$$$$	Over $280
$$$$	$200–$280
$$$	$120–$200
$$	$80–$120
$	Under $80

RESTAURANTS
An indication of the cost of a three-course dinner without drinks is given by **$** signs.

$$$$$	Over $80
$$$$	$50–$80
$$$	$35–$50
$$	$20–$35
$	Under $20

🍴 IMPERIAL HARBOURSIDE, DOUBLE BAY

$$
45A KNOX ST.
DOUBLE BAY
TEL 9326 2957

Not actually on the harbor, this nouvelle Chinese was created by restaurateur/architect Alfred Lai with an ambience of mango walls, curved granite bar, and Australian artworks. Menu has Peking panache, with a seafood accent: scallops in Harbourside sauce, salt and pepper mud crab, or lobster sashimi.

🔢 100 🚆 Train: Edgecliffe, Bus: 324, 325 🚭 💳 💳 All major cards

🍴 LA MENSA

$$
257 OXFORD ST.
PADDINGTON
TEL 9332 2963

A café that categorizes as Mediterranean, but crosses all boundaries: warm beetroot salad; grilled river trout with salsa verde; quince and pear tart. There is a communal table, indoor/outdoor dining, and groceries and vegetables for sale. Very hip, very popular.

🔢 75 🚌 Bus: 378, 380 🚭 💳 All major cards

KEY 🏨 Hotel 🍴 Restaurant ① No. of bedrooms 🔢 No. of seats 🚌 Transport 🅿 Parking 🕐 Closed 🛗 Elevator

🍴 MACLEAY STREET BISTRO
$$
73A MACLEAY ST.
POTTS POINT
TEL 9358 4891
Bistro-style fare with many influences including Modern Australian, Thai, and Spanish.
🔲 50 🚃 Train: Kings Cross
🕐 Closed Mon. L–Thurs.
🚭 🏧 All major cards

🍴 PRASIT'S NORTHSIDE ON CROWN
$$
413 CROWN ST.
SURRY HILLS
TEL 9319 0748
A very high standard of Thai food in a stylish restaurant, a delight in summer when it opens all its windows and is more outdoor than indoor.
🔲 90 🚃 Train: Central
🕐 Closed Sun. & Sat. L–Wed. 🚭 🏧 AE, MC, V

🍴 RAVESI'S ON BONDI BEACH
$$
CORNER OF CAMPBELL PARADE & HALL ST.
BONDI BEACH
TEL 9365 4422
Modern Australian cuisine with a seafood emphasis. Well, it would have to be, given the location with balconies overlooking Bondi Beach.
🔲 110 🅿 Voucher parking
🚌 Bus: 380, L82 🚭 🏧 All major cards

🍴 STAR BAR & GRILL
$$
155 VICTORIA ST.
POTTS POINT
TEL 9356 2911
Another of the Rockpool group of restaurants. This one serves rotisserie-roasted spice-rubbed meats, and dishes with a Mediterranean flavor such as squid ink risotto and stuffed shoulder of lamb.
🔲 110 🚃 Train: Kings Cross 🕐 Closed Sat. L–Tues. 🚭 🚭 🏧 All major cards

🍴 TRE SCALINI
$$
174 LIVERPOOL ST.
EAST SYDNEY
TEL 9331 4358
Busy, friendly Italian restaurant with a regular clientele in an area that abounds in Italian restaurants. Specialties include mud crab pasta with a tomato, cream, and brandy sauce; rolled fillets of veal filled with spinach, cheese, and parsley; tiramisù for dessert.
🔲 70 🚃 Train: Museum
🕐 Closed Sat. L & Sun. 🚭
🚭 🏧 All major cards

🍴 BAR COLUZZI
$
322 VICTORIA ST.
DARLINGHURST
TEL 9380 5420
Open from 5 a.m. until around 7 p.m., this little café with a big reputation serves very good coffee. It looks run-down, but decades of upscale custom have made it a Sydney institution.
🔲 14 🚃 Train: Kings Cross
🕐 Closed D 🏧 No credit cards

🍴 BILL'S
$
433 LIVERPOOL ST.
DARLINGHURST
TEL 9360 9631
Upscale café, small, light, sunny, and busy, with an eclectic menu. Try coriander noodle salad with seared salmon and a soy dressing. Also Bill's 2, 359 Crown St., Surry Hills, Tel 9360 4762; B.Y.O.
🔲 40 🚌 Bus: 389
🕐 Closed Sun. & D daily
🚭 🏧 All major cards

🍴 DOV
$
CORNER OF FORBES & BURTON STS.
EAST SYDNEY
TEL 9360 9594
Stylish café-restaurant serving a Modern Australian menu in a renovated sandstone building. Popular with the chic set. B.Y.O.

🍴 [continued]
🔲 50 🚃 Train: Kings Cross
🕐 Closed Sun. D 🏧 MC, V

🍴 ONDE
$
346 LIVERPOOL ST.
DARLINGHURST
TEL 9331 8749
Popular French bistro in a busy restaurant district. Sister restaurant Onzain overlooks Bondi Beach.
🔲 34 🚃 Train: Kings Cross
🕐 Closed L 🏧 All major cards

🍴 ORIGAMI
$
150 LIVERPOOL ST.
DARLINGHURST
TEL 9331 3733
One of the best and most affordable Japanese restaurants in Sydney, a long-time survivor in a competitive area.
🔲 120 🚃 Train: Museum
🕐 Closed Sat. L & Sun. 🚭
🏧 All major cards

🍴 RAW BAR
$
CORNER OF WAIROA & WARNERS AVES.
BONDI BEACH
TEL 9365 7200
It would have to be Japanese, and it is, with views to North Bondi Beach. This busy little place does sushi, tempura, and ramen, complemented by vegetarian options. B.Y.O.
🔲 60 🚌 Bus: 378, 380, L82
🚭 🏧 All major cards

🍴 ZIGOLINI'S
$
107 QUEEN ST.
WOOLLAHRA
TEL 9326 2337
Zigolini's does high standard Modern Australian fare and pays attention to details, such as providing a great range of teas (served in teapots). Stylish decor and atmosphere.
🔲 60 🅿 16 🚌 Bus: 327, 389
🕐 Closed Sun. D & Mon.
🚭 🏧 All major cards

HOTELS & RESTAURANTS

WESTERN SUBURBS

RESTAURANTS

🍴 BOATHOUSE ON BLACKWATTLE BAY
$$$
END OF FERRY RD.
GLEBE
TEL 9518 9011
Seafood is the dominant influence in the Modern Australian cuisine served at this superbly located restaurant overlooking Blackwattle Bay and the Sydney Fish Market.
🛏 100 🅿 40 🚍 Bus: 431; Sydney Light Rail to Wentworth Park 🕑 Closed Mon. 🄢 🄢 🄢 All major cards

🍴 BIRD, COW, FISH
$$
2/239 DARLING ST.
BALMAIN
TEL 9810 8281
An open kitchen, dark wood tables and chairs, white napkins, and crockery create a relaxed atmosphere. Owner Alan Saponari's seasonal menu changes daily. It might include roasted sea bass with saffron potatoes; duck confit with braised Puy lentils; and flourless chocolate torte with pistachio ice cream. B.Y.O.
🛏 45 🚍 Bus: 433, 452 🕑 Closed Sun., & L daily 🄢 🄢 All major cards

🍴 RAZOR'S EDGE
$$
129 ENMORE RD.
ENMORE
TEL 9557 5867
A personal favorite. Intimate atmosphere with a small but continually changing menu that caters half and half for vegetarians and carnivores. You might find celeriac and shallot soup; savory beetroot pudding with sultanas, raisins, dill, spinach, and orange zest; and baked quail with grape vinaigrette. B.Y.O.
🛏 80 🚍 Train: Newtown

🕑 Closed Sun.–Mon. & L daily 🄢 No credit cards

🍴 ROZELLE FISH BOWL
$$
580 DARLING ST.
ROZELLE
TEL 9555 7302
Seafood restaurant that offers great value and superb standards. Small and busy, especially on weekends, bench seating around the walls and in front of the open kitchen. Try Tandoori Atlantic salmon with cucumber and Spanish onion salsa; carpaccio of yellowfin tuna, salted cucumber, and trout roe; classic barbecued or beer-battered fish and chunky chips with lemon myrtle mayonnaise.
🛏 38 🅿 8 🚍 Bus: 500 🕑 Closed Sun.–Mon. & L daily 🄢 🄢 🄢 All major cards

🍴 BAR ITALIA
$
171 NORTON ST.
LEICHHARDT
TEL 9560 9981
One of the signature cafés of this Italian Quarter, where you can get industrial strength coffee, focaccia, gelato, and more while watching the beautiful people parade in the evenings.
🛏 250 🚍 Bus: 438, 436 🄢 🄢 No credit cards

🍴 BAY TINH
$
318 VICTORIA RD.
MARRICKVILLE
TEL 9560 8673
There are many Vietnamese restaurants in this area, but Bay Tinh is one of the best. Try beef and prawn pâté rolls barbecued and served with steamed rice noodles, salad, and hoisin sauce; marinated prawn, chicken, and onion hot pot served with rice papers, salad, and anchovy sauce. B.Y.O.
🛏 100 🚍 Bus: 423, 426 🕑 Closed Sun. L 🄢 🄢 Except on weekends 🄢 MC, V

🍴 BOROBUDUR
$
123–125 GLEBE POINT RD.
GLEBE
TEL 9660 5611
One of the Sydney institutions, Borobudur has been showing locals the best of Indonesian cuisine in a relaxed atmosphere and at an affordable price for the last 20 years.
🛏 120 🚍 Bus: 431 🕑 Closed Sun. & L daily 🄢 🄢 🄢 All major cards

🍴 ELIZABETH FARM TEA ROOM
$
70 ALICE ST.
ROSEHILL
TEL 9635 9488
A pleasant setting for indoor or outdoor dining, with good-value meals. This is the ideal lunch stop if you are sightseeing around Parramatta.
🛏 90 🚍 Train: Parramatta or Harris Park, or RiverCat then Parramatta Explorer bus 🕑 Closed D 🄢 🄢 MC, V

🍴 SUMALEE
$
BANK HOTEL, 324 KING ST.
NEWTOWN
TEL 9565 1730
It's not easy to find (downstairs at the back of the pub), it's all outdoor, and you have to line up to order your meal. However, the swarms of locals attest to the sheer quality of the Thai food offered on a street where every second restaurant is Thai.
🛏 300 🚍 Train: Newtown 🕑 Closed L Mon. 🄢 MC, V

🍴 THAI POTHONG
$
294 KING ST.
NEWTOWN
TEL 9550 6277
Contender for best Thai restaurant on King Street (and in Sydney), the Pothong is lively and popular yet affordably elegant. Extensive menu covers all tastes, with vegetarian, seafood, curry, stir fry, and Thai

salad dishes. Comprehensive wine list, also B.Y.O. Note: Reservations are vital on Friday and Saturday.
📅 280 🚆 Train: Newtown ⏰ Closed Mon. L 🚭 Except Fri. & Sat. 🅰 💳 All major cards

EXCURSIONS

PITTWATER

HOTELS

🏨 JONAH'S RESTAURANT 🍴 & ACCOMMODATION
$$
69 BYNYA RD.
PALM BEACH
TEL 9974 5599
FAX 9974 1212
Small, luxury boutique retreat on Sydney's Northern Beaches, an hour or so by car from the CBD. Peerless cliff-top site overlooking Whale Beach. The restaurant serves French-Mediterranean-style food with an emphasis on seafood.
🛏 8 🅿 40 🚭 🅰 💳 All major cards

🏨 PASADENA ON PITTWATER
$$
1858 PITTWATER RD.
CHURCH POINT
TEL 9979 6633
FAX 9979 6147
Situated on the water at Church Point, the Pasadena offers affordable accommodations in an idyllic setting with a fine restaurant attached.
🛏 14 🅿 30 🚭 🅰 💳 All major cards

RESTAURANTS

🍴 COTTAGE POINT RESTAURANT
$$$
2 ANDERSON PLACE
COTTAGE POINT
TEL 9456 1011
A slice of waterside heaven, this renovated boat shed overlooks the tranquil beauty of Cowan Waters and Coal &

Candle Creek in the Ku-ring-gai Chase National Park. Try the tuna carpaccio on shaved fennel with white truffle oil and Sevruga caviar, or oven-roasted guinea fowl, braised eschalots, and asparagus.
📅 95 ⛴ Ferry from Palm Beach, seaplane from Rose Bay ⏰ Closed D Mon. & Tues. 🅰 💳 All major cards

🍴 NEWPORT ARMS
$
KALINYA ST.
NEWPORT
TEL 9997 4900
Bistro, restaurant, or café—take your pick. There is plenty of seafood available to suit every budget, and pleasant views across the southern reaches of Pittwater.
📅 1000 🅿 60 ⏰ Closed Sun. 🚌 Bus: 187, L90 🅰 🚭 💳 All major cards

HAWKESBURY

HOTELS

🏨 WISEMANS FERRY COUNTRY RETREAT
$
OLD NORTHERN RD.
WISEMANS FERRY
TEL (02) 4566 4422
FAX (02) 4566 4613
Motel accommodations in a beautiful setting on the banks of the Hawkesbury River. A 9-hole golf course, tennis courts, pool, and restaurant.
🛏 30 🅿 100+ 🅰 🚭 🏊 💳 MC, V

FARTHER AFIELD

HUNTER VALLEY

HOTELS

🏨 THE CONVENT PEPPER TREE
$$$
HALLS RD.
POKOLBIN
TEL (02) 4998 7764
FAX (02) 4998 7323
The convent, built in 1909 in

PRICES

HOTELS
An indication of the cost of a double room without breakfast is given by **$** signs.
$$$$$	Over $280
$$$$	$200–$280
$$$	$120–$200
$$	$80–$120
$	Under $80

RESTAURANTS
An indication of the cost of a three-course dinner without drinks is given by **$** signs.
$$$$$	Over $80
$$$$	$50–$80
$$$	$35–$50
$$	$20–$35
$	Under $20

the New South Wales town of Coonamble, was saved from demolition and moved 600 km (375 miles) to the grounds of Pepper Tree Wines (see p. 210). The spacious rooms have high ceilings, most opening out onto a balcony or veranda. The decor is romantic with rich fabrics, gilt, and white cane furniture. A formal drawing room is furnished with antiques. Swimming pool, spa, tennis court, and mountain bikes for rent. Also here is Robert's restaurant (see p. 254).
🛏 17 🅿 20 🚭 🅰 🏊 💳 All major cards

🏨 PEPPERS GUESTHOUSE HUNTER VALLEY
$$$
EKERTS RD.
POKOLBIN
TEL (02) 4998 7596
FAX (02) 4998 7739
Deluxe guesthouse set among lush, fragrant gardens. Country rooms feature antique and rustic furnishings.
🛏 47 🅿 50 🅰 🏊 🏊 💳 All major cards

🚭 Non-smoking 🅰 Air-conditioning 🏊 Indoor/🏊 Outdoor swimming pool 🏋 Health club 💳 Credit cards   **KEY**

HOTELS & RESTAURANTS

🏨 VINEYARD RESORT
$$
CORNER OF BROKE
& MCDONALD RDS.
POKOLBIN
TEL (02) 4998 7600
FAX (02) 4998 7710
A wide range of affordable
accommodations to suit most
budgets. The resort has full
facilities in a parklike setting
with several wineries within
very short walking distance.
🛏 282 🅿 600+ 🚭 ♿
🛎 🏊 🎾 ♠ All major
cards

RESTAURANTS

SOMETHING SPECIAL

🍴 BLAXLANDS
An 1829 sandstone home-
stead set among the
grapevines. In summer dine
on the terrace overlooking
the rose garden. Relaxed
atmosphere, small seasonal
country-style menu. Try local
asparagus with a lime hol-
landaise sauce, lamb brains
thermidor, oven roasted duck
with caramelized apple, garlic
green prawn and scallop
mornay, and Jack Daniels
Tennessee mud cake. Hunter
Valley wines.
$$$
BROKE RD.
POKOLBIN
TEL (02) 4998 7550
🍴 80 🅿 50 🚆 Vine-
yard shuttle service 🚭
♿ ♠ All major cards

🍴 CASUARINA RESTAURANT
$$$
HERMITAGE RD.
POKOLBIN
TEL (02) 4998 7888
Set in a Lower Hunter Valley
vineyard, an elegant restaurant
with terra-cotta washed
walls, Victorian lighting, and
antique furnishings. The
Casuarina Country Inn is on
the same property. Chef Peter
Myer's eclectic Mediter-Asian

cuisine includes his renowned
flambés for two or more—
try chili lobster and prawn—
rabbit casserole, blueswimmer
crab cakes, grilled ocean trout,
and a superior Caesar salad.
An extensive wine list, all of
Hunter Valley wines and one
vintage of Moet!
🍴 110 🅿 60 🚆 Vineyard
shuttle service 🕐 Closed L
Mon.–Sat. 🚭 ♿ ♠ All
major cards

🍴 CHEZ POK
$$$
PEPPERS GUESTHOUSE
EKERT'S RD.
POKOLBIN
TEL (02) 4998 7596
Popular and highly acclaimed
restaurant with an emphasis
on local produce in a country-
style setting with French
influences. Good for anything
from a coffee to a banquet.
🍴 100 🅿 60 🚆 Vineyard
shuttle service 🚭 ♿
♠ All major cards

🍴 ROBERT'S AT PEPPER TREE
$$$
HALL'S RD.
POKOLBIN
TEL (02) 4998 7330
Adjoins National Trust-listed
Pepper Tree Cottage (built
1876) on Pepper Tree Wines
estate (see p. 210). From a
wood-fired oven fueled by
vine clippings, chef Robert
Molines produces dishes such
as pheasant with wild mush-
rooms or suckling rack of
lamb with baby aubergine, and
desserts such as pear and
mascarpone tart or wild
berry waffles. Wine list
showcases Hunter Valley
vineyards.
🍴 90 🅿 🚆 Vineyard
shuttle service 🚭 ♿
♠ All major cards

🍴 COTTAGE RESTAURANT
$$
109 WOLLOMBI RD.
CESSNOCK
TEL (02) 4990 3062

Modern Australian cuisine,
with its eye firmly on local
wines, in the Lower Hunter's
major town. Elegant and
sophisticated setting.
🍴 65 🚆 Vineyard shuttle
service 🕐 Closed Sun.–
Mon. & L daily 🚭 ♿
♠ All major cards

CENTRAL COAST

HOTELS

🏨 RAFFERTY'S RESORT
$$
7 RAFFERTY'S RD.
CAMS WHARF
TEL (02) 4972 5555
FAX (02) 4972 5253
Very comfortable detached
and duplex cottage accom-
modations on the shores of
Lake Macquarie, 70 miles
(112 km) north of Sydney.
Units have verandas, stoves,
dishwashers, TV and VCR,
washers and dryers, and air-
conditioning. Set amid 35
acres (14 ha) of native flora
on the shores of Lake
Macquarie, the resort has
three swimming pools (one
heated), barbecue facilities,
tennis courts, canoes and
dinghies, and a boat ramp.
The English chef does a
menu of seafood, steaks,
pasta, homemade breads, and
ice cream.
🛏 61 🅿 70 🚭 ♿ 🏊
♠ AE, MC, V

🏨 SURFSIDE PALM BEACH RESORT
$
56–58 OCEAN PARADE
THE ENTRANCE
TEL (02) 4333 1902
FAX (02) 4334 5888
Fourteen self-contained
vacation units—some
budget, some deluxe—in a
quiet tropical garden 100
yards (91 m) from The
Entrance beach and the
channel to Tuggerah Lake.
Solar-heated pool and spa,
and a game room.
🛏 14 🅿 14 🚭 🏊
♠ AE, MC, V

🏨 COUNTRY COMFORT INN TERRIGAL
$

154 TERRIGAL DR.
TERRIGAL
TEL 02 4384 1166
FAX 02 4385 1480

First-class motel overlooking the Pacific Ocean with the restaurants, shopping, and vacation entertainment of Terrigal within walking distance.

ⓘ 47 🅿 50 🚭 ❄ 🏊
🅰 All major cards

BLUE MOUNTAINS

HOTELS

SOMETHING SPECIAL

🏨 CLEOPATRA

There are only five suites in this National Trust house, built circa 1880. It is the acme of elegance, with a beautiful garden and much-vaunted restaurant (see p. 256). Packages comprise dinner and bed-and-breakfast. Weekends are more expensive. There is a tennis court, and all the Blue Mountains attractions are close by.

$$$$

118 CLEOPATRA ST.
BLACKHEATH
TEL (02) 4787 8456
FAX (02) 4787 6238

ⓘ 5 🕐 Closed Jan. 🚭
🅰 All major cards

🏨 LILIANFELS BLUE 🍴 MOUNTAINS
$$$

LILIANFELS AVE.
ECHO POINT
KATOOMBA
TEL (02) 4780 1200
FAX (02) 4780 1300

Multi-award winning hotel with superb views of the Jamison Valley. The original National Trust-protected grand colonial house and gardens contain function rooms and a restaurant. The airy, spacious rooms are in a newer redbrick wing that echoes the Victorian opulence of the main building. There is also a huge lounge with floor-to-ceiling windows, piano, and open fire in winter. For the energetic horseback riding, golf, bush walks, and mountain bike rides are all nearby. Chef Ralph Potter cooks country-style with an emphasis on meats and game at Darley's, and lighter food with an Asian-Mediterranean influence at Lillian's. The wine list at both features wines from Cowra, Mudgee, Orange, and the Hunter Valley.

ⓘ 86 🅿 50 ❄ 🚭 🏊
🏊 🍸 🅰 All major cards

🏨 ECHOES
🍴 **$$$**

3 LILIANFELS AVE.
ECHO POINT
KATOOMBA
TEL (02) 4782 1966
FAX (02) 4782 3707

This modern guesthouse was built to capitalize on splendid views of the Jamison Valley. The foyer has cathedral ceilings, while the upstairs restaurant and lounge have sofas and open fires in winter overlooking the valley. Upstairs rooms have balconies, downstairs they open onto verandas and the lawn. The restaurant serves a relaxed lunch on the terrace overhanging the valley, weather permitting, and a formal dinner of country fare with a French flavor: poached chicken breast with quince and lemon thyme; roast saddle of lamb with white bean ragout, Savoy cabbage, and spring onions. Wine list emphasizes small local wineries.

ⓘ 12 🅿 14 🚭 ❄
🅰 All major cards

🏨 FAIRMONT RESORT
🍴 **$$$**

1 SUBLIME POINT RD.
LEURA
TEL (02) 4782 5222
FAX (02) 4784 1685

Large imposing resort hotel, built high on a ridgetop overlooking the rugged Jamison Valley. Spacious rooms, family accommodations, and suites overlook the valley, grounds, or nearby Leura golf course. The restaurant offers a fixed-price buffet and formal dining several nights a week.

ⓘ 210 🅿 200 ❄ 🚭 ❄
🏊 🏊 🍸 🅰 All major cards

🏨 JEMBY-RINJAH LODGE
$$

336 EVANS LOOKOUT RD.
BLACKHEATH
TEL (02) 4787 7622
FAX (02) 4787 6230

Situated on the road to Evans Lookout, this resort operates to stringent environmental principles and offers a beautiful bushland setting. Restaurant operates on weekends and some week nights. Walking trails at the door.

ⓘ 10 Cabins with kitchens
🅿 10 🚭 🅰 All major cards

🏨 MOUNTAIN HERITAGE 🍴 COUNTRY HOUSE RETREAT
$$

CORNER OF APEX & LOVEL STS., KATOOMBA
TEL (02) 4782 2155
FAX (02) 4782 5323

Grand turn-of-the-century guesthouse, in a secluded spot but close to Katoomba's pubs and antique and gift shops. Family-run for the past 20 years, it is set on a hill with wonderful views. Its light and spacious rooms and suites have beautiful heritage decor, with handmade furniture made from recycled timbers. All have private bathrooms, some with spas and open fires. Lounge and dining room have open fires in winter and valley views. Seasonal, reasonably priced menu from cardamom tuna fillet smoked on the premises to spicy marinated kangaroo loin char-grilled rare with bok choy greens, oyster mushrooms, and pumpkin with a mild curry

---

sauce. Try the strawberries Romanoff or hot apple and rosella tartlet.

🛈 40 🅿 50 Ⓢ Ⓢ 🏊
Ⓢ All major cards

🏨 ROWAN BRAE
$$
282–285 GREAT WESTERN HWY.
BLACKHEATH
TEL (02) 4787 8296
FAX (02) 4787 7888
Affordable elegance in a delightful mountain home built circa 1896. Warm and helpful hospitality. Croquet on the lawn is an amusing diversion.

🛈 9 🅿 9 Ⓢ Ⓢ AE, MC

🏨 LEURA GARDENS IBIS RESORT
$$$
44 FITZROY ST.
LEURA
TEL (02) 4784 1331
FAX (02) 4784 1813
First-class motel amid four acres (2 ha) of award-winning landscaped gardens. Rooms feature country-style furnishings.

🛈 78 🅿 80 Ⓢ Ⓢ 🏊
🍴 Ⓢ All major cards

🍴 CLEOPATRA
$$$
118 CLEOPATRA ST.
BLACKHEATH
TEL (02) 4787 8456
Award-winning chef Dany Chouet draws on regional French cuisines, using the finest Australian produce with much-acclaimed finesse and lightness of touch. In winter there will be duck livers with a maize pancake, rabbit pie, or a cassoulet of beans, pork, duck confit, and sausage. In the summer, try lunch in the garden: spatchcock with grapes, and individual pear tart with cognac ice cream. B.Y.O.

🍽 50 🚆 Train: Blackheath, then taxi 🕐 Closed L Mon.– Sat. Ⓢ Ⓢ All major cards

🍴 AVALON
$$
98 MAIN ST.
KATOOMBA
TEL (02) 4782 5532
Upstairs over an old shop in downtown Katoomba, run by artists Glen Puster and Gail Pollard with an individual dash. Buzzing on weekends, quieter mid-week. Eclectic menu, daily specials. Try Glen's lamb loin fillet rolled in garlic and thyme, wrapped in bacon with red wine sauce and a lime glaze; or warm chicken tenderloin panfried with capsicum, marinated eggplant, and warm orange and ginger dressing tossed with lettuce and sprinkled with parmesan; or Gail's delicious desserts: rich chocolate cheesecake, warm sticky date pudding, or open meringues topped with fresh berries. B.Y.O.

🍽 80 🚆 Train: Katoomba 🕐 Closed L Mon.–Wed. & Sat. Ⓢ Ⓢ MC, V

🍴 CAFÉ BON TON
$$
192 THE MALL
LEURA
TEL (02) 4782 4377
Located in a mountain garden setting in a former butcher's shop, this café serves light lunches and beautiful tea and cakes. But the real action is in the evening when the log fire and hearty meals come into their own.

🍽 75 🅿 6 🚆 Train: Leura 🕐 Closed D Tues. Ⓢ Ⓢ AE, MC, V

🍴 MOUNT TOMAH BOTANIC GARDENS RESTAURANT
$$
BELL'S LINE OF RD.
MOUNT TOMAH, VIA BILPIN
TEL (02) 4567 2060
Superb Modern Australian fare with indoor and outdoor dining and views that extend forever. It's unlicensed, so buy a bottle before setting out as there are no outlets anywhere nearby. Reservations only.

🍽 170 🅿 450 🕐 Closed D (except Sat.) Oct.–March Ⓢ Ⓢ MC, V

🍴 ARJUNA INDIAN RESTAURANT
$
16 VALLEY RD.
KATOOMBA
TEL (02) 4782 4662
Classic north Indian and tandoori cuisine comes with spectacular Megalong and Jamison Valley views. Spicy menu with ample vegetarian options. B.Y.O.

🍽 80 🅿 10 🚆 Train: Katoomba 🕐 Closed Tues.–Wed. & L daily Ⓢ Ⓢ AE, MC, V

SOUTH COAST

HOTELS

SOMETHING SPECIAL

🏨 MILTON PARK

Grand old country house hotel set on more than 300 acres (120 ha). The original house has a lounge with open fires in winter, and a restaurant with vaulted ceilings, rich tapestries, and warm colors. Guest rooms, in a newer wing, display period furniture and original paintings. The seasonal menu has European and Asian influences; mainly Australian wine list includes current releases as well as classic vintages.

$$$$
HORDERNS RD.
BOWRAL
TEL (02) 4861 1522
FAX (02) 4861 4716
🛈 40 🅿 100 Ⓢ 🏊
Ⓢ All major cards

🏨 JERVIS BAY HOUSE
$$
1 CAROLINE ST.
VINCENTIA
TEL (02) 4441 7476
FAX (02) 4441 7476
Luxury bed-and-breakfast accommodations on the

beach close to the main town of Huskisson, with sweeping views from the balconies and pool out over Jervis Bay.
ℹ️ 3 🅿️ 5 ☲ 💳 MC, V

SADDLEBACK MOUNTAIN HOUSE
$$
SADDLEBACK MOUNTAIN RD.
VIA KIAMA
TEL (02) 4232 3969
FAX (02) 4232 2248
Magnificent views out to sea and over scenic dairy pastureland for nearly 100 miles (160 km) to the north, south, and east. This bed-and-breakfast (with restaurant) has enclosed verandas, elegant sitting rooms, and exquisite antique furniture. The beach is a short drive from the house.
ℹ️ 5 🅿️ 25 ❄️ 🚭
💳 MC, V

BEACH HOUSE MOLLYMOOK
$
3 GOLF AVE.
MOLLYMOOK
TEL (02) 4455 1966
FAX (02) 4455 3841
Comfortable and affordable B&B accommodations in a beachfront location overlooking the Pacific Ocean and with a golf course at the door.
ℹ️ 15 🅿️ 15 ☲ 💳 MC, V

SOUTHERN HIGHLANDS

HOTELS

PEPPERS MANOR HOUSE MOUNT BROUGHTON
$$$
KATER RD.
SUTTON FOREST
TEL (02) 4868 2355
FAX (02) 4868 3257
First-class hotel in an idyllic rural setting, next to a golf course, with all facilities and considerable old-style opulence and charm. All packages include breakfast; minimum stay two nights on weekends.

ℹ️ 43 🅿️ 45 ☲ 💳 All major cards

BERIDA MANOR COUNTRY HOTEL
$$
6 DAVID ST.
BOWRAL
TEL (02) 4861 1177
FAX (02) 4861 1219
Old-style guesthouse with full facilities in a parklike setting adjacent to the Royal Bowral Golf Course.
ℹ️ 55 🅿️ 60 🚭 ❄️ ☲
🏋️ 💳 All major cards

CANBERRA

HOTELS

HYATT HOTEL CANBERRA
$$$
COMMONWEALTH AVE.
YARRALUMLA
TEL (02) 6270 1234
FAX (02) 6281 5998
Art deco-style building that was formerly (and to an extent still is) the favored watering hole of the city's power brokers. Accommodations are elegant and stylish.
ℹ️ 249 🅿️ 270 🚭 ❄️ 🚭
☲ 🏋️ 💳 All major cards

CHIFLEY ON NORTHBOURNE
$$
102 NORTHBOURNE AVE.
BRADDON
TEL (02) 6249 1411
FAX (02) 6249 6878
First-class motel accommodations on one of the main roads a couple of blocks from downtown. Poolside rooms open onto balconies.
ℹ️ 78 🅿️ 80 🚭 ❄️ 🚭
☲ 🏋️ 💳 All major cards

CAPITAL PARKROYAL
$$
1 BINARA ST.
CANBERRA CITY
TEL (02) 6247 8999
FAX (02) 6257 4903
Top-notch accommodations in the business district with the Canberra casino nearby.

Built in 1986, rooms are larger than usual and most overlook the green lawns of a park. Public areas are light and spacious with an atrium roof.
ℹ️ 293 🅿️ 202 🚭 ❄️ 🚭
☲ 🏋️ 💳 All major cards

RESTAURANTS

🍴 FRINGE BENEFITS
$$
54 MARCUS CLARKE ST.
CANBERRA CITY
TEL (02) 6247 4042
Upscale Modern Australian with the usual Asian and seafood influences thrown in. Convivial atmosphere. Budget travelers can still find reasonably priced dishes.
🍽️ 40 🕐 Closed Sun. & Sat. L 🚭 Outside tables for smokers 💳 All major cards

🍴 MANUKA DELI
$$
STYLE ARCADE
FRANKLIN ST.
MANUKA
TEL (02) 6295 0755
One of many eateries in this chic shopping precinct. Modern Australian cuisine with influences from Asia and the Mediterranean in the café-style menu. Winner of architectural awards for design as well as for regional café food.
🍽️ 40+46 🚌 Bus: 238, 265, 310, 311 🕐 Closed Sat.–Sun. & D Mon.–Thurs.
🚭 ❄️ 💳 MC, V

🍴 TU DO
$
7 SARGOOD ST.
O'CONNOR
TEL (02) 6248 6030
Vietnamese restaurant, in rather ordinary premises, but setting a high standard with the food. Try paper rolls with pork, prawns, and herbs; lemongrass and chili chicken; satay king prawns.
🍽️ 50 🚌 Bus: 307 🚭 ❄️
💳 All major cards

SHOPPING

Names, names, names. A walk through Sydney's main shopping strips can sometimes be little different from a shopping trip in New York, Tokyo, or Paris. All the big names in fashion and jewelry are represented, which isn't much help if you're looking for things to take home that have a distinctly Australian flavor. But there are several items that are definitely worth seeking out. Jewelry is the obvious first stop—with exquisite South Pacific pearls, dazzling opals, diamonds, and gold sourced from around the country and its seas. Aboriginal art and artifacts are extremely popular, and the best items are highly prized on the international market. Australian wines make great gifts, as well as a welcome addition to a harborside picnic. Finally, you can outfit yourself in genuine Outback clothing so you'll not only look the part, but you can handle the worst the climate can throw at you.

Specialty shops are usually open nine to five (to noon Saturdays, closed on Sundays), but in popular tourist areas you'll find they are considerably more flexible, and are often open all day and into the night seven days a week.

ANTIQUE & AUCTION HOUSES

Christie's
180 Jersey Rd., Woollahra
Tel 9326 1422
International auction house specializing in Australian, European, and Southeast Asian paintings, plus Aboriginal art, jewelry, antiques, decorative arts, books, and memorabilia.

Lawsons Fine Art Auctions
212 Cumberland St.
Tel 9241 3411
Regular auctions of decorative art, fine jewelry, books, maps and prints, antique and modern silver, tribal art, and fine wines.

Sotheby's
Level 1, 118–122 Queen St.
Woollahra
Tel 9362 1000
International auction house specializing in Australian and European paintings and sculpture, Aboriginal and Oceanic art, jewelry, antiques, and decorative and Oriental works of art.

Sydney Antique Centre
531 S. Dowling St.
Surry Hills
Tel 9361 3244

A collection of antique stores all under one roof. Extensive stock ranging from small collectibles to large pieces and historically significant furniture.

ARCADES & MALLS

Chifley Plaza
Chifley Square
Corner of Hunter & Philip Sts.
Tel 9221 4500
Upscale arcade area with the emphasis on international clothing and jewelry names.

Harbourside Shopping Complex
Darling Harbour
Tel 9281 3999
Gift-oriented shopping, including some significant Aboriginal operations. Budget eateries and bars also abound.

King Street Shopping Precinct
King St., Newtown
One of the most bohemian and stylish of the city's shopping areas. There are antique shops, second-hand bookshops, and clothing stores among the Thai restaurants and hairdressers.

MLC Centre
Corner of King & Castlereagh Sts.
Tel 9224 8333
Upscale arcade area with the emphasis on international clothing and jewelry names.

Paddington Shopping Precinct
Oxford & Queen Streets
Paddington
Food, clothing, houseware, and jewelry stores among the numerous cafés, pubs, and restaurants, catering to a chic Eastern Suburbs clientele.

Pitt St. Mall
Pitt St.
Boutiques, music stores, and bookshops, plus the Olympic Store. Many Victorian facades. Entrance to Strand Arcade, Skygarden Arcade, Centrepoint, and Grace Bros. department store.

Queen Victoria Building
455 George St.
Tel 9264 1955
Elegant, multi-level shopping gallery specializing in local and international designer wear and jewelers, plus giftware and stylish cafés (see p. 111).

Skygarden
77 Castlereagh St.
Tel 9231 1811
Arcade with stores selling local and international clothing labels and jewelry.

Strand Arcade
193 Pitt St.
Tel 9232 4199
Step back in time in this graceful Victorian arcade. Four levels of trendy Australian designer-label clothing, jewelry, antiques, cafés, unique gift shops, and beauty salons. The Strand Hatters (for a genuine Australian fur-felt Akubra or the finest quality Ecuadorean panama) and the Old Sydney Coffee Shop have been there since the arcade opened in 1892.

AUSTRALIAN CRAFTS & GOODS

Australian Craftworks
127 George St., The Rocks
Tel 9247 7156
Housed in the historic Old Police Station. A retail and exhibition gallery representing

400 Australian craftspeople: ceramics, glass, hand-turned wood, textiles, jewelry, leather, prints, Aboriginal art.

Object-Centre for Contemporary Craft
3rd Floor, Customs House, 31 Alfred St., Circular Quay
Tel 9247 9126
Not-for-profit showcase for Australian craft and design. Exhibition spaces, a publishing section, studios—and a retail section on the ground floor.

Dorian Scott
105 George St., The Rocks
Tel 9221 8145
Sydney International Airport
Tel 9317 2881
Australian-made products: Drizabone oilskins, hand knit and Coogi sweaters, Helen Kaminski handwoven raffia hats, Maggie Shepherd women's after-five wear, children's wear, Rossi boots.

BOOKS & PRINTS

Angus & Robertson Bookworld
Imperial Arcade, 168 Pitt St.
Tel 9235 1188
Located in the Pitt Street Mall, this is one of the city's two main bookstores, with an incredible range of subjects, guides, general titles, fiction, and a good magazine section.

Dymocks Booksellers
424–430 George St.
Tel 9235 0155
The second of Sydney's largest bookstores, with a great range of stationery, guides, specialty and general titles, plus local and international fiction.

Ken Duncan Gallery
73 George St., The Rocks
Tel 9241 3460
Limited edition panoramic Australian landscape photographs by Ken Duncan, also a range of books, posters, postcards, etc., featuring his work.

Ken Done Gallery
1–5 Hickson Road, The Rocks
Tel 9247 2740
A large selection of original oils on paper and canvas, both framed and unframed; limited edition screen prints; and a small gallery shop selling posters, cards, and other Done merchandise.

CAMERAS

Paxton's Camera & Video
285 George St.
Tel 9299 2999
Still, digital, and video cameras and accessories.

Ted's Camera Store
254 Pitt St.
Tel 9264 8422
SLR, digital, and video cameras and accessories, professional cameras and accessories, darkroom equipment, a secondhand section, and a mini-lab processing service.

CLOTHING & ACCESSORIES

Bally
40 Grand Walk, Queen Victoria Building, 455 George St.
Tel 9267 3887
Women's and men's shoes, handbags, briefcases, travelbags, belts, men's leather jackets, and business suits.

Chanel
70 Castlereagh St., Tel 9233 4800
Chanel-label clothes, jewelry and watches, fragrances, cosmetics, leather goods, sunglasses.

Country Road
Queen Victoria Building
142–44 Pitt St.
Tel 9394 1818
Australian-designed men's and women's clothing labels. The emphasis is on quality and understated style. There are houseware lines as well.

Done Art & Design
123 George St., Tel 9251 6099
Queen Victoria Building, 455 George St., Tel 9283 1167;

Sydney International Airport, Tel 9667 0996.
Art on clothing that uses icons such as Sydney sailboats and the Opera House as motifs for vibrant designs. Men's and women's beach and casual attire.

Double Bay Shopping Precinct
Double Bay
Upscale clothing and jewelry stores catering to the discerning and seriously well-to-do.

Alfred Dunhill
74 Castlereagh St.
Tel 9231 5511
Men's clothing, from casual and sportswear to tailored and ready-to-wear suits, plus watches and fragrances.

Emporio Armani
4 Martin Place
Tel 9231 3655
Less formal clothing from the international design house, including jeans, T-shirts, casual wear, and evening wear.

Giorgio Armani
137 Elizabeth St.
Tel 9283 5562
Stylish men's and women's formal and evening wear from this internationally known Italian house of couture.

Gucci
Shop 7, MLC Centre, King St.
Tel 9232 7565
Castlereagh St., The Rocks
Tel 9252 1663
Boutiques selling the Gucci label handbags, small leather goods, luggage, belts, footwear, homeware, jewelry, sunglasses, watches, scarves, and neckties. The Rocks shop also sells men's and women's clothing.

Hermès Paris
Skygarden, 77 Castlereagh St., Tel 9223 4007;
Regent Hotel, 199 George St., Tel 9247 1396
Hermès brand men's and women's ready-to-wear clothing, bags, scarves, shoes, leather goods.

Hunting World
MLC Centre, corner of King
& Castlereagh Sts.
Tel 9223 8870
Regent Hotel, 199 George St.
Tel 9241 3762
Men's and women's ready-to-
wear clothing, leather goods,
watches, and luggage.

Luggageland
397 George St.
Tel 9299 6699
All luggage items tax free to
visitors. Hard and soft luggage,
briefcases, leather goods. Large
stock of Zero Halliburton and
Samsonite luggage.

Mambo
17 Oxford St., Paddington
Tel 9331 8034
Hip and groovy clothing
emporium popular among the
surfing set, noted for its
distinctive, humorous, and
irreverent designs. Teenagers
and twentysomethings love it.

**Lower Oxford Street
Shopping Precinct**
Oxford St., Darlinghurst
A precinct of restaurants and
mid-market clothing stores for
men and women, covering a
range of lifestyles.

**R.M. Williams Bushman's
Outfitters**
389 George St.
Tel 9262 2228
Shop 1, 2 Chifley Plaza, corner
of Hunter & Phillip Sts.,
Tel 9223 1949
Finest quality Australiana for
Outback cow cockies and Pitt
Street farmers: men's and
women's elastic-sided riding
boots, dress boots, moleskin
skirts and trousers, oilskins,
women's jodphurs, men's dress
trousers, and much more.

Weiss Art
85 George St., The Rocks
Tel 9241 3819
A range of quality goods with
the Weiss brand. Australian-
made 100 percent cotton
T-shirts, children's and babies'
wear, cotton and polycotton

sweatshirts, and golfing products—towels, tees, balls, etc.

DEPARTMENT STORES

Argyle Stores
12 Argyle St., The Rocks
Tel 9251 4800
Next door to The Rocks Centre
and offering jewelry, clothing,
art, and souvenirs aimed at
international visitors.

David Jones
Corner of Elizabeth
& Market Sts.
Tel 13 3357
Self-described "world's most
beautiful store"; two buildings
with local and international
clothing, cosmetics, appliances,
homeware, and a stunning food
hall with several outlets for
oysters, coffee, tea, and more.

Gowings
Corner of George & Market Sts.
Tel 9264 6321
This smaller department store is
an institution in Sydney, specializing in menswear but with a
great selection of such eclectica
as Swiss Army knives and
Akubra hats (the Australian
equivalent of Stetsons).

Grace Bros.
Sydney Central Plaza,
Corner of Pitt, Mall, & Market Sts.
Tel 9238 9111
Major city department store
with a large range of local and
international clothing, appliances,
cosmetics, and more.

FOOD & WINE

Airport Fine Foods
Departure Level, International
Terminal, Sydney Airport,
Tel 9669 2740
Retail outlet selling Australian
beef, pork, kangaroo, turkey,
live lobsters, crabs, abalone,
scallops, salmon, tuna, wines,
cheeses, and canned and
bottled foods.

Australian Wine Centre
1 Alfred St., Circular Quay

Tel 9247 2755
Upscale bottle shop with
1,000 different Australian wines
in stock. They conduct tastings,
deliver to most places world-
wide, and have a wine bar next
door for those who would like
to try a glass.

Sydney Fish Market
Blackwattle Bay, Pyrmont
Tel 9660 1611
Everything under the sea (not to
mention rivers and estuaries).
Retail and wholesale businesses
operate from the early hours.
Numerous restaurants are also
on the premises. Look for
sashimi tuna and salmon, fresh
oysters, and Atlantic salmon.

GIFTS

Aussie Bear & Friends
41 Argyle St., The Rocks
Tel 9251 2901
About 5,000 teddy bears from
all the major designers. Also
teddy bear-related products and
a range of plush, handmade
cuddly Australian animals.

Cartier
43 Castlereagh St.
Tel 9235 1322
Watches, jewelry, leather bags,
wallets, pens, lighters, scarves, all
with the Cartier brand.

Clocktower Square
Corner of Argyle &
Harrington Sts., The Rocks
Tel 9247 6134
Jewelry, clothing, art, and
souvenirs aimed at Sydney's
international visitors.

DFS Australia
155 George St., The Rocks
Tel 9258 7657
Duty-free and tax-free goods
including alcohol, watches,
leather goods, ready-to-wear
clothing, cosmetics, opals, food
items, and souvenirs.

The Rocks Centre
18 Argyle St., The Rocks
Jewelry, clothing, art, and
souvenirs aimed at visitors.

Sydney Tower Duty/Tax Free Centrepoint
Corner of Castlereagh, Market, & Pitt Sts.
Tel 9231 6955
Watches, opal jewelry, leather goods, perfumes, cosmetics, souvenirs, knitwear, T-shirts. There is also a coffee shop and restaurant with a Hungarian flavor.

Woollahra Galleries
160 Oxford St., Woollahra
Tel 9327 8840.
Eclectic collection of antique furniture, jewelry, paintings, glassware, silver.

JEWELRY & GEMS

Angus & Coote Duty Free
Departures Concourse, Sydney International Airport
Tel 9667 0990
Watches from $A29 up to $A6,000; gold and silver jewelry, a range of opals, diamonds, cultured pearls, and some crystal glassware.

Flame Opals
119 George St., The Rocks
Tel 9247 3446
Extensive range of solid stones set in 18-carat gold or sterling silver.

Gemtec
51 Pitt St. (corner of Dalley St.)
Tel 9251 1599
Opal jewelry, mainly set in yellow and white gold, also loose opals. Gemtec is unusual in that it mines and cuts its own stones. For those interested in the progress from raw stone to opal ring, Gemtec has a store-front cutting and polishing room.

Makers Mark
Chifley Plaza, Corner Phillip & Hunter Sts., Chifley Sq.
Tel 9231 6800
Exciting designs from Australia's leading studio jewelers, silver-smiths, and craftspeople. Time-less classics and outrageous fashion statements, from silver coffee pots to distinctively Australian jewelry featuring

everything from industrial offcuts to pink Argyle diamonds and exquisite South Sea pearls.

Opal Fields
155 George St., The Rocks
Tel 9247 6800
Solid Australian opal stones and jewelry featuring the collections of seven designers, mostly set in white and yellow gold and platinum, but also many set in silver. See, too, their museum of opal fossils and specimens.

Paspaley Pearls
142 King St.
Tel 9232 7633
Outlet for Australia's leading supplier of South Sea pearls to the world—among the finest to be found anywhere.

Percy Marks
60–70 Elizabeth St.
Regent Hotel, 199 George St.
Hotel Inter-Continental,
    117 Macquarie St.
75½ George St., The Rocks
    Tel 9233 1355
Local jeweler specializing in the finest Australian opals, diamonds, and South Sea pearls.

The Rocks Opal Mine
Clocktower Sq., Argyle St.
The Rocks
Tel 9247 4974
A showroom selling opal stones and jewelry from $A10 to several thousand dollars, a lifesize model of a working opal mine (a small fee to enter), and an opal dig where you can fossick for your own rough opals (once again, small fee).

Rox Gems & Jewelry
Strand Arcade, 193 Pitt St. & 412–414 George St.
Tel 9232 7828
Rox has two in-house designers who specialize in distinctive contemporary pieces, often featuring platinum, diamonds, pearls, and unusual gemstones.

Tiffany & Co.
Chifley Plaza, Corner of Hunter & Phillip Sts., Chifley Sq.
Tel 9235 1777

Flagship Australian store for the famed American company. Fine jewelry, watches, and giftware.

MARKETS

Balmain Markets
St. Andrews Church, corner of Darling St. & Curtis Rd., Balmain
Tel 0418 765736
Typical range of clothing, jewelry, and art, much of it secondhand, but with the occasional gem among the trinkets.

Glebe Markets
Glebe Public School
Glebe Point Rd., Glebe
Tel (02) 4237 7499
One of the city's large and bustling weekend markets with a leaning toward the more bohemian end of the clothing and jewelry spectrum.

Paddy's Markets
9 Hay St., Haymarket
Tel 1300 361 589;
www.paddysmarkets.com.au
Bustling weekend market with everything from clothing to electrical goods to live poultry, pets, fruit, and vegetables.

Paddington Bazaar
Uniting Church, corner of Oxford & Newcombe Sts. Paddington
Tel 9331 2646
Extraordinary range of clothing, jewelry, and art stalls, plus food, massage, cosmetics, and some electrical goods. Very popular with the locals.

The Rocks Market
Upper George St., The Rocks
Tel 9255 1717
A boost to the local outlets on the weekends—all manner of souvenirs, clothing, jewelry, and art available.

ENTERTAINMENT & ACTIVITIES

It may be on the opposite side of the world from just about everywhere, but Sydney can dazzle most visitors with the range and quality of its arts and entertainment. The Sydney Opera House is the obvious focus for the arts—plays, opera, classical music, pop concerts, and more. There is certain to be something to see during even the shortest visit to Sydney. Farther afield, there are theaters, cinemas, and performance spaces in the suburbs, with sports arenas and racetracks dotted around the greater metropolitan area. All through January the city is in entertainment mode with the Sydney Festival comprising performances of every type, many of them free. Every Friday the *Sydney Morning Herald* newspaper has details of what's on in the city over the weekend and following week.

Two major ticketing agencies for theater and sports events with outlets throughout the city area are: **Ticketek,** Tel 9266 4800 and **Ticketmaster,** Tel 13 6100.

BALLET & OPERA

Australian Ballet, Sydney Opera House, Tel 9223 1088
The best of contemporary and classical works from Australia's national ballet company.

Opera Australia, Sydney Opera House, Tel 9319 9522
The third busiest opera company in the world, their repertoire spans opera from Handel and Monteverdi to Britten, Janacek, and Berg.

Sydney Dance Company, Wharf Theatre, Pier 4, Hickson Rd., Walsh Bay; and Sydney Opera House, Tel 9221 4811
Australia's leading contemporary dance company. It has toured overseas to considerable acclaim.

CINEMA

Academy Twin Cinema, 3A Oxford St., Paddington Tel 9361 4453
Venue for a mixture of mainstream, foreign-language, and non-mainstream films. The Academy hosts the Gay and Lesbian Film Festival which takes place during Mardi Gras.

Dendy Cinemas, 261 King St., Newtown Tel 9550 5699

624 George St.
Tel 9264 1577
19 Martin Place
Tel 9233 8166
Cinemas screening an eclectic range of nonmainstream and art theater films from Australia and around the world. The Martin Place location has a trendy bar/restaurant.

Greater Union Cinemas, 525 George St.
Tel 13 3456
232 Pitt St.
Tel 13 3456
Major cinemas showing mostly mainstream films, including Australian films. George St. venue has six screens and shows the latest releases.

Hoyts Cinemas, 505 George St., Tel 13 27 00
All the latest blockbusters are shown here on huge screens.

Verona Cinema, 17 Oxford St., Paddington, Tel 9360 6099
Venue for mainly art theater films. Very popular designer bar/café on the second floor.

Village Cinemas, 545 George St., Tel 9264 6701
Six-screen cinema showing mainstream films, including Australian films and blockbusters.

ENTERTAINMENT CENTERS

Sydney Entertainment Centre, Harbour St., Haymarket, Tel 1900 957333

Venue for everything from basketball games to pop concerts, all indoor and with audiences exceeding 10,000.

Sydney Opera House, Bennelong Point, Tel 9250 7777
Not just for opera, this is the premier venue in the city for music, drama, dance, and more.

Sydney Symphony Orchestra, Sydney Opera House, Tel 9334 4644
The principal orchestra of the city, performing everything from the great classics to contemporary music. The orchestra performs free in The Domain as part of the Sydney Festival in January.

Sydney Town Hall, 483 George St., Tel 9265 9007
The emphasis on performance may have shifted to the Opera House, but quite a lot still goes on here. Occasional dance nights, especially during the Sydney Festival, and free lunchtime organ recitals.

NIGHTLIFE

The Albury, 6 Oxford St., Paddington, Tel 9361 6555
Probably the best known gay bar in the city, although there is plenty of competition in this section of Oxford Street.

Banta Room, 163 Oxford St., Darlinghurst, Tel 9360 2528
Among numerous bars and restaurants here, this nightclub has dance music for the less gay members of the local community.

The Basement, 29 Reiby Place, Circular Quay, Tel 9251 2797
One of the city's leading jazz venues, with top local and international acts. Dinner and show packages, or show only with limited seating.

The Cauldron, 207 Darlinghurst Rd., Darlinghurst, Tel 9331 1523
A popular and stylish nightclub; the patrons are as interesting as the music and dancing.

Club 77, 77 William St.,
Darlinghurst, Tel 9361 4981
The major lesbian club in the city.

Comedy Store, 450
Parramatta Rd., Petersham,
Tel 9564 3900
Pub performance venue a short
distance from the city specializing
in comedy. Shows six nights a
week; show only or dinner/show.

DCM, 31–33 Oxford St.,
Darlinghurst, Tel 9267 7380
A popular dance club, predomin-
antly but not exclusively gay.

Enmore Theatre, 130 Enmore
Rd., Enmore, Tel 9550 3666
Popular performance space a
short distance from the city with
comedy, music, and revues.

Harbourside Brasserie,
Pier 1, Hickson Rd., Walsh Bay,
Tel 9252 3000
A mix of musical styles at this
venue on the water almost
under the Harbour Bridge.

Harold Park Comedy Hotel,
115 Wigram Rd., Glebe, Tel 9552
2999
Boutique hotel offering local or
international comedy acts most
nights. Show only, or dinner/show.

Marble Bar, Sydney Hilton
Hotel Basement, 259 Pitt St.,
Tel 9266 2000
Ornate and stylized rococo bar—
a bit like the interior of the State
Theatre on a small scale.
A popular watering hole well
worth a visit, often with live music
on Friday and Saturday nights.

Metro Theatre, 624 George
St., Tel 9264 2666
Ideally sized pop and rock music
venue that hosts a range of high-
profile local and international
acts in an intimate atmosphere.

Midnight Shift, 85 Oxford St.,
Darlinghurst, Tel 9360 4319
A long-established gay bar in this
section of Oxford Street.

Riva Night Club, 130
Castlereagh St., Tel 9286 6666

Located in the Sheraton on the
Park, Riva is a sophisticated
nightclub with a dance floor, a
cabaret/jazz club, and a lounge.

SOHO Bar, 171 Victoria St.,
Potts Point, Tel 9358 6511
Popular bar in the Kings Cross
area for the chic (read dressed
in black) set.

Soup Plus, 383 George St.,
Tel 9299 7728
A popular jazz venue that also
operates as a restaurant.

Star City, 80 Pyrmont St.,
Pyrmont, Tel 9777 9000 (Star
City Infoline: 1300 300711)
The city's only legal casino, with
restaurants, bars, the Lyric
Theatre, accommodations, and,
of course, hundreds of gaming
tables and machines.

State Theatre, 49 Market St.,
Tel 13 6100
This venue is as interesting as
the performances (see p. 104).
The wide variety of events
includes the Sydney Film Festival
(Tel 9660 3844) in June.

THEATER

Bell Shakespeare Company,
88 George St., The Rocks,
Tel 9241 2722
As the name suggests, the main
work of this company is that of
the Bard. When the company is
not on tour, it usually performs
at the Opera House (address is
for head office). Several plays are
staged each year.

Belvoir Street Theatre,
25 Belvoir St., Surry Hills,
Tel 9699 3444
Highly regarded small theater
complex; the base for Company
B, which puts on international
and Australian plays, modern
works, and classics.

Capitol Theatre, 13 Campbell
St., Haymarket, Tel 9320 5000
Venue for a range of theatrical
events, usually long-running
musicals with special performances filling the gaps.

Ensemble Theatre,
78 McDougall St., Kirribilli,
Tel 9929 0644
An intimate theater beside the
harbor on Sydney's Lower North
Shore. Mostly new works, but
also classics performed by some
of Australia's leading actors. Dine
in the waterside restaurant.

Her Majesty's Theatre,
107 Quay St., Haymarket,
Tel 9212 3411
Venue for a range of events
including plays and musicals.

Marian Street Theatre,
2 Marian St., Killara,
Tel 9498 3166
In a leafy northern suburb.
Specializes in comedies, thrillers,
and Broadway plays. Also a
restaurant and children's theater.

Seymour Theatre Centre,
City Rd. & Cleveland St.,
Chippendale, Tel 9364 9400
Major theatrical venue on the
edge of the city, with several
performance spaces for full
productions through to readings
of new local works.

Theatre Royal, MLC Centre,
King St., Tel 13 6100
Venue for a range of events
including plays and musicals, with
special performances.

Wharf Theatre, Pier 4,
Hickson Rd., Walsh Bay,
Tel 9250 1777
Major venue for part of the
Sydney Theatre Company's and
the Sydney Dance Company's
seasons. Spectacular site below
the western pylon of the
Harbour Bridge.

ACTIVE SPORTS

DIVING
Dive 2000, 2 Military Rd.,
Neutral Bay, Tel 9953 7783
Retail scuba diving and under-
water photography equipment.
They also train divers and under-
water photographers, and
provide underwater images.

ENTERTAINMENT & ACTIVITIES

Pro Dive, 27 Alfreda St., Coogee, Tel 9665 6333 or 9232 5733
School for divers. Dives at Port Stephens and Jervis Bay, about three hours' drive north and south of Sydney, also trips farther afield for experienced divers.

GOLF
Bondi Golf Links, Military Rd., North Bondi, Tel 9130 1981
Small 9-hole golf course on the headland of Bondi Beach.

Leura Golf Club, Sublime Point Rd., Leura, Tel (02) 4782 5011
Pleasant 18-hole course set among the Blue Mountains.

Moore Park Golf Club, Corner of Anzac Parade & Cleveland St., Moore Park, Tel 9663 4966
Large golf course, the closest to the city, and a night driving range.

KAYAKING
Sydney Kayak Centre, The Spit Bridge, Mosman, Tel 9969 4590
Single and double kayaks for rent in a sheltered area of Middle Harbour.

SAILING
Eastsail, New Beach Rd., Rushcutters Bay, Tel 9327 1166
One of several yacht and cruiser charter companies in the city (see pp. 84–85).

Northside Sailing School, The Spit, Mosman, Tel 9969 3972
Middle Harbour-based sailboat and sailboard rental.

SQUASH
Hiscoes Squash and Fitness Centre, 525 Crown St., Surry Hills, Tel 9699 3233
Accessible venue for squash close to the city.

SWIMMING
Andrew (Boy) Charlton Pool, Mrs. Macquarie's Rd., The Domain, Tel 9358 6686 (closing April 2001 for renovations)
Harborside pool in The Domain. Lap swimming areas, speed lanes, open swimming areas.

North Sydney Olympic Pool, Alfred St. South, Milsons Point, Tel 9955 2309
Harborside pool. Very popular at lunchtime and during the week; less busy on weekends. Covered and heated in winter.

Prince Alfred Park Pool, Chalmers St., Surry Hills, Tel 9319 7045
Pool close to a railway station on the southern edge of the city.

TENNIS
Parklands Sports Centre, Corner of Lang Rd. & Anzac Parade, Moore Park, Tel 9662 7033
A large tennis complex next to Centennial Park.

The Palms Tennis Centre, Quarry Rd., Paddington, Tel 9363 4955
A medium-size well-presented tennis center in the Eastern Suburbs with great views.

SPECTATOR SPORTS

BASKETBALL
Sydney Kings (men) & Sydney Flames (women) Basketball, Superdome at Homebush Bay, Tel 9319 7777
City's premier basketball teams, competing in the Australian national league.

CRICKET
Sydney Cricket Ground, Driver Ave., Moore Park, Tel 9360 6601
Usually the venue for at least one Test cricket match each year, it also stages state cricket matches and one-day games.

FOOTBALL
Australian Rules Football, Cricket Ground, Tel 9360 6601
The Sydney Swans play at the Cricket Ground alternate winter weekends in the national competition of this Australian game.

Rugby League, Tel 9339 8500; and **Rugby Union**
Two of the major sporting codes in the country. Sydney stages

games at club, state, and international level.

Soccer, Tel 9380 6099
The world game has a fairly low profile in Australia, but Sydney has club, state, and international games at a range of venues.

GREYHOUND RACING
Wentworth Park, Wentworth Park Rd., Glebe, Tel 9660 4308
There's a meet every Saturday and Monday night throughout the year. Major events in the fall.

HARNESS RACING
Harold Park Paceway, Ross St., Glebe, Tel 9660 3688
Meetings held Tuesday day and night and Friday night through-out the year. Carnival in the fall.

HORSE RACING
Canterbury Park, King St, Canterbury, Tel 9930 4000
Seven miles (11 km) south of the city. Bimonthly mid-week day meetings, some night meetings. Air-conditioned betting area and the whole track is visible to the naked eye.

Rosehill Gardens Race-course, Grand Ave., Rosehill, Tel 9930 4000
Fourteen miles (23 km) west of the city. Modern stands, bars, and restaurants; betting ring under cover. Spring and fall carnivals and regular Saturday meetings.

Royal Randwick Racecourse, Alison Rd., Randwick, Tel 9663 8425
A sweeping turf course, a blend of charming old structures and modern stands; excellent dining and bars. Classic races such as the Doncaster, the AJC Derby, and St. Leger Stakes (the oldest race in Australia). Frequent Saturday and mid-week meets.

Warwick Farm Racecourse, Corner of Hume Hwy. & Gov. Macquarie Dr., Tel 9602 6199
Rural atmosphere, tree-lined grounds; popular with family picnickers as well as regular racegoers. Mainly mid-week.

ILLUSTRATIONS CREDITS

Abbreviations for terms appearing below: (t) top; (b) bottom; (l) left; (r) right; (c) center.

Cover, (tl) SuperStock Ltd. (tr) PowerStock/Zefa Photo Library. (bl) Tony Stone Images. (br) Pictor International, London. 1, Corbis/Jan Butchofsky. 2/3, Jean-Paul Ferrero/Auscape. 4, Tony Stone Images. 9, Medford Taylor. 11, Tony Stone Images. 12/13, Greg Hard/Wildlight. 15, Ron Ryan/Coo-ee Picture Library. 16/17, Carolyn Johns/Wildlight. 18, Reg Morrison/Auscape. 19, Ron Ryan/Coo-ee Picture Library. 21, Jean-Paul Ferrero/Auscape. 22, Jean-Paul Ferrero/Auscape. 23, Anthony Blake Photo Library. 24/25, Michael Jensen/Auscape. 26, Royal Geographical Society, London, UK/Bridgeman Art Library. 26/27, State Library of NSW/Auscape. 28, Mitchell Library, State Library of NSW/Bridgeman Art Library. 30/31, National Library of Australia, Canberra/Bridgeman Art Library. 32/33, David Mariuz/Australian Geographic. 34, Carolyn Johns/Wildlight. 35, Tony Stone Images. 37, Greg Barrett/Bangarra Dance Theatre. 38/39, Done Art & Design. 41, Steve Day/AA Photo Library. 42, Steve Day/AA Photo Library. 44/45, Images Colour Library. 47 (t), Steve Day/AA Photo Library. 47 (b), Steve Day/AA Photo Library. 48/49, Ron Ryan/Coo-ee Picture Library. 49, Steve Day/AA Photo Library. 50 (t), Jean-Marc La Roque/Auscape. 50 (b), Ray Joyce/Museum of Sydney. 51, Steve Day/AA Photo Library. 52/53, Steve Day/AA Photo Library. 53, Steve Day/AA Photo Library. 54/55, Tom Keating/Wildlight. 56, Steve Day/AA Photo Library. 57, Art Gallery of NSW. 59 (t), Elioth Gruner "Spring Frost," 1919, oil on canvas, 131.0 x 178.7 cm, Gift of F.G. White 1939, Art Gallery of New South Wales. 59 (b), artist unknown large Buddha figure, marble, 210 cm height, Art Gallery of NSW Foundation Purchase 1997, Art Gallery of New South Wales. 61 (t), National Gallery of Victoria. 61 (b), Eugène Von Guérard "Sydney Heads," 1865, oil on canvas, 56.0 x 94.0 cm, Bequest of Major H.W. Hall 1974, Art Gallery of New South Wales. 62, Steve Day/AA Photo Library. 63, Nature Focus. 66, Steve Day/AA Photo Library. 67, Steve Day/AA Photo Library. 68, Steve Day/AA Photo Library. 69, Steve Day/AA Photo Library. 70, Steve Day/AA Photo Library. 71, Steve Day/AA Photo Library. 72, Philip Quirk/Wildlight. 73, Steve Day/AA Photo Library. 75, Jean-Paul Ferrero/Auscape. 76, Steve Day/AA Photo Library. 77, P.Kenward/AA Photo Library. 78/79, Steve Day/AA Photo

Library. 80, Steve Day/AA Photo Library. 81, Sandy Nicholson/Wildlight. 84/85, Philip Quirk/Wildlight. 86/87, Sandy Nicholson/Wildlight. 87, Steve Day/AA Photo Library. 90, Jim Rice/Wildlight. 92, Pavel German/NHPA. 92/93, Coo-ee Picture Library. 94/95, Jean-Paul Ferrero/Auscape. 95, Jean-Paul Ferrero/Auscape. 96, Jean-Paul Ferrero/Auscape. 97, Jean-Paul Ferrero/Auscape. 98, Jean-Paul Ferrero/Auscape. 101, Steve Day/AA Photo Library. 103 (t), Ron Ryan/Coo-ee Picture Library. 103 (bl), Image Library, State Library of NSW. 103 (br), Steve Day/AA Photo Library. 104, Jean-Paul Ferrero/Auscape. 105, Steve Day/AA Photo Library. 106, P.Kenward AA Photo Library. 109, Jean-Paul Ferrero/Auscape. 110, State Theatre. 111, Ron Ryan/Coo-ee Picture Library. 112 (l), Steve Day/AA Photo Library. 112 (r), Philip Quirk/Wildlight. 113, David McDonald. 114, A.Baker/AA Photo Library. 116, Jean-Paul Ferrero/Auscape. 117, Steve Day/AA Photo Library. 118, Steve Day/AA Photo Library. 119, Steve Day/AA Photo Library. 121, Steve Day/AA Photo Library. 123, Philip Quirk/Wildlight. 125, Geoff Friend/Powerhouse Museum. 127, Philip Quirk/Wildlight. 128/129, Steve Day/AA Photo Library. 129, Jean-Paul Ferrero/Auscape. 130/131, Greg Hard/Wildlight. 132, Steve Day/AA Photo Library. 133, Greg Hard/Wildlight. 134, Jean-Paul Ferrero/Auscape. 136, Steve Day/AA Photo Library. 137, Steve Day/AA Photo Library. 138/139, Sydney Jewish Museum. 140, Tom Keating/Wildlight. 140/141, Renee Nowytarger/Reuters Popperfoto. 141, Renee Nowytarger/Reuters Popperfoto. 143, Jean-Paul Ferrero/Auscape. 145, Steve Day/AA Photo Library. 146/147, Jean-Paul Ferrero/Auscape. 148, Jean-Paul Ferrero/Auscape. 149, Grenville Turner/Wildlight. 150, Penny Tweedie/Corbis UK Ltd. 151, Sydney Aboriginal Discoveries. 152/153, Andrew Rankin/Wildlight. 155 (t), Philip Quirk/Wildlight. 155 (bl), Grenville Turner/Wildlight. 155 (br), Jay Sarson/Lochman Transparencies. 156, National Aboriginal Cultural Centre. 157, David Malangi (Australian, b.1934, Yathulumurru/Ramingining Munharrngu tribe), "Two blue-tongued lizards," 1983, bark painting, Art Gallery of NSW. 158, R. van Starrex/Wildlight. 159, Steve Day/AA Photo Library. 162/163, Steve Day/AA Photo Library. 163, Steve Day/AA Photo Library. 164/165, Steve Day/AA Photo Library. 165, Steve Day/AA Photo Library. 166, SOCOG/Allsport (UK) Ltd. 166/167 Photography Courtesy of the Olympic Co-ordination Authority. 169, Steve Day/AA Photo Library. 171, Photography Courtesy of the Olympic Co-ordination Authority. 172, Carolyn Johns/Wildlight. 173, Andrew Rankin/Wildlight. 174, Steve Day/AA Photo

Library. 176, Steve Day/AA Photo Library. 177, Steve Day/AA Photo Library. 178/179, Jean-Paul Ferrero/Auscape. 180, Steve Day/AA Photo Library. 181, Steve Day/AA Photo Library. 182/183, Jean-Paul Ferrero/Auscape. 184, Mike Braham/Lochman Transparencies. 185, Jiri Lochman/Lochman Transparencies. 188/189, Philip Quirk/Wildlight. 189, P.Kenward/AA Photo Library. 190/191, Steve Day/AA Photo Library. 191, P.Kenward/AA Photo Library. 192, Steve Day/AA Photo Library. 194, Steve Day/AA Photo Library. 195, Brett Gregory/Auscape. 197, Brett Gregory/Auscape. 198 (t), Bill Belson/Lochman Transparencies. 198 (c), Erwin & Peggy Bauer/Bruce Coleman. 198 (b), Steve Day/AA Photo Library. 199 (t), Jorg & Petra Wegner/Bruce Coleman. 199 (tc), Reg Morrison/Auscape. 199 (bc), Jiri Lochman/Lochman Transparencies. 199 (b), Hans & Judy Beste/Lochman Transparencies. 200 (t), Hans & Judy Beste/Lochman Transparencies. 200 (tc), Mary Plage/Bruce Coleman. 200 (bc), C. Andrew Henley/Auscape. 200 (b), D. Parer & E.Parer-Cook/Auscape. 201 (t), Wayne Lawler/Auscape. 201 (tc), Mary Plage/Bruce Coleman. 201 (bc), Jean-Paul Ferrero/Auscape. 201 (b), John Cancalosi/Auscape. 202 (t) Peter Marsack/Lochman Transparencies. 202 (tc), Hans & Judy Beste/Lochman Transparencies. 202 (bc), M.P. Kahl/Auscape. 202 (b), Jean-Paul Ferrero/Auscape. 203 (t) Jean-Paul Ferrero/Auscape. 203 (c) Clay Bruce/Lochman Transparencies. 203 (b), Jeff Foott/Bruce Coleman. 205, Dennis Sarson/Lochman Transparencies. 208/209, Wildlight. 209 (t), Steve Day/AA Photo Library. 209 (b), P.Kenward/AA Photo Library. 211, Steve Day/AA Photo Library. 212, Mitchell Library, State Library of NSW/Bridgeman Art Library. 213 (t), Wade Hughes/Lochman Transparencies. 213 (c), Milton Wordley/Wildlight. 213 (b), Jean-Paul Ferrero/Auscape. 214, Steve Day/AA Photo Library. 215, Brett Gregory/Auscape. 216, Steve Day/AA Photo Library. 217, Brett Gregory/Auscape. 218/219, Grenville Turner/Wildlight. 219, Coo-ee Picture Library. 220, Tom Keating/Wildlight. 221, Brett Gregory/Auscape. 222/223, Grenville Turner/Wildlight. 223, Brett Gregory/Auscape. 225, Jean-Paul Ferrero/Auscape. 226, Bradman Museum. 227, Jean-Paul Ferrero/Auscape. 228/229, Michael Jensen/Auscape. 230, National Gallery of Australia. 231, Steve Day/AA Photo Library.

The publisher would like to thank HarperCollins Publishers for their kind permission to reprint one verse from "Five Bells" by Kenneth Slessor from *Selected Poems*.

Published by the National Geographic Society
John M. Fahey, Jr., *President and Chief Executive Officer*
Gilbert M. Grosvenor, *Chairman of the Board*
Nina D. Hoffman, *Senior Vice President*
William R. Gray, *Vice President and Director, Book Division*
David Griffin, *Design Director*
Elizabeth L. Newhouse, *Director of Travel Publishing*
Barbara Noe, *Associate Editor*
Caroline Hickey, *Senior Researcher*
Carl Mehler, *Director of Maps*
Joseph F. Ochlak, *Map Coordinator*
Kristin M. Edmonds, *Editorial Consultant*
Gary Colbert, *Production Director*
Richard S. Wain, *Production Project Manager*
DeShelle Downey, *Staff Assistant*

Edited and designed by AA Publishing (a trading name of Automobile
Association Developments Limited, whose registered office is Norfolk
House, Priestley Road, Basingstoke, Hampshire, England RG24 9NY.
Registered number: 1878835).
Betty Sheldrick, *Project Manager*
David Austin, *Senior Art Editor*
Rachel Alder, *Senior Editor*
Bob Johnson, *Designer*
Simon Mumford, *Senior Cartographic Editor*
Nicky Barker-Dix, Helen Beever, *Cartographers*
Richard Firth, *Production Director*
Picture Research by Zooid Pictures Ltd.
Drive maps drawn by Chris Orr Associates, Southampton, England
Cutaway illustrations drawn by Maltings Partnership, Derby, England

Library of Congress Cataloging-in-Publication Data
McHugh, Evan.
    The National Geographic Traveler. Sydney / Evan McHugh.
    p.   cm.
    Includes index.
    ISBN 0-7922-7435-0
    1. Sydney (N.S.W.)—Guidebooks. I. Title. II. Title: Sydney.
    DU178.M39   1999
    919.44'10466—dc21   99-40370
                                                   CIP

Printed and bound by R.R. Donnelley & Sons, Willard, Ohio.
Color separations by Leo Reprographic Ltd, Hong Kong
Cover separations by L.C. Repro, Aldermaston, U.K.
Cover printed by Miken Inc., Cheektowaga, New York.

Visit the Society's Web site at http://www.nationalgeographic.com

The information in this book has been carefully checked and to the best
of our knowledge is accurate. However, details are subject to change, and
the National Geographic Society cannot be responsible for such changes,
or for errors or omissions. Assessments of sites, hotels, and restaurants
are based on the author's subjective opinions, which do not necessarily
reflect the publisher's opinion. The publisher cannot be responsible for
any consequences arising from the use of this book.

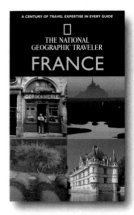
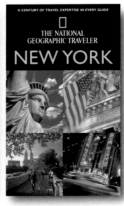
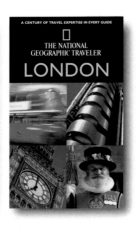